AND WROTE
MY STORY
ANYWAY

BLACK SOUTH AFRICAN WOMEN'S NOVELS AS FEMINISM

BARBARA BOSWELL

WITS UNIVERSITY PRESS

Published in South Africa by:
Wits University Press
1 Jan Smuts Avenue
Johannesburg 2001

www.witspress.co.za

Copyright © Barbara Boswell 2020
Published edition © Wits University Press 2020

First published 2020

http://dx.doi.org.10.18772/12020096185

978-1-77614-618-5 (Paperback)
978-1-77614-622-2 (Hardback)
978-1-77614-619-2 (Web PDF)
978-1-77614-620-8 (EPUB)
978-1-77614-621-5 (Mobi)

For the Miriam Tlali portrait photograph: *Photograph by Adrian Steirn, courtesy
of 21 Icons South Africa*

Project manager: Elaine Williams
Copyeditor: Lynda Gilfillan
Proofreader: Inga Norenius
Indexer: Elaine Williams
Cover design: Hybrid Creative
Typeset in 10.5 point Plantin

Dedicated to
Noel Madden, with love

CONTENTS

Acknowledgements

I am grateful to my patchwork quilt of transnational community that has supported my work, read various drafts of the manuscript, and engaged in edifying conversations, encouraging me to complete this book. I am thankful to Miriam Tlali, Lauretta Ngcobo, Sindiwe Magona, Gladys Thomas, Yvette Christiansë, Gabeba Baderoon, Diana Ferrus, Malika Ndlovu, A Lynn Bolles, Deborah Rosenfelt, Elsa Barkley Brown, Merle Collins, Angel David Nieves, Bonnie Thornton Dill, Deborah McDowell, Carol Corneilse, Angel Miles, Kimberlee Staking, Bianca Laureano, Jing Song, Pumla Dineo Gqola, Tyler Fleming, Dennis Tyler, Shanna Smith, Jennifer Bacon, Renetta Garrison Tull, Wendy Carter-Veale, Makhosazana Xaba, Athambile Masola, Floretta Boonzaier, Zoë Marks, Yaliwe Clarke, Polo Moji, Nadia Davids, Mandisa Haarhoff, Sindiswa Busuku, Kharnita Mohamed, Sandy Young, Cassie Premo Steele, Harry Garuba, Christopher Ouma, Roshan Cader, Lynda Gilfillan, Elaine Williams, Natasha Diedricks, Precious Sharon Sinovuyo Bikitsha, and Letlhogonolo Mokgoroane, who were all part of my writing community, reading various drafts of this work, and holding space for me as I completed it. I am also thankful for the input of the anonymous peer reviewers, whose comments refined and improved this book. I acknowledge the financial support of the Fulbright Foundation, the American Council of Learned Societies (ACLS), the Carter G Woodson Institute for African-American and African Studies at the University of Virginia, and the University of Cape Town in bringing this project to fruition. Finally, I am grateful to my family for their unfailing love and support, especially my son, Jesse Meintjes, and my mother, Una Boswell.

Author's Preface

*I forcefully created for myself, under extremely hostile conditions,
my ideal life. I took an obscure and almost unknown village
in the Southern African bush and made it my own hallowed
ground ... My work was always tentative because it was always
so completely new: it created new worlds out of nothing.*

Bessie Head
— *A Woman Alone: Autobiographical Writings*

*I have always reserved a special category for myself, as a
writer – that of pioneer blazing a new trail into the future.*

Bessie Head
— *A Woman Alone: Autobiographical Writings*

Imagine one possibility of this future Bessie Head conjures. It is
1994. A young woman – me – designated 'coloured' by apartheid
law, and about to come of age in the new, democratic South Africa,
working as a trainee journalist at an alternative newspaper in Cape
Town. I'm assigned a work of fiction to review, *The Cardinals, with
Meditations and Short Stories*, by a writer unfamiliar to me: Bessie
Head. Extremely conscious of her agency as a writer, and wishing to
leave a legacy, Head had been writing into a future she could neither
have predicted nor anticipated. Yet our meeting on the page was an
encounter she must have foreseen; writing, as she did, across time
and space. Meeting her like this knocked my world off its axis.

As a child who'd grown up during the last decade of formal apartheid, I'd received an education in accordance with my designated place in South Africa's racial hierarchy. An avid reader, my literary diet had consisted of books borrowed from a government library, and literature prescribed by apartheid bureaucrats for language instruction in school. Black writers of any gender were excluded from these works, since most of them – and their work – had been banned.

The political changes in South Africa leading to the first democratic election in 1994 unleashed a flood of previously banned literature. It was at this moment that I became acquainted with Head's first novella, *The Cardinals*, written in the early 1960s and published posthumously in 1993. It was her only published work of fiction set and written in Cape Town, before she was 'endorsed out' of South Africa in 1964 on an exit permit that would exile her to Botswana for the rest of her life, prohibiting her return to the land of her birth.

The experience of reading Head's work was profoundly unsettling. Try as I might, I was unable to produce the required book review for my newspaper's art pages. Head's writing confounded me in two ways: this was the first time I'd experienced the city where I was born and had lived in on the pages of a work of fiction. In *The Cardinals*, Head had vibrantly and intimately rendered the place that I loved, my home city. She had written a love letter to a place I was about to inhabit, for the first time, as an autonomous, liberated citizen. As a black girl who had been prohibited by apartheid law throughout my life from entering certain public spaces in Cape Town, I was acutely aware of how space was opening up to me. I went everywhere I could, determined to experience everything the city had to offer. The place she had sketched in her novella some thirty years prior was the same living, breathing city I was now exploring daily.

The experience of having my world depicted in this way was, at the time, alien. Until then, the worlds I had entered through fiction had always existed elsewhere. While I enjoyed being transported to foreign places, it had never occurred to me that my own world could be the subject or setting for fiction. The literature I'd previously read had always centred some other place, elsewhere, or the subjectivity of someone who didn't look like me. Discovering my home town, in all its beauty and ugliness, as a central character in a work of fiction drew me into the text in a completely new way. Here was a new space – the discursive – opening up to me, which I explored with as much zest as the physical geography of the city.

The Cardinals intrigued and mystified me on another level, too. Its main character, Mouse, was a young black woman who had just started working as a journalist. She wrote fiction in her spare time, and the novella was a *kunstlerroman* (artist's novel) illuminating Mouse's internal struggles as she mastered the art of writing. Unsure of her talent and unsure of her voice or whether she even had anything to say, she nevertheless carried on writing. As a fledgling writer myself, I connected deeply with this character. Though acutely aware of my power to represent people in the way 'news' was constructed, I was simultaneously afraid of this power. The character's struggles with finding her voice thus resonated deeply on a personal as well as political level. Never before had I encountered the subjectivity of a young coloured woman at the centre of a novel. The message I had received through twenty years of fiction reading was that the interiority of a young black woman embedded within apartheid's social relations was simply not a subject worthy of literature.

Head's work jolted me awake, I realised, because I had not thought it possible that a black woman could be a writer. My education and socialisation had led me to believe that producing art – the production of a beautiful object, for no reason other than the pleasure of creating – was an activity that I, or someone like me, should not consider a possibility. Reading *The Cardinals* crystallised for me the fact that a black woman who had lived under apartheid, in similar conditions to mine, had succeeded in carving out a creative life – a fact that, until then, had not been a possibility I'd been remotely aware of.

What Head had 'forcefully created' (*A Woman Alone*, 28) through her writing was not only her 'own hallowed ground', but also a space into which I could enter, dream different dreams, and imagine myself as a creative being. In 'creat[ing] new worlds out of nothing' (28), Head also remade the world for me, conjuring a host of new possibilities. I have been guided by these possibilities in writing this book.

Head's fiction and essays reveal great insights and self-conscious reflection on the transgressive nature of writing as a black South African woman. Her writing informs the perspective I bring to the work of constructing this history of black South African women's fiction. Born Bessie Amelia Head in the South African province of Natal in 1937, Head's talent as a fiction writer and essayist came to fruition during her exile in today's Botswana, where she'd fled in 1964. The product of an interracial, and, under South African law, illegal relationship between a wealthy white woman and a black man thought to be the family's stable hand (Nixon 1993), the circumstances of her birth, and her racial classification as coloured meant a childhood of disavowal and rejection, spent in foster care and an orphanage.

Intensely preoccupied with race, as were most other black writers of her time, Head has left a lasting legacy of non-fiction writing on the ways in which apartheid hindered creativity and cultural production. Head succeeded in becoming one of Southern Africa's most prolific black women writers, with an oeuvre that includes *When Rain Clouds Gather* (1968), the first novel to be published in English by a black South African woman writer, *Maru* (1971); *A Question of Power* (1973); *The Collector of Treasures and other Botswana Village Tales* (1977); *Serowe: Village of the Rain Wind* (1981); *A Bewitched Crossroad: An African Saga* (1984); and *The Cardinals, With Meditations and Short Stories* (1993). While Head had worked as a journalist for the *Golden City Post* in Cape Town, her creativity as a writer truly blossomed only once she'd left South Africa in 1964 for the former Bechuanaland.

Though Head's life was certainly marked by tragedy – the circumstances of her birth, her maternal family's rejection of her because of her race, her biological mother's suicide, her exile from and inability to return to her homeland, her own mental health problems which led to her being committed to a psychiatric hospital in Botswana, and her untimely death at the age of 49 – reading her fiction only in relation to these 'tragedies' risks diminishing the space of creative articulation her writing opened up. For Rob Nixon, Head's life became the crucible in which her conceptualisation of creativity was forged. Being disavowed first by her biological family, and then by her country, Head sought alternatives to the naturalised categories of family, race and nation upon which selfhood rests.

It was this process of seeking alternative ways of being in the world, and carving out a space of belonging in a geographic area that ignited her creativity and became the catalyst for her theorising, through fiction, African women's creativity. Desiree Lewis has identified creativity as an ongoing concern in Head's fiction, 'a productive power that she constantly celebrates through her extraordinary metaphors and fictional strategies' (Lewis 2007, 33). In 'forcefully creat[ing]' her own world, where she could 'dream dreams a little ahead of the somewhat vicious clamour of revolution and the horrible stench of evil systems', Head displays what Carole Boyce Davies (1994, 36–37) has named 'migratory subjectivity', relating not only to 'the many locations of Black women's writing, but also to the Black female subject refusing to be subjugated'. In her awareness of her agency in the analysis of her own life, and the interplay between the different ideological and geographical spaces she inhabits as a writer, Head embodies 'migratory subjectivity'. She writes that same subjectivity for her women characters.

The story of Mouse in *The Cardinals* mirrors that of Bessie Head, who herself worked as a reporter and agony aunt for the *Golden City Post* in Cape Town between 1960 and 1962. That her first, unfruitful attempt at novel writing concerns a young 'mixed-race' woman with literary aspirations is no accident, as Head used the discursive space of the novel to map out the developing artistic consciousness of a black woman writer.

In *Maru*, as in *The Cardinals*, Head offers a mode of accessing creativity and artistic production through a character, this time the figure of Margaret, who is a developing artist. *Maru* offers a heretofore unparalleled (in African fiction) meditation on women's creativity and the woman artist's struggle for mastery. The novel's meditations are compelling: they offer, for the first time in the African novel in English, a glimpse into the creative life of an African woman, written by an African woman. Head's theorising from a black, African woman's standpoint constitutes a rare and precious instruction on cultivating and nurturing creative expression from the position of an oppressed woman, located on the bottom rung of the racial hierarchy within which society places her. Margaret's paintings leave the reader in no doubt that she is a gifted visual artist. Her themes were chosen 'from the ordinary, common happenings in the village as though those themes were the best expression of her own vitality. The women carried water buckets up and down the hill but the eye was thrown, almost by force, towards the powerful neck, and the animated expressions and gestures of the water-carriers as they stopped to gossip' (107). The language of vitality in the artwork's description, and the way the paintings force the eye towards the artist's intended focal points, are textual markers of visual excellence. This passage in *Maru* describing Margaret's painting resonates with a vignette from *The Cardinals*, where Johnny instructs Mouse on how to write from the vantage point of Table Mountain, overlooking the city of Cape Town.

> Look at that town the way an artist must look at it. He has to concentrate, in a compact and simplified form, its vastness, its mood, its purpose and the flow and rhythm of its life. He is lost if he concentrates on detail, the same way a writer gets lost if he starts picking at bits and pieces of life. Life is not in bits and pieces. It is a magnificent, rhythmic, pulsating symphony ... While you look at that town with the eye of an artist, look at it also with the eye of a writer and let there be no difference between the artist and the writer. (134–135)

For Head, there is no difference between the visual and literary artist. Both must take in the world, analyse it, and remake or artistically render it for a larger aim – to be 'of some use to someone, somewhere' (*The Cardinals*, 108). The assignment Johnny gives Mouse in the above passage is actualised by Margaret in *Maru*. Margaret's work is filled with a compelling vitality – she has mastered her craft by being able to successfully communicate a mood or message through her art; that is, convey a universal truth to an intended audience. This ability is confirmed when Maru savours the paintings Margaret has produced, analysing them intellectually and emotionally:

Thus the message of the picture went even deeper to his heart: 'You see, it is I and my tribe who possess the true vitality of this country. You lost it when you sat down and let us clean your floors and rear your children and cattle.' (109)

In this way Margaret's art, depicting Masarwa experience so as to convey an impression of life, including oppression, ultimately moves Maru to outlaw the enslavement of the Masarwa by the Motswana. The artwork, created in good faith, finds its intended audience, and performs a dual function: aesthetically pleasing, it also conscientises its recipient to create a more just social order. Reflecting on her creative process, Margaret says: 'I drew all the pictures from pictures from my mind. I first see something as it looks but it looks better when it reappears again as a picture in my mind' (104). Here, Head offers insight into the process of envisioning a different world, taking the ugliness of the existing social order and fashioning it into something 'better'. This is one way of discerning the magical quality with which she sought to imbue her work – the creative vision that enables the artist to envision better worlds, for the greater good of humanity.

Head's *kunstlerroman* reveals a clear vision regarding the responsibility of the artist in an unjust, rapidly modernising world. Johnny muses early on in *The Cardinals* that Africa, on the crest of a wave of decolonisation, is entering a new phase of history, one where nationalism will lead to irrevocable change. Though writers should have loyalty neither to continent, nor political ideology nor nation, Johnny argues that there is, nevertheless, a role for them in the psychological liberation that follows national liberation: 'It is the duty of the conqueror to abuse you, and treat you like an outcast and alien, and to impose false standards on you. Maybe we [writers] can help throw some of those imposed standards overboard. It is a great responsibility to be a writer at this time' (71–72).

Head clearly saw the role of the writer – and her role specifically – as aiding the struggle of Africans to interrogate and discard oppressive ideologies. Creative articulation was the gift Head honed in order to achieve this aim; she consciously left a legacy and a model for artistic production which, through her unshakable faith, 'found' others, in an unknown future, who needed such instruction. This is instruction I take gladly. In this book, I use it as a guide in examining the work of Head's imagined literary heirs – the women writers for whom, I believe, she blazed a trail into the future.

Acronyms

ANC	African National Congress
Codesa	Convention for a Democratic South Africa
Cosaw	Congress of South African Writers
FSAW	Federation of South African Women
MK	Umkhonto we Sizwe
TRC	Truth and Reconciliation Commission
WNC	Women's National Coalition

Introduction: 'And Wrote My Story Anyway': Black South African Women's Novels as Feminism

Black women have always been involved in the creation and performance of our literature, especially oral literature ... We have been writing for a long time; it is now that these writings are beginning to come out in the open.

Lauretta Ngcobo — *Let It Be Told*

What are the uses of feminist literature and theory? What possibilities for knowing and understanding ourselves might feminist literary theory offer the postcolonial, post-apartheid subject? More than 20 years after the transition to democracy in South Africa, power and dominance have seemingly shifted, yet have reformulated themselves along racial configurations strikingly similar to those produced by the apartheid state. For those who are economically abjected by local and global structures shaped by a neoliberal global world order, can theory offer liberatory ways of seeing, or transgressive modes of engaging with, and being in, the world? In a social order where the majority of citizens have found the fulfilment of basic human and socioeconomic rights receding almost beyond reach, are we justified in looking towards texts – fiction, theory, criticism – for signposts towards achieving fully actualised, dignified lives for those for whom 1994 meant the deferment of freedom?

And Wrote My Story Anyway: Black South African Women's Novels as Feminism takes, as a point of departure, the fundamental power of stories to shape and transform lives. It asks what we can learn from the literary output of those most negatively impacted by colonialism and apartheid – black women – if we consider their writing as a set of theories that produce a praxis towards a more just social order. Literature has the capacity to remake worlds and to imagine alternatives to 'what is': political and social orders that oppress, and which limit freedom. Black South African women historically wrote fiction as a way of fighting the gross inhumanity of the apartheid system, creating a canon that, as its foundational preoccupation, interrogated power in its most brute forms. It is within this tradition that post-apartheid black women's writing situates itself.

Consequently, this book examines the novels of black South African women writers during and after apartheid as a site of theory production: each novel is not only a set of literary narrations, with its own aesthetic, but also a political blueprint that enables us to ask critical questions of the nation, and to analyse the intersectional nature of black women's locations within apartheid and democratic South Africa.

Cultural critic Edward Said (1994, 80) has noted that 'the capacity to represent, portray, characterize and depict is not easily available to just any member of just any society'. South African society, structured in recent history by the oppressive and exploitative systems of colonialism and apartheid, has historically been organised in a way that systematically excluded black women from writing and other forms of cultural production. These systems worked on multiple levels not only to disenfranchise black women and black subjects in general, but also to repress creativity and the capacity to dream. By curtailing the educational opportunities available to black women, politically disenfranchising them, and responding to anti-apartheid activism through censorship, imprisonment, violence and banning, the apartheid government effectively prohibited black women from the realm of literary production. Despite all this, black women writers insisted upon rendering creative accounts of life, political events, human relations, and the struggles they faced.

During the transition to democracy and beyond, black women writers' creativity has flourished. No longer constrained by laws such as the Publications Act of 1963, the Suppression of Communism Act of 1950, or an apartheid imaginary that conceived of black subjects as devoid of culture, black women have been prolific, producing novels, plays and poetry that are often at the vanguard of social change. Pumla Gqola (2009 a, 214) notes that 'the most dramatic shift in the South African literary scene has occurred in relation to women's place within written and performed poetry'. But it is also in writing novels that black women have seized a space previously denied them to render worlds hitherto unseen in South African literature.

This book analyses the ways in which selected black South African women writers, in daring to write, construct the South African nation in their novels. It analyses the fiction of Miriam Tlali, Lauretta Ngcobo, Sindiwe Magona, Zoë Wicomb, Agnes Sam, Farida Karodia, Zukiswa Wanner, Yvette Christiansë, Rayda Jacobs and Kagiso Lesego Molope in an attempt to map the ways in which these writers conceived of – and reconfigured – the South African nation in the late twentieth and early twenty-first centuries. I have selected these particular writers because, in many ways, their works and lives present us with a series of firsts: Tlali, for example, was the first black South African woman to publish a full-length work of fiction within the borders of South Africa; Ngcobo was the first black woman to produce an intersectional analysis of South African women's oppression as situated within a matrix of white supremacist ideology and African patriarchy; Magona and Wicomb are the first black women writers to interrogate, in fiction, the nation-building project of the South African Truth and Reconciliation Commission (TRC); and Agnes Sam and Farida Karodia are foundational writers in their depictions of South African Indian women's and girls' subjectivities. Christiansë and Jacobs are the first black South African women writers to pen neo-slave narratives which, I argue, produce discursive resonances with the transitional, democratic nation, while Wanner and Molope uncover new literary terrain in their depiction of black queer subjectivities in the developing nation. These writers' texts have been chosen because each speaks to a particular historical moment in the apartheid and post-apartheid nation, interrogating the taken-for-granted constitution of the nation-space.

I argue that those daring to write under the repressive regime of apartheid display what Carole Boyce Davies (1994, 36) names 'migratory subjectivity'. In her theorisation of the ways in which black women's writing renegotiates their identities, Davies argues that, for black women, writing can be likened to a migratory experience: the acts of writing and migration both involve psychological and physical boundary-crossing, as well as the constant renegotiation of black women's identities. Black women's writing therefore signals personal agency, since the act of writing, for a black woman, consists of a series of boundary-crossings requiring an active agent to do such crossings. In South Africa, this migratory subjectivity of black women writers is particularly salient, given that these women wrote in resistance to a system of political and patriarchal repression which sought, at its most basic level, to rob them of their full humanity and to limit most forms of expression. Similarly, black women writing in post-apartheid South Africa are engaged in a series of boundary crossings – surpassing the thresholds of expectation that view them as non-suitable producers of art, given their collective historical relegation to the realm of physical labour and non-intellectual work.

Chimamanda Ngozi Adichie, in a well-circulated TED talk (2009), cautions on the dangers of a 'single story'– reductive narratives that flatten out African subjectivity and humanity, producing stereotypes, and ultimately contributing to economic and discursive imbalances of global power. Stories, however, also have the power to heal, to restore humanity where it has been denied, and to point to a feminist praxis that has the potential to liberate. A fundamental underpinning of my book is its insistence on reading black women's writing not only as creative, but also as theory. Since black women have been historically – and, to a differing degree, are currently – denied access to sites of formal theory-making, their fiction can be viewed as a site of prodigious theoretical production, as a discursive 'place' where they critique an existing unjust political order, and imagine an alternative, more socially just world (Lewis, 2003).

And Wrote My Story Anyway thus approaches black women's literature produced during and after apartheid as theory – and, in the words of bell hooks, as theorising 'as a location for healing' (hooks 1994, 59). Directing their literature as a theory towards healing is characteristic of many black South African women's creative work.

Consider Gcina Mhlophe's short story, 'The Toilet', published in 1987, at the height of apartheid's repression. In this semi-autobiographical story, the young African woman who is the first-person narrator relates her journey from a worker in a clothing factory in Johannesburg, where her job is to cut loose threads from garments, to a writer of poems and stories. Under apartheid law, the protagonist lives 'illegally' in a suburb of Johannesburg designated 'whites only', together with her sister who is a domestic worker for a white family. The family does not know that the main character lives in the servant's quarters with her sister, and she consequently hides for most of her life so as to avoid detection.

Part of the unnamed character's development as an artist is possible because she discovers a public toilet in a park; there, she locks herself in for several hours each day in order to compose her poems and stories in a notebook. The problem with this temporary writing haven however, is that the toilet is reserved for whites, and the narrator's use of this space is a dangerous transgression of apartheid law, punishable by imprisonment and 'deportation' to a homeland, were she to be discovered.

Yet, in transforming the toilet to function as what Virginia Woolf (1929) refers to as a room of her own, Mhlophe's character not only flouts apartheid law, but also transgresses apartheid's ideological code – which produced an educational system that deliberately excluded women from the realm of cultural and literary production. The aim was, after all, to position African women as 'hewers of wood and drawers of water' within the apartheid political economy. Yet in Mhlophe's story, the narrator uses the space of the toilet as an incubator for her dreams of being a performer and writer:

> I was really lucky to have found that toilet because the winter was very cold ... Also, the toilet was very small – the walls were wonderfully close to me – it felt like it was made to fit me alone. I enjoyed that kind of privacy. I did a lot of thinking while I sat there on that toilet seat. I did a lot of daydreaming too – many times imagining myself in some big hall doing a really popular play with some other young actors. (1987, 3)

The story ends when the narrator one day arrives at her toilet, only to find it locked. Somehow she has been found out, and she is barred entry to her creative space. This exclusion could potentially be a moment of defeat, discouragement, or deterrence. Yet the character perseveres in her quest to write: 'For the first time I accepted that the toilet was not mine after all. Slowly I walked over to a bench nearby, watched the early spring sun come up, and wrote my story anyway' (13).

Mhlophe, here, is engaged in much more than entertaining storytelling: 'The Toilet' effectively produces a theory of literary production, a theory that is specifically alert to the materiality of race and gender in the protagonist's life. The subject Mhlophe conjures here is an African woman with dreams, aspirations and critical faculties – the antithesis of the image of the oppressed, unthinking African woman constructed by apartheid ideology; the latter is, indeed, an image that confronts the reader in much early African literature in English by writers such as Chinua Achebe and Alan Paton. Mhlophe's protagonist, who has both a working life and a family life, balances the two under the constraints of one of the most oppressive political systems known to mankind. She reflects upon these, and produces strategies for creating a better life. She is creative, reconfiguring her space and rethinking her abject status, and becomes the creator of her own literary worlds. Mhlophe also theorises space and apartheid spatiality, engaging in what Katherine McCittrick (2006) names a critical black feminist geography – a heuristic tool for mapping the subversive place-making practices of black subjects who inhabit the margins of discursive and geographical space. Mhlophe thus theorises space as a non-neutral commodity: in Mhlophe's formulation, space is always racialised, always gendered.

So, too, is literary production. Who gets to write, and under what circumstances they are allowed to publish, are deeply political issues, infused with power differentials based on race, gender, sexual orientation, and one's place in the world. Here, 'place' denotes both geographic location and the designated 'place' society assigns an individual, whether as a domestic worker, cultural worker, labourer or thinker.

Mhlophe's theory of racialised and gendered space, and its impact on literary production, also demonstrates the strategy which I term black women's 'creative re-visioning' (Boswell 2017, 414). Mhlophe's character takes the space of the toilet – usually associated with scatology, repulsive bodily functions and unpleasant smells – and transforms this unsavoury space into a place that nurtures creativity. She creates the 'room of her own' in which to write and dream, and in this way transforms her world by transforming herself from factory worker to writer, artist and intellectual. She offers here a theory of liberation to others who occupy a similarly constrained position, and does so by subverting the tools of oppression designed to stifle her humanity and creativity, using them to create an alternative vision and life for herself. For black women, especially, the story invites an entry into the world of creativity, of (re)writing the self, and of authoring alternative visions of the world.

Mhlophe's short story functions not only as narrative, but also as a theory which works on three levels: it assesses black women's position in apartheid South Africa; it offers a strategy for resisting the oppression that produces this positionality and it offers a theory of literary production.

This book examines the ways in which black South African women like Mhlophe have analysed and theorised the nation, and black women's position within it, in mostly novelistic terms. It maps the narratives and counter-narratives these writers have used to express their exclusion from dominant constructs of that nation by analysing *Muriel at Metropolitan* (1975) by Miriam Tlali, *And They Didn't Die* (1990) by Lauretta Ngcobo, Farida Karodia's *Daughters of the Twilight* (1986), *Jesus is Indian and Other Stories* (1989) by Agnes Sam, *David's Story* (2000) by Zoë Wicomb, *Mother to Mother* (1998) by Sindiwe Magona, *The Slave Book* (1998) by Rayda Jacobs, Yvette Christiansë's *Unconfessed* (2006), Zukiswa Wanner's *Men of the South* (2010), and *This Book Betrays my Brother* (2012) by Kagiso Lesego Molope. In so doing, this book aims to make visible a body of literature – black South African women's fiction in English – which, until recently, has largely been ignored in mainstream criticism of South African, African and postcolonial literatures.

Why the narrow focus on one nation, at a time when black and African diasporic literary criticism has taken a distinctly transnational, pan-Africanist turn? One answer is that the history of black women's literary production in South Africa which I attempt to map has, quite simply, not been told, and as long as it is subsumed within larger transnational movements, it risks remaining untold. While many of the works of fiction critically analysed here would be well placed within transnational, comparative criticism, there is a productive tension in holding them within the framework of apartheid and the transitional nation-space. South Africa is a nation singularly inflected by apartheid and an ostensibly peaceful transition to democracy, and the literature produced by black women during these historical periods opens a view into the workings of nationalisms and gender within first, a highly oppressive and, then, a transitional nation. This view allows us to understand writing as resistance – an important form of agency on the part of those deliberately excluded from circuits of political and economic power, as well as cultural expression.

The 'nation', postcoloniality and black South African women's writing

Cultural articulations contribute to the construction of nations, and the novel as a cultural product is implicated in the creation of ideologies that maintain nations. Within modernity, nations have emerged as contested and ambivalent spaces, brought into coherence as much by culture and ideology as by physical borders. Althusserian interpretations of the nation-state hold that ideology plays as large a role in buttressing national formations as more concrete state apparatuses (Althusser 1971). Ideology represents the 'imaginary relationship of individuals to their real conditions of existence': a narrative of 'reality' which keeps subjects in a state of subjection by making them accept certain interpretations of their lives (Althusser 1971, 187). Narratives woven by ideology, or by those who hold ideological power, thus construct the nation, and reproduce it by maintaining existing power relations.

Anderson (1991, 6) defines the nation as an 'imagined political community' and argues that the idea of the nation as an organising political force gained credence in eighteenth-century Western Europe during the rise of the Enlightenment and the waning of religious influence. The concept of 'the nation' flourished, according to Anderson, partly because of the invention of print-capitalism, which provided concrete textual means – the novel and the newspaper – by which members of the 'imagined communities' of nations could conceive of those fellow citizens whom they would never meet, but with whom they shared a bond of belonging to the same nation. 'These forms provided the technical means for "re-presenting" the kind of imagined community that is the nation' (Anderson 1991, 25). Print-capitalism, and particularly the novelistic form, thus buttressed the formation of nations in Western Europe, making it possible for national subjects to see themselves in relation to other citizens.

Edward Said's examination of culture and imperialism similarly acknowledges the novel as an important cultural form in the creation of imperialist national cultures. Novels are not produced in a cultural vacuum, argues Said (1994, 71), who demonstrates what he calls 'the novel's consolidation of authority'. For imperial Britain, this authority made governance and social power 'appear both normative and sovereign, that is, self-validating in the course of the narrative' (Said 1994, 77). In these ways, writing as a form of cultural production is implicated in constructing the nation, and often, too, in constructing dominant nationalist discourses of the nation.

Recent postcolonial and feminist theorising of the nation has contested Western, Eurocentric concepts of the nation by examining nationalisms as they emerge in so-called Third World contexts. Feminist postcolonial scholars have illuminated the ways in which nationalisms are often constructed through the exclusion of certain subjects, notably women, from citizenship. In so doing, this body of scholarship by writers such as Said, Homi Bhabha, Gayatri Spivak, Mary Layoun, Anne McClintock, Nira Yuval-Davis, Partha Chatterjee and Sangeeta Ray complicates the Eurocentric focus of foundational works on nationalism by theorists like Anderson and Althusser.

Bhabha, for example, provides a more complex formulation of 'the nation' and ideology's role within it than does Althusser. For

Bhabha (1990) the nation is a liminal space haunted by ambivalence. Bhabha (1990, 1) reads the nation semiotically, as that which signifies ambivalence: its temporality inscribes 'a much more transitional social reality' than unitary nationalist discourses would have it signify. Thus, reading the nation as text, as it is written, is valuable in that it displays 'the wide dissemination through which we construct the field of meanings and symbols associated with national life' (Bhabha 1990, 3).

Mary Layoun (2001) similarly reads the nation as narrative, but with an added focus on the ways in which ideologies of gender construct such narratives. In *Wedded to the Land? Gender, Boundaries and Nationalism in Crisis*, Layoun (2001, 18) examines the intersections of gender, culture, and nationalism in territories displaying what she calls 'nationalism in crisis'. Layoun (2001, 10) defines the function of nationalism as follows:

> Nationalism – at any given time, in a specific space, and in the name of particular nationally defined and constituted peoples – constructs and professes a narrative of the nation and of its relation to a projected potential or already existing state. In doing this, nationalism lays claim to a privileged national perspective of the 'nation' and thus justifies its own capacity to narrate – to organize and link the diverse elements of – the nation.

In functioning as a narrative, nationalism thus privileges its own rendering of reality as narrative. Layoun's analysis expands that of Bhabha's by inserting gendered analyses into examinations of the nation and nationalism.

Feminist scholarship such as Layoun's has done a great deal to counter androcentric theories of the nation and statehood by critically examining the gendered ways in which the nation constructs its citizens: specifically, how women are discursively constructed and made to stand as sign for the nation, and how deployments of these constructions of women function in the articulation of nationhood. In their theorising of nationalism and gender, Nira Yuval-Davis and Floya Anthias (1989, 1) have noted that 'the central dimensions of the relationships between collectives and the state are constituted around the roles of women'. McClintock

(1995, 352), through an explication of Afrikaner nationalism and its creation of the trope of the 'mother of the nation' in South Africa, argues that 'all nationalisms are gendered, all are invented, and all are dangerous'. Moreover, because nationalism positions male subjects in the same relation to the nation as they stand to women, McClintock (1995, 353) argues convincingly that 'nations have historically amounted to the institutionalization of gender difference'. Similarly, Sangeeta Ray (2000) has critiqued masculinist theories of nationalism that continue to use Ernest Renan's 1882 articulations of nationalism as a framework, despite a number of feminist interventions into such androcentric discourses of the nation. Through an analysis of several novels that centre India, Ray demonstrates one of her central arguments around nationalism as it has been deployed by both colonisers and the indigenous peoples of India: 'woman' becomes a sign for the nation in imperial, independence and postcolonial nationalist discourses. Ray further argues that the figure of the woman is invoked as a stabilising mechanism by means of which national identities and notions of unitary national cultures – destabilised in recent times by postmodernist reconfigurations of culture as influenced by transnational elements – are consolidated. Chatterjee (1993) further cautions that woman-as-sign of the nation is often also deployed by colonial discourses as part of their 'civilising mission' through, in the case of India, ostensibly seeking to protect Indian women from atrocities committed by indigenous men in the name of culture or religion. In other words, in the formulation of Spivak, colonial logic often deploys woman as sign of the nation in order to justify white men's acts of violence against brown men as 'saving brown women from brown men' (Spivak, 2001). acts of violence against brown men.

Feminist critic Elleke Boehmer has pointed to the ways in which patriarchy and nationalism buttress each another. Boehmer (1991, 7) argues that 'two mutually reinforcing cases can be made for the relationship between patriarchy and nationalism. The first identifies in both nationalism and patriarchy a unitary, monologic vision, a tendency to authorise homogenising perceptions and social structures and to suppress plurality. Nationalism, like patriarchy, favours singleness.' Since national identity is overwhelmingly gendered male, excluding women from constructs of national identity, Boehmer (1991, 9) contends that, for women, writing can be a way of fracturing this exclusive masculinist conception of national identity: 'In writing, women express their own reality and so question received notions of national character and experience.'

I have focused here on certain canonical theories of nationalism and nation formation, as well as important epistemological interventions generated by feminist theorists who have examined women and gender in relation to narratives of the nation. Most male theorists have been rightly faulted for the scant attention they pay to the way nationalism interpellates and utilises women as sign for the nation, and feminist theory has sought to redress this lacuna. Furthermore, most discussions about nation centre around either western or postcolonial nations, the latter category of nations having attained independence from various imperial forces during the twentieth century, with their heterogeneity subsumed under the rubric of 'the postcolonial', 'the third world' or 'the developing world'. However, theories of the nation, and the relationships of women to various nationalisms, sit especially uneasily in relation to a country like South Africa, until fairly recently marked by legislated racial separation and discrimination.

The nascent South African nation first coalesced when the British parliament passed the South Africa Act in 1909, creating the Union of South Africa in 1910 from the British colonies of the Cape of Good Hope and Natal, together with the Orange River Colony and the Transvaal (the two latter colonies were former Boer Republics, occupied and annexed by Britain after the second Anglo-Boer War). The Act, and the Union it created, entrenched white settler political and economic dominion over black populations, thereby setting up white South Africa to produce the 1913 Natives Land Act, which in turn dispossessed the vast majority of black South Africans of their land. While South Africa achieved 'independence' from Britain by becoming a Republic in 1961, this independence had, as its defining characteristic, the ideology of apartheid, whose policies rendered the majority of South Africans non-citizens on the basis of race. The nation formed in 1961 thus defined itself through exclusion of the majority from citizenship, thus strengthening white hegemony and enabling the extreme economic exploitation of people categorised as African, Indian or coloured.

The existence of the apartheid nation founded, in one sense, on the 1913 Land Act that disqualified all African people from owning land, throws into relief a number of questions about nations, nationalisms and postcolonialism. Could apartheid South Africa be considered a postcolonial state? What sort of a postcolonial nation was a country that based nationhood on the exclusion of the majority of subjects living within its geographical boundaries? Did the disenfranchised constitute 'nations within a nation'? Is present-day South Africa – arguably rid of the scourge of formal apartheid – a postcolonial or merely a post-apartheid state? How do conflicting, oppositional strains of nationalism, as constructed by the apartheid government and the anti-apartheid liberation movements, shape the nation today? And, most significantly, how are women positioned in relation to the ascension of African nationalisms as metanarrative of South African society and the waning hegemony of white nationalisms? How does the nation-building project (which in 1994 styled South Africa as the 'Rainbow Nation' – Archbishop Desmond Tutu's post-apartheid coinage) and its political economy deploy women as the signs of this multicultural society? How have black women conceived of the nation, inserted themselves into the national discourse, and reimagined the nation in their writing?

This study seeks to answer some of these questions, using the lens of black women's fiction to interrogate the notion of the nation. The feminist works mentioned above are especially helpful in pondering how nationalisms deploy and designate women. My concern here, however, is the corollary of this examination: it is, rather, the way subaltern women, those doubly disavowed in South Africa by apartheid on the grounds of their race and gender, have constructed the nation through representations of themselves, their realities, and the nation in both apartheid and post-apartheid South Africa. The focus here is not on imaginings or constructions of women by dominant imperialist or nationalist discourses: instead, it inverts this focus to examine how such women read their nation/nationlessness, and imagine that nation through counter-narratives. Since apartheid rendered black women essentially without a nation, making them exiles within their own country, I focus on the ways in which black women writers inscribed the nation and made sense of their position in it.

This book privileges the novel in English as a form of narrating the nation. I argue that the novels written by black South African women, examined here, represent what Gayatri Spivak terms the 'subaltern speaking', even though such speaking, entailing 'a distanced decipherment by another, which is, at best, an interception', was not always heard by those in power (Spivak 2001, 2207).

Race and subjectivity: defining black women

Deconstructing and unravelling the various rudiments of identity, especially in a country burdened by centuries of institutionalised racism, is a project fraught with complexity. Identity, always fluid and dynamic, 'measured' or defined, represents, at best, a momentary freeze-frame, a composite of experience and subjectivity as temporal as the moment in which it is defined. For black (American) feminist theorists (Crenshaw 1989; hooks 1990; Collins 1990; Davies 1994; Zinn and Dill 1996) the multiple interwoven strands in black women's identity – race, gender, class, sexuality and location – are not easily untangled for scrutiny: these markers intersect to delineate and circumscribe the realities, experiences and opportunities for actualisation in black women's lives. Gendered identities cannot be examined without noting the intersectionality (Crenshaw 1989) of gender with race, class and sexuality; an analysis of racial identity would fall short if it did not interrogate the various differences in the material conditions experienced by women writers.

My examination of race departs from the ideological standpoint that race and racial categories are socially constructed. I use the signifier 'black' to incorporate the work of women categorised African, Indian and coloured under apartheid taxonomies. The use of the term 'black' as a racial and identity marker gained currency as a political and descriptive term in the United States, the United Kingdom, the Caribbean and South Africa during the 1960s and 1970s, when it was used to assert a subversive black identity. As Davies (1994, 6) points out, 'In most contexts, the term "black" resonated unabashed acceptance of African identity, located in history and culture ("blackness") as powerful or beautiful in a world of cloying, annihilating whiteness.' The term 'black' as a marker of identity gained credence in South Africa during the late 1960s and 1970s through the Black Consciousness Movement, spearheaded by the charismatic leader, Steve Biko. It was in 1971 that Biko (1978, 12–13) first proposed the adoption of a radical black identity as the antithesis to white racism:

> Being Black is not a matter of pigmentation – being Black is a reflection of a mental attitude … By merely describing yourself as Black you have started on a road towards emancipation, you have committed yourself to fight against all forces that seek to use your blackness as a stamp that marks you out as a subservient being.

Biko's proposition was an attempt to galvanise and unite oppressed South Africans against the divide-and-rule strategy of the apartheid regime effected by the promulgation of the Population Registration Act of 1950, which subjected all South Africans to racial classification as determined by the apartheid government. This strategy confined black people to the constructed racial categories African, Indian and coloured, and restricted people thus classified to living within prescribed geographical locations. Social, sexual and marital interaction between these 'races' was criminalised.

A large part of the segregation project was to 'divide and rule' black South Africans. Accordingly, the non-white population was categorised into three separate, legally constituted races: the category African, subdivided into eight separate ethnicities; Asiatics, or people of Asian descent, including Indians; and coloureds, descendants of the indigenous first people, various enslaved peoples, as well as Africans, who were constructed as mixed-race. This racial taxonomy was also hierarchical, so that the white race was seen as the pinnacle of humanity, with Africans ranked lowest, and Asiatics and coloureds positioned somewhere between these two racial categories.

Because the South African racial category 'coloured' is heterogenous and highly contested, I briefly discuss here the origins of the term and the group it represents. Mohamed Adhikari (2005, 2) notes that in the period following the end of formal British slavery at the Cape in 1838, 'coloured' identity started forming when the heterogeneous labouring class in the Cape Colony cohered around shared socioeconomic status, with assimilation into the lower ranks of colonial society at the Cape:

> The emergence of a fully fledged Coloured identity as we know it today was precipitated in the late nineteenth century by the sweeping social changes that came in the wake of the mineral revolution. Not only did significant numbers of Africans start coming to the Western Cape from the 1870s onwards but assimilated colonial blacks and a wide variety of African people who had recently been incorporated into the capitalist economy were thrust together in the highly competitive environment of the newly established mining towns. These developments drove acculturated colonial blacks to assert a separate identity in order to claim a position of relative privilege to Africans on the basis of their closer assimilation to Western culture and being partly descended from European colonists.

What Adhikari's research shows is the formation of a highly fluid racial and cultural identity, shaped by political, social and economic forces, in the crucible of a rapidly intensifying capitalist economy during the decades following the end of legal slavery at the Cape. The category 'coloured' was further forged by political exclusion during the first half of the twentieth century in the Cape– such as the denial of the right of coloured people to be elected to the parliament of the Union of South Africa– and finally solidified into a legal identity by apartheid law in the 1950s.

The category was thus legally constructed, through the Population Registration Act, to position coloureds as 'not white enough to be white and not black enough to be black' (De la Rey and Boonzaier 2002, 80). Economic and social privileges were embedded within this hierarchical taxonomy: coloureds, for example, had less freedom of movement or political freedom, as well as fewer educational opportunities, than whites, but were relatively well off compared to Africans, whose lives were far more viciously circumscribed by apartheid laws. Though both the African and coloured groups were disadvantaged and oppressed by apartheid policy, coloureds experienced certain forms of privilege, such as employment preferences in certain low- and unskilled forms of labour. Creating the racial category coloured thus resulted in social and psychological alienation from other 'races', producing the borderland of a racial identity neither white nor black – privileged, but with no claim to citizenship or rights. It was in an attempt to transcend these divisive apartheid identities that Biko and the Black Consciousness Movement proffered the ideal of a unified, politically conscious, activist black identity.

Racial identity has become much more fluid in post-apartheid South Africa. Yet Nthabiseng Motsemme (2002, 647) points out that while the collapse of apartheid has opened up 'spaces for new identities to be negotiated and created', it is also the case that 'the collapse of the meta-narrative of apartheid has called historically and politically-defined identities into crisis' (2002, 673). This 'crisis of identity' has manifested itself in many ways. In a study examining the way black women gender activists in the Western Cape subjectively experience race, Cheryl De la Rey and Floretta Boonzaier (2002, 77) have found that divisions fostered by apartheid race categorisation linger on, and that 'contemporary experiences of division between coloureds and Africans in the Western Cape are remnants of apartheid strategies and policies that explicitly sought to divide black South Africans'.

Writing on coloured identity in the 'new' South Africa, Zoë Wicomb points to the ways in which many coloured people, who had previously disavowed the term, have begun to reassert collective coloured identity as a vehicle for making citizenship demands from the state. Though coloureds were consigned to a liminal racial identity during the years of apartheid they – ironically – embraced this identity as political emancipation became a reality for South Africans of all races. In doing so, many coloureds have continued to inhabit a space of racial liminality, with many constructing racial identity in relation to lack: not white, not black. In her introduction to *Coloured by History, Shaped by Place: New*

Perspectives on Coloured Identities in Cape Town, Zimitri Erasmus (2001, 18) points out that, in post-apartheid South Africa, this liminality has often manifested itself in a coloured discourse of disavowal and exclusion, and a conceptualisation of coloured identity as 'residual'. Erasmus (2001, 21–22) argues for the reconceptualisation of coloured identity beyond such notions, positing that these identities need to be reimagined as 'cultural identities comprising detailed bodies of knowledge, specific cultural practices, memories, rituals and modes of being', and understood as a 'creolised cultural identity'.

In a similar manner, the South African racial category Indian, which had its genesis in the arrival of Indian indentured labourers in Natal from 1860, has had its heterogeneity flattened through colonial and apartheid racial classification. Arushani Govender (2019) sees the racial category 'South African Indian' as reductive of the heterogeneity of the contemporary population so named or self-identifying as such. For Thomas Hansen (2013, 203), Indian identity is indelibly inflected by various systems of oppression which have been imposed on this community since 1860:

> Indians in South Africa remain ... 'in suspension' – in a provisional and indeterminate space: with a history of forced removals, non-recognition, of economic success against many odds; of being at the mercy of powerful forces beyond their own control ...

In examining the reconstitution of racial identity in post-apartheid South Africa, Gqola (2003, 74) points also to the appropriation of 'trendy Blackness' by certain white South Africans, who linguistically appropriate black culture, and, in the 'new' South Africa, attempt to link their identities ancestrally to blackness. Such attempts foreclose the possibility of reckoning with South Africa's past, and redressing social injustices that continue to flow from apartheid:

> These fashionable and opportunistic white appropriations of Blackness in South Africa trivialise precisely what they ostensibly celebrate. In conflating Africanness, Blackness and linked

identities with the presence of an aboriginal African ancestor, they depoliticise race and ahistoricise power relations. They undermine the discursive social and political constructions of race. In this manner, attempts by progressive white and Black South Africans to meaningfully come to terms with the country's racial past in order to forge forward are thwarted. (Gqola 2003, 74)

Additionally, Erasmus (2001, 20) warns of the dangers of 'rainbow nationalism', which, as an ideology eager to build a united new South Africa, reads all South African racialised identities as merely 'different', thus depoliticising and ahistoricising the ways in which these identities were deployed at different political and historical moments.

The term 'black' (as with other racial categorisations in post-apartheid South Africa) thus remains a contested one in contemporary South African culture. Although its meanings are fluid, there is a danger of expediently appropriating blackness as a means of flattening out the complexities of inequality that is apartheid's legacy. As Erasmus (2001) warns, identifying colouredness as blackness may deny complicity with apartheid hierarchical racial taxonomies, from which those categorised coloured indisputably benefited. However, in examining women's work here, I am not yet prepared to forsake the signifier 'black'. My use of the term 'black' in this examination of the literature of black South African women writers subsumes coloured, Indian and African identities. I thereby follow on from the Black Consciousness politics of Steve Biko as a way of categorising the work of a group of women whose voices and artistic expression were invisibilised by the apartheid metanarrative of white supremacy. Given the small number of women not categorised as white, who were able to write and publish fiction in South Africa's recent past, it makes analytic sense to group the works of some of the most important counter-hegemonic women writers under the rubric 'black women's writing'. However, while 'black' here is used as an analytical category to group together the literature of subaltern South African women in a distinct body of work, this project attempts also to attend to the heterogeneity of these writers by applying an intersectional analysis to their lives.

Fredric Jameson (1971, 404) has argued that part of the work of a critic involves uncovering meanings that lie beneath the censorship and omissions of the dominant culture: 'The process of criticism is not so much an interpretation of content as it is a revealing of it, a laying bare, a restoration of the original message, the original experience beneath the distortions of the various kinds of censorship that have been put upon it.' *And Wrote My Story Anyway* aims to 'lay bare' or make visible the works of black women whose literary production has been ignored by androcentric and racist critical traditions in South African literature. The project aims to chart a historiography of black women's fiction in South Africa, tracing their writing mainly through the genre of the novel.

Gay Wilentz (1992, xiii) argues that 'committed critics of oppressed people's literatures agree that we cannot separate the literature from the historical or cultural context in which it was written'. Locating the production of literature within its historical, political and cultural contexts requires an interdisciplinary approach which relies not only upon reading, analysing and interpreting texts, but also upon an excavation of the material conditions under which such texts were produced. To this end, my analysis examines historical events and the impact of these events upon the lives of the writers included in this study.

The scope of this book is limited in two particular ways. First, I focus mainly on novels, and to a lesser extent, short stories, produced in English. While black women writers have written and published in indigenous South African languages, most of the literature they produced during apartheid centred on exposing the inhumanity of the system to an outside audience of anti-apartheid sympathisers and exiled South Africans. South African feminist critic Desiree Lewis (2001, 163) has argued that many narrations of the nation during the 1970s and 1980s, most notably life histories of black women, were explicitly published and circulated to 'codify, distribute and in certain cases produce mediating and testimonial texts that could effectively transmit the stories of apartheid to readers who were physically, politically and culturally very far away from it'. It is my contention that novels by black South African women published during the 1980s and 1990s served a similar purpose of explicating black women's lives under the apartheid system, and raising awareness within a national and international community about the effects of apartheid. Thus, the majority of such fiction was written and published in English to make it accessible to audiences on a global scale. I therefore examine only English-language novels, as these are most likely to have been written with the intention of reaching the largest possible audience.

The second limitation follows from my decision to focus mainly on the genre of the novel. While examples of plays, protest poetry and short fiction abound in the apartheid and post-apartheid era, my analysis focuses primarily on novels. One exception to this is the analysis of Agnes Sam's collection of short stories in Chapter Three. There, I focus specifically on the short story 'Jesus is Indian', since its engagement with and production of South African Indian girlhood and subjectivity is almost unparalleled in its texture and richness. It is a literary first which theorises girlhood and intricately sketches the interiority of a girl negotiating multiple sites of oppression.

The rest of this book focuses exclusively on novels. In *Culture and Imperialism*, Said (1994, xii) argues that the eighteenth-century European novel was 'immensely important in the formation of imperial attitudes, references and experiences'. For Britain and France, in particular, novelistic narrations served the function of buttressing the nation as well as its expansion into 'other' spaces. In addition, the narratives by which such expansions were justified became part of a 'novelistic process' (Said 1994, xii), so that 'the novel's consolidation of [national] authority is not simply connected to the functioning of social power and governance, but made to appear both normative and sovereign, that is, self-validating in the course of the narrative' (Said 1994, 77).

From discussions with some of the writers whose work features in this book, the novel as a genre might be said to have chosen them – thereby propelling their writing. Miriam Tlali (interview, 2006), for example, shared with me that she'd never consciously chosen the form for her first published work, *Muriel at Metropolitan*: 'I had a lot to say ... and I didn't care to write a short story.' The novel form enabled her to transform a story that was autobiographical, to embroider on its events and enlarge its cast of characters. Similarly, while Lauretta Ngcobo had previously written some poetry and prose, her foray into serious writing came in the form of a novel, as she made clear during my interview with her:

> A novel allows you space to say, right, this happened. If it hadn't happened, what else could have happened? What could I have done, what could have happened if it didn't happen that way? What else? I could have two, three, four alternative narratives. When a memory or an event takes place, I have a way of exploring other possibilities. (Ngcobo interview, 2006)

In privileging black women's novelistic outputs within the broader South African literary tradition, I examine how those most oppressed within a nation conceive of that space, and construct counter-discourses from a subaltern position. In choosing the novel as the primary unit of analysis, I model my work somewhat on Gay Wilentz's comparative study of African and African-American women writers. Wilentz (1992, xvi–xvii) holds that these two forms 'are the most approachable in terms of reconstructing social values and as vehicles for social change; moreover, the world represented in these forms often reflects the culture in more direct ways than in forms such as poetry'. The black woman's novel thus provides a fruitful vehicle for analysing discourses that simultaneously construct and fracture dominant nation-building narratives.

The novel, as produced by black women especially during apartheid, can also be conceived of as an engagement with modernity. Consider the following passage from Miriam Tlali's pioneering novel, *Muriel at Metropolitan*:

> 'Yes, we Africans are undergoing change,' I replied. 'We are fast acquiring the white man's way of life – we have to in order to fit into this modern world. As different tribes in the past we had a few cultural differences, but these minor distinctions are a thing of the past. They may be put down on record and preserved, stored away in the museums and archives so that coming generations may read about them and know them, but they now belong to

an age we shall never go back to, an age we cannot go back to whether we like it or not.' (1975, 44)

Rendered through her title character, Muriel, Tlali here indicates black women's inextricable imbrication within modernity. Though other black women writers, specifically Ngcobo, also valued oral traditions, Tlali's position makes clear the intractability of a writerly embeddedness within modernity, and shows an urgency to engage with it so as to leave a legacy in written, published form.

Ngcobo (1987, ix) declares: 'Black women have always been involved in the creation and performance of our literature ... We have been writing for a long time; it is now that these writings are beginning to come into the open.' She, too, references this engagement with modernity as a mode of expression which black women writers must inevitably embrace if they do not wish to be further silenced by the narrativisation of a history replete with androcentrism and racism.

The novels and their synergies

Chapter One of this book locates black South African women writers within their place and time in South African history. I chart the ways in which the apartheid policy and its major laws affected women's lives politically and economically. I also locate black women's resistance to these policies, and review their literary production during this period as a form of resistance to apartheid.

Chapter Two considers the ways in which Miriam Tlali and Lauretta Ngcobo reimagine and reconfigure space, and, by extension, the nation, in their pathbreaking novels, *Muriel at Metropolitan* (1975) and *And They Didn't Die* (1990). I demonstrate how Tlali and Ngcobo both use space in these novels as a means to 'write' the nation from a subaltern standpoint. Both of these iterations of the nation-space offer readers new ways of reading and understanding the nation as a space that is not only racialised, but also gendered in very specific ways.

Chapter Three examines daughterhood and female Indian subjectivity during apartheid through the fiction of Farida Karodia and Agnes Sam. It pays particular attention to the ways in which contact with colonial power and the apartheid system positions young Indian women protagonists in *Daughters of the Twilight* (1986) and 'Jesus is Indian' (1989), and how the vantage point of the subaltern girl-child is used to critique the nascent nationalism of the soon-to-be 'new' South Africa. The chapter also illustrates how both Karodia and Sam attempt to make visible the history of Indians in South Africa, including the history of indentureship.

Ideologies and interpretations of motherhood are examined in Chapter Four, which critically explores Sindiwe Magona's *Mother to Mother* (1998) and her deployment of the subject position of motherhood to challenge emerging nationalist discourses. I argue that she strategically uses the partriarchally sanctioned authorial position of motherhood in order to subvert patriarchal, nationalist discourses. This chapter additionally offers an intertextual reading of Zoë Wicomb's *David's Story* (2000) and testimonies submitted to the South African Truth and Reconciliation Commission (TRC). It argues that Magona and Wicomb's novels each represent an important intervention into the ways in which the TRC processes constructed the women who testified before it as secondary victims of apartheid atrocities. Focusing on narratives of rape as produced by the TRC and by Wicomb's novel, I contend that *David's Story* interrogates and challenges the silences surrounding the treatment of women guerrillas by the ANC during the anti-apartheid struggle, effectively drawing attention to the omissions in public discourse around the ANC's treatment of women within its own military ranks.

Chapter Five examines a relatively new genre in black South African women's writing, the neo-slave narrative. Reading Yvette Christiansë's *Unconfessed* (2006) comparatively with Rayda Jacobs's *The Slave Book* (1998), I argue that these novels both point to the origins of the coloured population's presence in South Africa, using the nation's democratic rebirth as a way to reconstitute the shame that, it has been argued, often accompanies coloured identity.

In Chapter Six I examine Zukiswa Wanner and Kagiso Lesego Molope's engagement with black masculinities in their respective novels *Men of the South* (2010) and *This Book Betrays my Brother*

(2012), with a particular focus on their treatment of violent masculinities. I argue that both writers, in their critique of hegemonic black masculinities and domestic violence, propose alternative masculinities that are crucial for the development of a nation so far marred by unacceptably high levels of violence against women.

In conclusion, Chapter Seven offers a theory of black South African feminist criticism. I consolidate the ways in which black women's fiction could be regarded as theory, and thus constitutes a black South African feminist criticism while also offering the concept as an analytical lens for reading black women's fiction.

1

Writing as Activism: A History of Black South African Women's Writing

Black South African women's literary production should be under-stood within the wider political context which, in the period reviewed in this book, was dominated by apartheid. Though colonial South Africa was always racially segregated and marked, as with other colonial societies, by the exploitation of colonised bodies and the decimation of indigenous cultures and history, apartheid ideology became legally entrenched when the white Afrikaner National Party ascended to power in 1948. This chapter surveys South Africa's history during the twentieth century in relation to black women's literary production, focusing on the ways in which the apartheid doctrine and its policy of racial segregation affected black women's lives, both politically and as producers of writing. This history is structured in three broad sections: the segregation era, before formal apartheid (1910–1948); the apartheid era (1948–1990); and the post-apartheid era. For each historical period, I survey the laws and conditions that structured black South Africans' lives; docu-ment women's resistance to forms of injustice and oppression; and survey the types of literatures black women produced as a result of, and in reaction to, the prevailing political conditions.

While male critics and writers such as James Matthews, Njabulo Ndebele, Michael Chapman and Richard Rive, among others, have created taxonomies of black literary output during apartheid – the *Drum* School of writing of the 1950s, the protest literature of the late 1950s and 1960s, and Black Consciousness writing of the 1970s and 1980s, others have taken issue with the reductive nature of the concept of 'protest literature'. Writing in 1991, at the beginning of the transition to democracy, Mbulelo Mzamane asserted the following:

Now more than ever, it has become reductionist to categorise all African literature as protest. Protest literature is writing by the racially oppressed addressed to readers of the ruling class in an attempt to solicit their sympathy and support against discriminatory laws and practices ... Protest springs from a feeling of being a ward: it is the activity of apprentices, and it is the action of subordinates who see themselves as such. It is both solicitous and moderate. (In Narismulu 1998, 197)

I follow Mzamane by refusing to neatly situate early black women's writing within the 'protest' category, since the multivalence of their work addresses multiple aspects of black life. In any case, black women writers defy easy categorisation within these androcentric schemas.

Women were largely excluded from publishing in *Drum* magazine, one of the primary publication vehicles for black journalists and creative writers during the 1950s. Furthermore, black women's writing straddles the classificatory divide between protest literature – critiqued by Ndebele (1986) as overdetermined by the spectacle of apartheid – and the more nuanced interpretations of black life and interiority characteristic of Black Consciousness writing. Consequently, this book declines to rigidly compartmentalise black women's writing within certain literary and political periods. Instead, I aim to offer a chronological account of black women's literary output as informed and shaped by the broad political events of their times.

Black women's writing during the segregation era: 1910–1948

Although legally implemented during the 1940s and the 1950s, apartheid's genesis was a series of segregationist laws enacted earlier under British colonial rule. These laws include the South Africa Act passed by the British House of Commons in 1909, which in 1910 established the Union of South Africa. This Union was predicated upon the exclusion of black South Africans from citizenship, as the law which established it removed the limited parliamentary rights that a small section of the black population had held prior to its enactment. White political power was further buttressed by the Natives Land Act of 1913, which made it illegal for Africans to buy or lease land anywhere in South Africa, or live anywhere outside of specially designated reserves. The Act effectively secured over 80 per cent of South African land for whites, who made up less than 20 per cent of the population.

The African National Congress (ANC) became the primary extra-parliamentary opposition to these segregationist policies. Formed as an anti-colonial organisation in 1912 (then known as the African Native National Congress) in direct reaction to the formation of the Union of South Africa in 1910, the ANC was aimed chiefly at securing political and land rights for Africans who were disenfranchised, and would soon be systematically removed from their land.

During this period a number of male African intellectuals rose to prominence as writers. Sol T Plaatje's *Native Life in South Africa*, published in 1916, illuminated the devastation wrought by the Natives Land Act. Plaatje later published *Mhudi* (1930), an epic love story set against the historical backdrop of the war between the Ndebele and Baralong in the early nineteenth century. Written between 1917 and 1920 according to Laura Chrisman (1997), *Mhudi* was the first novel to be published by a black South African in English, though this would only occur in 1930. A year later, Thomas Mofolo's *Chaka*, a translation of the original Sesotho version of 1909, was published. Other prominent black male writers during the earlier half of the twentieth century include SEK Mqayi, JJR Jolobe, HIE Dhlomo, RRR Dhlomo, BW Vilakazi and AC Jordan, who formed part of an educated literary elite closely aligned with the then African Native National Congress (Chapman 1996). These writers were important precursors of, and influences upon, black women writers during the latter half of the century.

Though there was a dearth of published writing by black women during the pre-apartheid era, a number of black women's works written during this time have been excavated and re-recorded for posterity, thanks to the publication of the anthology *Women Writing Africa: The Southern Region* (Daymond et al. 2003). In an attempt to retrieve the often subsumed voices of South African women writers, the editors of the anthology gathered various oral and written forms of expression, such as political speeches, petitions, essays, court depositions, as well as oral and published poetry and storytelling. The editors point out that black women who expressed themselves in the public domain, whether in writing or speech, were generally able to do so through their membership of a relatively elite group who had gained literacy through colonial education.

The history of black South African women's literacy and education is not only complex but also contested. Christian missionaries were the first to offer black women limited access to formal education, steeping them in ideologies of domesticity and femininity, models of womanhood that were often unattainable to these women because of their race (Daymond et al. 2003, 25). Megan Healy-Clancy (2014), in her history of Inanda Seminary, a mission school for African girls, shows how the school was founded by missionaries to provide suitable wives for mission-educated African men – wives who would be good domestic companions as well as mothers. Employment opportunities for these women were, in the late 1800s, confined to teaching or domestic work. An example of the gendered ideologies produced by mission schools is provided in Phyllis Ntantala's autobiography, *A Life's Mosaic* (1993): having grown up to be an intellectual, Ntantala (1993, 30) describes the colonial education she received as a young girl in the 1920s at a school at Colosa in the Eastern Cape as 'brainwashing'.

Mission education accounts, in part, for what is considered the first publication of a black woman's writing in South Africa: Adelaide Dube's poem, 'Africa My Native Land', in the Zulu language newspaper, *Ilanga Lase Natal* (Daymond et al. 2003, 161). Published in 1913, the year of the Natives Land Act, the poem laments Africans' loss of access to their ancestral land.

In print, the earliest body of poetry by a black woman is the work of Nontsizi Mgqwetho, a migrant from the Eastern Cape to Johannesburg, who, from 1920 to 1929, produced a substantial corpus of poetry in isiXhosa in the Johannesburg-based newspaper, *Umteteli wa Bantu*. Her poems were overtly political, commenting on politics within the African Native National Congress, and containing appeals for black solidarity in the face of white oppression (Daymond et al. 2003, 176). Translations of her *Umteteli* poems, collected by Jeff Opland and published in 2007 as *The Nation's Bounty: The Xhosa Poetry of Nontsizi Mgqwetho*, marked a radical departure from the oral modes of black women's composition and expression of poetry.

Black women also published novels and novellas in isiXhosa during the early twentieth century. The earliest of these were Lillith Kakaza's *Intyantyambo Yomzi* (1913) and *UThandiwe wakwaGcaleka* (1914); the latter is the first known novel written by a woman in isiXhosa. Another such work is Victoria Swartbooi's novella, *UMandisa*, published in 1934, which emphasises the importance of ubuntu through the coming-of-age story of Mandisa, the protagonist (Daymond et al. 2003, 206). *UMandisa* has been hailed as a proto-feminist novel: Hoza (2012, 63), for example, reads it as a 'self-consciously crafted feminist-oriented novel', while for Daymond et al., it offers an alternative vision of Xhosa femininity – one that prizes education for women over marriage and immersion into patriarchal culture.

Black women's political resistance during apartheid: 1948–1990

The introduction of formal, legislated apartheid by the National Party in 1948 significantly thwarted the development of a black literary tradition. After coming to power, the National Party government instituted a number of laws that entrenched white economic and political hegemony, disenfranchised all black South Africans, and legitimated the continued exploitation of black South African labour. White economic privilege and political power were entrenched through a series of segregationist laws enacted between 1948 and the early 1950s. The notion of white superiority was central to the ideology and workings of apartheid. The Bantu Education Act of 1953, for example, aimed, in the words of Prime Minister Hendrik Verwoerd, to

> reform [education] so that Natives will be taught from childhood that equality with Europeans is not for them ... Racial relations cannot improve if the wrong type of education is given to

Natives. They cannot improve if the result of Native Education is the result of frustrated people who have expectations in life which circumstances in South Africa do not allow to be fulfilled. (In Wheeler 1961, 250)

Other primary laws buttressing apartheid included the Population Registration Act of 1950, which required all South Africans to be classified into four broad racial groups: 'Europeans, Asiatics, persons of mixed race or coloureds, and "natives" or "pure blooded individuals of the Bantu race"' (Bowker and Star 1999, 197). The Group Areas Act of 1950 determined where people were allowed to work and live, based on their racial classification. Another key law upholding apartheid was the 1951 Bantu Authorities Act, which created separate homelands or reserves where Africans were forced to live, and dispossessed them of land outside these areas. The 1950 Suppression of Communism Act outlawed the Communist Party of South Africa and gave the government the authority to ban publications supportive of communism. This law became one of the key mechanisms for suppressing information and banning literary and other writing opposed to apartheid, which was automatically classified as supportive of communism.

Black women felt apartheid's devastation in uniquely gendered ways. In 1952, the government passed what were arguably the two most detrimental pieces of legislation to African women. Commonly known as the 'pass laws', the first was the Native Laws Amendment Act, which made it illegal for any African person to be in an urban area for more than 72 hours ('Effects of Apartheid', 1980) unless they had legal permission, had previously lived there continuously for more than fifteen years, and had worked for one employer for more than ten years. This law was specifically aimed at bolstering the existing 'influx control' policy, which set out to halt the urbanisation of African women by confining them to the rural reserves.

The second such law was the 1952 Natives Abolition of Passes and Coordination of Documents Act (The Role of Women in the Struggle, 1980). Until this point, South African law required all African men over the age of 16 to carry passes, which legally enabled them to work and move around in urban areas. Contrary to what its name – Abolition of Passes – suggests, the law's intention was to extend control by issuing reference books containing personal details. It eventually extended the compulsory carrying of passes to African women in 1956. Until this law was passed, African women had been exempt from carrying passes in urban areas. The Union government had once before, in 1913 in the Orange Free State province, tried to impose passes on women, but was met with fierce resistance and was forced to shelve the plan.

The extension of these pass laws to women meant the destruction of African family life, since African men who were needed as cheap labour in the cities now had to leave their families behind in the reserves. The 1952 Act meant that African women could not join or live with their husbands in urban areas. Women were confined to the rural reserves designated 'homelands' by the government. There, the apartheid state expected them to survive as subsistence farmers, care for the elderly and their children, and produce future labourers (Meer 1985).

The African National Congress and aligned organisations vehemently resisted all such legislated segregation. In 1952, the ANC and the South African Indian Council initiated the Defiance Campaign in reaction to the amended pass laws and other discriminatory legislation. Politically active black women responded in a gendered way to these apartheid mechanisms and the oppressive structures they produced. Politicised by the two pass law amendments and their implications, black women became increasingly involved in the ANC Women's League formed in 1943 to involve women more formally in Congress activities. In response to the threat of the extension of the pass laws to African women, women of all races came together in 1954 and founded the Federation of South African Women (FSAW), South Africa's first autonomous national women's organisation.

Chaired at its inception by Ida Mntwana, the federation authored the Women's Charter, whose stated aim was 'striving for the removal of all laws, regulations conventions and customs that discriminate against us as women, and that deprive us in any way of our inherent right to the advantages, responsibilities and opportunities that society offers to any one section of the population' (FSAW 1954). In 1956, FSAW initiated the largest women's protest against the extension of the pass laws to African women. On 9 August 1956, 20 000 women of all races from around the country marched to the apartheid government's seat of power, the Union Buildings in the capital city, Pretoria. The women's petition not only opposed the extension of passes to women, but demanded the repeal of all pass laws, including those circumscribing the movements of African men.

In addition to this massive protest, FSAW also initiated key campaigns such as the sustained protest against compulsory passes for African women; bus boycotts, which were successful in lowering transportation costs for workers; and protests against sub-standard housing for black South Africans. With a membership of approximately 230 000, FSAW mobilised women nationally for key demonstrations and campaigns, and placed women's demands for adequate housing, just labour laws, access to education, and the abolition of the pass system within the framework of the struggle for black political rights. Despite FSAW's resistance and political action, the South African government continued to issue passes to African women. Given the dire consequences for women if they were found without passes – imprisonment and deportation back to their designated homelands – many had no choice but to acquiesce to the pass laws. However, despite widespread resistance, 75 per cent of all adult African women had, by 1960, been forced to carry passes (Schmidt 1983).

The year 1960 signalled a radical change in the way apartheid was administered, and how anti-apartheid activists responded to the state. While the government regularly imprisoned or banned its most vocal critics, until that year, organisations such as the ANC, FSAW and the ANC Women's League had been tolerated and allowed to operate as civil society organisations. But on 21 March 1960, apartheid police opened fire on a group of township activists peacefully protesting the pass laws in Sharpeville, killing 69 protestors, including 40 women and 8 children. About 80 per cent of those killed or injured were shot in the back ('Effects of Apartheid' 1980). Sharpeville marked a change in the nature of the government's response to anti-apartheid protesters. The ANC, the main liberation movement, was banned, and many of its leaders arrested under the first State of Emergency declared by the government.

Most of the leaders of FSAW, who were members of the ANC, were also banned, prohibiting them from appearing in public places, addressing groups of people or organising any political activities. Though FSAW itself was never banned, the imprisonment and banning of key leaders meant it could no longer function effectively. The only autonomous national movement for women thus stopped all political activity.

With no political base from which to organise, activist women continued to work within the ANC for social and political change. Given that the ANC had been driven underground, most women within the movement worked covertly, or joined the ANC outside the country during the 1960s and 1970s. While in exile, the ANC Women's League disbanded, and was replaced by the ANC's Women's Section, which had its headquarters in Lusaka and was politically headed by the Women's Secretariat (Hassim 2004). The role of the Women's Section in exile during this period was deemed mostly supportive, and 'functioned as a network of solidarity rather than as a mobilising agency' (Hassim 2004, 435).

From these precarious positions, activist women continued to demand a more just and inclusive society for South African women and men, even though these demands could not legally be voiced as public protest within South Africa. As apartheid became increasingly repressive during the 1960s and 1970s, conditions worsened, particularly for black women, who strategically adapted their resistance. On 16 June 1976, apartheid police again lashed out, this time at children protesting the introduction of Afrikaans as the compulsory language of instruction in schools. At least four children, including thirteen-year-old Hector Pieterson, were killed by police bullets, unleashing student riots across the country. In the ensuing violence, police killed over 1 000 black people – many of them children of school-going age. In the aftermath of the uprising, the South African police stepped up efforts to repress children's activism, since the youth were becoming increasingly militant in their demands for a free South Africa.

Apartheid's blatant brutality against children led a number of young black South African women to leave the country and join Umkhonto we Sizwe (MK), the ANC's military wing, which was engaged in guerrilla warfare against the state. Young women who

had witnessed the events of the 1976 uprising, or who were subsequently detained and tortured by police, led the influx into the
armed wing of the ANC. Makhosazana Njobe reported to exiled
ANC women that the 1976 massacres had led to a reinvigoration
of the struggle against apartheid, and that young women especially
were eager to participate as soldiers in the fight against apartheid.
Njobe (1978) warned the apartheid government that 'the 1956
babies [present at the pass law protest] are now 22 years and older.
When next the women come to the Union Buildings, [it] shall not
witness music by our women but sounds from the barrel of a gun.'

Despite the militant rhetoric circulating among exiles, inside
South Africa activists were severely curtailed in their responses to
the 1976 violence. Another round of arrests and bannings followed
the uprising, and among those arrested and detained in the aftermath of the 1976 killings were ANC leader Winnie Mandela;
sociologist and anti-apartheid activist Fatima Meer; Joyce Seroke
of the South African Young Women's Christian Association;
Sally Motlana, vice-president of the South African Council of
Churches; and Mamphela Ramphele, a medical doctor working
with rural women. Many of these women were also banned upon
their release from prison (Njobe 1978).

The 1976 violence increased black women's militancy and
resolve to end apartheid. But with virtually all political organisations
banned, and with many prominent leaders of the women's movement
either in prison or banned, most black women found it difficult to
organise themselves and work collectively against apartheid. The
methods employed by the apartheid state during the 1970s and
1980s determined to a large extent the type of resistance women
could offer. During the latter part of the 1970s and the early half of
the 1980s, increased apartheid repression meant that large, mass-
based protests such as those organised by FSAW in the 1950s were
rarely seen.

Black women's literary output during apartheid

The implementation of formal apartheid, including the oppression
and brutalisation of black citizens, severely curtailed the development of a black literary tradition. As playwright, novelist and

critic Richard Rive observed (1982, 14), the Suppression of Communism Act rendered South African writing in English 'virtually ... White by law'. As many as 146 black writers living abroad were banned in 1966 under the Suppression of Communism Act (Chapman 1996, 243).

Coupled with the Suppression of Communism Act and the 1953 Bantu Education Act, a third law curtailed the intellectual development of black South Africans: the Extension of University Education Act of 1959. This law prohibited black people from attending universities designated white, making it illegal for them to register at a previously open institution without the permission of the Minister of Internal Affairs. It proposed and eventually inaugurated separate tertiary institutions for different ethnic groups, effectively excluding the majority of the populace from tertiary education. The Act effectively excluded all but the elite from tertiary education, as educationist John Wheeler (1961, 248) graphically demonstrates:

> At the end of 1960, approximately 30 000 European students were attending the Universities of Stellenbosch, Witwatersrand, Cape Town, Rhodes, Natal, Potchefstroom, Orange Free State, Pretoria, and South Africa. In contrast, approximately 600 African, Coloured, and Indian students were attending Fort Hare University College ... At least 100 Africans, Coloureds, and Indians are permitted to take correspondence courses from the University of South Africa.

With the majority of black South Africans excluded from tertiary education and, consequently, the opportunity to publish, literary production was, for the majority, a domain almost impossible to access. Collectively, the Bantu Education Act, the Suppression of Communism Act, and the Extension of University Education Act account for the fact that, by the end of the 1980s, only six novels had been published by black South African women.

The 1960s and 1970s

Despite these extreme restrictions, black women wrote their stories anyway, choosing writing as one form of resistance to apartheid.

Autobiography predates full-length works of fiction published in English. Noni Jabavu, born in 1919, became the first black South African woman to publish book-length works in English in London. *Drawn in Colour: African Contrasts* (1960), an autobiography, was reprinted five times within its first year of publication, and was republished in the USA in 1961, as well as being translated into Italian (Xaba 2009). A follow-up autobiography, *The Ochre People: Scenes from a South African Life*, was published in 1963, the success of which 'put Noni way ahead of other women in the country of her birth' (Xaba 2009, 218).

For feminist critic Athambile Masola, Jabavu's work remains relevant to contemporary South Africa, especially to the lived experience and representation of black women. Masola (2017) argues that Jabavu is an important literary figure not merely because she was the 'first': 'her work is relevant because it continues to ask difficult questions about what it means to be human beyond the limitations and impositions of identity'.

In the realm of imaginative writing, 'Black women … [were] latecomers relative to black men as well as white writers' (Hunter 1994, 113). Bessie Head was the first black South African woman to publish a full-length novel in English, but significantly did so as an exile in Botswana. *When Rain Clouds Gather* appeared in 1968, followed by *Maru* in 1971, and *A Question of Power* in 1973. Head's subsequent works, which are all collections of short stories and essays, include *The Collector of Treasures and Other Botswana Village Tales* (1977); *Serowe: Village of the Rain Wind* (1981); *A Bewitched Crossroad: An African Saga* (1984); and *The Cardinals, With Meditations and Short Stories* (1993). Tellingly, Head was able to produce these novels only once she had left South Africa in 1964 on an exit permit which would permanently prohibit her return to the country of her birth. Head (1990, 61–62) described the effect of apartheid on her creativity as stultifying:

Twenty-seven years of my life was lived in South Africa but I have been unable to record this experience in any direct way, as a writer. A very disturbing problem is that we find ourselves born into a situation where people are separated into sharp racial groups. All the people tend to think only in the groups in which they are and one is irked by the artificial barriers. It is as though with all those divisions and signs, you end up with no people at all. The environment completely defeated me as a writer.

Head's description of her psychic space elucidates the extent to which black subjects, and black women in particular, were excluded not only from the spheres of citizenship and education, but also from the arena of literary creativity.

Head's work defies classification within black South African literary taxonomies. Richard Rive (1982) has delineated three major trends in black South African writing: 1) Early literature, produced between 1928 and 1942; 2) Protest literature, 1942 to 1970; and 3) Black Consciousness writing, 1976 to 1982. Early literature, produced by authors like Sol Plaatje and RRR Dhlomo, was produced during and before World War II, and consisted of writing that Rive (1982, 12) characterises as 'imitative of writing by Whites and tend[ing] to be stilted and banal. The chief motive behind its creation seemed to have been to impress on a patronising White readership the measure of sophistication achieved by the Black author.' The genre of choice for this period was the novel, with no short stories and very few critical essays produced. Literary production by black South Africans during this period was exclusively the province of men.

Protest literature, according to Rive, can be divided into two schools: the *Drum* School, which features black writing produced between 1942 and 1970, and the Soweto School of writing produced between 1971 and 1976. Writers from the *Drum* School were strongly influenced by the Harlem Renaissance, especially by writers such as Langston Hughes and Richard Wright. Rive (1982, 12) contended that the *Drum* School was 'defined loosely as writing by blacks describing their situation to Whites whom they felt had the power to effect change. Such an approach was essentially a negative one, a literature about victimization, but, unlike Liberal literature, written by the victim himself.'

Though Head was a contemporary of many of the *Drum* writers, and wrote for its subsidiary, *The Golden City Post* (MacKenzie 1990), she cannot be categorised as part of the *Drum* School of protest writing. In her earlier writing, Head differed in her choice of genre, the novel – a sign of the relative security and creative freedom she enjoyed outside of the borders of the apartheid state. In contrast, the genre of choice for most of the *Drum* School was the short story, which, says Rive (1982, 12), was easier to write 'by comparison with the novel which requires a much longer period and a more temperate political climate'. Protest writing was aimed at expounding the conditions of black life under apartheid and drawing attention to the indignities and hardship suffered by the oppressed majority. Head's work, by comparison, seems almost apolitical and was labelled as such by her contemporaries writing from within South Africa during this period of increased state repression. Her literary output, as characterised by her three novels, *When Rain Clouds Gather, Maru* and *A Question of Power*, paradoxically places the 'ordinary' – friendships, love triangles, communal cooperation, people's relationships with their neighbours and to the land – in the service of larger, universal themes; among these are the irrationality of racism, the dichotomy between good and evil, and the human being's relation to God, themes that transcend the narrow focus characteristic of South African protest writing.

Head's writing also broke with the masculinist 'Jim-comes-to-Jo'burg' tradition which was a feature of earlier black novels (Rive 1982, 13). This tradition, popularised by novelists like Peter Abrahams and AS Mopeli-Paulus, may be described as the black bildungsroman, where a boy from the country moves to a city (usually Johannesburg) and becomes a man, within the constraints of apartheid segregation. Head's writing transcends both the gendered and urban biases that had previously defined much black South African writing. Her novels unselfconsciously draw the focus away from the southern African city, which is spatially gendered male in black protest writing. All of her novels are set in small rural villages in Botswana, and emphasise the land, people's dependence on it and their relations to it. While Head's earlier novels – *When Rain Clouds Gather* and *Maru* – seem to privilege male experience, her female characters Margaret and Dikeledi in *Maru*, and especially Elizabeth in *A Question of Power*, carve out a discursive space for black southern African women where none had previously existed.

Women writers' narrativisation of black dispossession within South Africa continued with Miriam Tlali's publication of *Muriel at Metropolitan* in 1975. This was the first novel published in English by a black woman within the borders of the country and was quickly banned 'on the grounds of language derogatory to Afrikaners' (*Between Two Worlds* 2004, dust jacket). The novel is aimed largely at elucidating the labour conditions of black South Africans and crystallises the racist attitudes, demonstrated as the norm for this period, apparent in most white South Africans. In both tone and content – the detailed dissection of apartheid – the novel seems aimed at a white South African and international audience, though Tlali later noted that her 'prime responsibility' was 'the raising of the level of consciousness of blacks ... I must go deeper into them, their feelings, try to make them understand their hopes, desires and aspirations as a people' (Rolfes 1981, 63). The novel is path-breaking not only because it was the first to be published by a black woman in South Africa – it was also the first South African novel to locate its point of view from within the subjectivity of a black woman.

Black poet Gladys Thomas is another writer who gained prominence during the 1970s. One of her most significant works is the collection of poetry, *Cry Rage!*, which was jointly published with James Matthews in 1972. Thomas's poem, 'Fall Tomorrow', condemns the apartheid government's Group Areas Act of 1950, legislation that resulted in the forced removal of hundreds of thousands of 'non-white' South Africans from suburbs that were now reserved as white residential areas. Focusing on the ensuing chaos wrought upon family structures and the destruction of communities, Thomas notes the dehumanisation implicit in such apartheid laws:

Let our sons dazed in eye
rape and steal
for they are not allowed to feel.
Let our men drink,
let them fight,
let what is said about them
then be right,
for they are not allowed to think. (In Daymond et al. 2003, 335)

The poem, which predicts the fall of apartheid, is one of Thomas's best-known works: 'You that remade us/ your mould will break/ and tomorrow you are going to fall!' (in Daymond et al. 2003, 335) It also poignantly foreshadows the criminality and, particularly, the sexual violence that would become part of the post-apartheid social fabric, and that can be attributed to the brutalising and dehumanising effect on black subjects of the apartheid policy. *Cry Rage!* was immediately banned upon publication, thus becoming the first anthology of poetry to be censored. Thomas would go on to become a significant voice against the apartheid regime, with her 1987 play *Avalon Court: Vignettes in the Life of the 'Coloured' People on the Cape Flats of Cape Town* becoming a major indictment of the Group Areas Act.

Black protest theatre became another avenue where black women could present their writing to a larger audience during the 1970s and 1980s. Fatima Dike wrote and staged two plays during the late 1970s: *The Sacrifice of Kreli*, performed at the Space Theatre in Cape Town in 1976, and *The First South African*, staged at the Space Theatre in 1977 and published by Ravan Press in 1979. Dike started writing plays after witnessing the aftermath of a particularly brutal child rape and murder in Guguletu in 1975; as she recalls: 'I had something to say to my people for that' (Gray 1980, 157). After working at the Space Theatre as a stage manager for a year, Dike started writing plays in 1976, and soon thereafter produced *The Sacrifice of Kreli*. Based on events surrounding the ninth frontier war between the British and the Gcaleka people in the eastern Cape towards the end of the nineteenth century, *The Sacrifice of Kreli* centres on the political drama surrounding the exiled king of the Gcaleka, Kreli, who died in 1902. Dike was motivated to write the play in order to restore a sense of pride in black history:

[W]hat made me write this play is that one day I woke up and realised that there were eighteen million black people in this country who had no past, because whatever past we had as a nation was oral history – it was not written down; and it was wiped out by the written history which the white people in South Africa had written against what we had to say. And when I discovered this I realized that here was a part of my history, my past. From then onwards I felt if I had a past, a present, I could also have a future. (In Gray 1980, 159)

Dike was able to stage the elaborate play with the help of a patron who spent around R15 000 (a substantial sum at the time) on the production. From there, she soon went on to write and stage *The First South African* at the Space Theatre. Pointing to the absurdity of apartheid race classification, the play dramatised the true story of a man born to a black mother and a white father, who looked like a white man, but lived in a township, Langa, and spoke isiXhosa. In an interview, Dike indicated that, although she had experienced many hardships as a black woman, she would never exchange the hardships of her life for the luxury and finery to which whites had access. She went on to conceptualise the liberatory nature of a black South African woman who dares to create through writing, even under the most oppressive of conditions: 'I do not feel in any way that I am deprived of anything, because I've freed myself from that. Because, you know, I have my writing – I can do anything with my writing. Nobody can ever take my writing away from me; I've got that' (in Gray 1980, 163).

The 1970s also saw the publication of one of the first autobiographies by a black woman in English, Joyce Sikakane's *A Window on Soweto* (1977), published by the International Defence and Aid Fund in London. The narrative describes life in Soweto from a detached point of view, without immediately using the first-person 'I' to enrich description. Sikakane describes a general day-in-the-life of a Soweto resident, and only later touches on her own family history and her exile. Carole Boyce Davies, writing on black women's autobiography transnationally, reads this mode of narration as constructing a 'self synonymous with political struggle' (Davies 1991, 279), thereby decentring the individuality of the woman telling the story and focusing on larger political explication.

The 1980s

This decade saw the publication of six book-length works of fiction by black women writers: Miriam Tlali's *Amandla* (1980); Lauretta Ngcobo's *Cross of Gold* (1981); Farida Karodia's *Daughters of the Twilight* (1986) and *Coming Home and Other Stories* (1988); Zoë Wicomb's short story collection, *You Can't Get Lost in Cape Town* (1987); and Agnes Sam's *Jesus is Indian and Other Stories* (1989). Diane Case's young adult novel, *Love, David* (1986), also appeared. This paucity of writing caused Ngcobo (1989, ix) to note in her introduction to Tlali's *Soweto Stories*: 'A South African woman writer in the 1980s is a rare find.' Ngcobo (1989, xv) saw Tlali as 'part of an important band of [black] women' brave enough to hold and express an opinion: 'She dared not only to speak out against the South African system, but also against the dominance of male writing, which had attended black literature from the very beginning. She struck out bold and fearless.'

Tlali's second novel, *Amandla* (1980), a graphic depiction of the Soweto uprising of 1976, was also banned. *Amandla* differed significantly from Tlali's first novel in style, tone and pace. Where *Muriel at Metropolitan* tightly narrates the constricted, claustrophobic space of an apartheid furniture store to demonstrate the day-to-day workings and humiliations of apartheid, *Amandla* is at once an intimate, expansive and polyvocal rendering of the 1976 student uprising. Steeped in Black Consciousness ideology, *Amandla* follows the student leader, Pholoso, as he survives the police shootings of 16 June, goes underground to conscientise young people about disciplined militant opposition to apartheid, is arrested and tortured in prison, and eventually flees South Africa for Swaziland.

Much more militant in tone than her previous novel, *Amandla* employs a radically different style. Through the figure of Pholoso, Tlali shows how 'the revolution is spearheaded by ... the youth' (134), and likens the struggle against apartheid to the biblical narrative of the Israelites' persecution while enslaved in Egypt. Despite the centrality of Pholoso as heroic freedom fighter and saviour of the nation, the voices and experiences of other characters are clearly heard as they narrate the uprising and its aftermath. The most significant of these are women like Felleng, Pholoso's girlfriend; his grandmother, Mumsy; and Nana, a beloved aunt. These women and their musings are often vehicles for illustrating the precariousness of black womanhood within the liberation struggle and Black Consciousness discourse, with Tlali demonstrating the difficulties black women encountered in negotiating the unique forms of racism and sexism generated by apartheid during the volatile 1970s.

In assessing Black Consciousness as an ideology and a movement that fostered black writing, Pumla Gqola (2001) has argued that, although BC was liberatory in intent, it problematically flattened out differences such as gender, class and sexual orientation within black subjectivity by asserting that racial oppression was the primary, if not only, form of oppression facing black South Africans. In *Amandla*, Tlali ably negotiates Black Consciousness ideology by producing a stringent critique of apartheid rooted in Black Consciousness, while simultaneously problematising the discourse by revealing the multivarious, gendered experiences of black women's subjectivities during the 1976 uprising. That she bears testimony in this novel to domestic violence experienced by a black woman at the hands of her black husband within a community that remains very much united against the common enemy of apartheid, shows her commitment to refusing to allow women's stories and experiences to be relegated to secondary status.

On account of the censorship, these two novels were more widely read abroad than in South Africa. Locally, both were unenthusiastically received by critics, with Nadine Gordimer decrying Tlali's 'analytical naivety' (Lockett 1989, 277). Both black and white critics took issue with Tlali's literary output: 'Lionel Abrahams, for example, calls *Muriel at Metropolitan* "modest" and Peggy Crane speaks of "the simplicity of the telling", while Marie Dyer complains of the "unpatterned" and "formless" quality of the novel' (Lockett 1989, 278). Tlali's response to these criticisms of especially *Amandla* is, however, unapologetic:

It is said that *Amandla* is not a novel but a statement. I wonder what a novel is. In my writings, I never try to copy somebody or adopt principles set down by scholars. I have read quite a lot of literature. I have always remarked that I'd like to present my stories with the Black audience in mind and I have never really intended to write for a white audience. I don't think it's important at this point. (In Seroke 1988, 307)

One year after the publication of Tlali's *Amandla*, Lauretta Ngcobo published her first novel, *Cross of Gold*, in 1981. Like Head, Ngcobo was able to write and publish this novel and her next, *And They Didn't Die* (1990), only once she had left South Africa. Her husband's arrest and imprisonment for his political involvement led her into exile in Swaziland, Tanzania and Zambia in the 1960s. She eventually settled in England, where both her novels were written. Ngcobo (1987, 134) had found herself creatively stifled and unable to produce literary work in a country which was 'muzzled breathless':

There was a relentless persecution of those writers and journalists who dared speak the truth. In their reports of the self-mutilating ghettoes, they exposed what the system was doing to destroy the lives of men and women. The government launched a witch-hunt against all so-called agitators – and there are no better agitators than those who wield the pen. Most of those writers and journalists were finally forced to leave the country and face exile. So was I.

Also published during the second half of the 1980s was Zoë Wicomb's *You Can't Get Lost in Cape Town* (1987). A collection of interrelated short stories that also functions as a *kunstlerroman*, it deals extensively with coloured identity under apartheid, interrogating issues such as class divisions between coloureds as well as gender relations and the differences generated by urban versus rural life experiences. The collection follows Frieda Shenton from girlhood through young adulthood, while tracing the development of her growing artistic and political consciousness. Where Frieda starts off politically naïve about the ways in which her life is circumscribed by apartheid, the collection ends with her as a politically conscientised young woman who becomes a writer, living in self-imposed exile from South Africa. Farida Karodia's *Daughters of the Twilight* (1986), a coming-of-age novel, follows two Indian sisters, Meena and Yasmin, at the height of apartheid as they negotiate the system in their small rural town. Narrated by young Meena, the novel shows the inhumanity of apartheid laws, including the Group Areas Act, which sees the girls' family forcibly evicted from their home and compelled to start over in a tiny settlement. The family has to negotiate South Africa's racial classification system in order to secure Meena's education by reclassifying her as coloured instead of Indian, as well as having to deal with the aftermath of Yasmin's rape and impregnation by a wealthy white farmer's son. This confluence of events – the family's eviction and forced removal, the rape and the ensuing pregnancy – results in the disintegration of Meena's family. Additionally, the novel deals with Indian and Muslim identity in South Africa, pointing to an often-forgotten aspect of the country's history: the indentured labour of Indians who relocated to South Africa to work, only to suffer appalling economic exploitation in the pre-apartheid, colonial capitalist system.

A second collection, Angus Sam's *Jesus is Indian and Other Stories*, published in 1989, elucidates similar themes. In the title story, 'Jesus is Indian', Sam uses a similar first-person narrator, the sassy Angelina, who humorously and poignantly relates how she negotiates (South African) Indian culture while being pressured to assimilate into her Catholic School, run by foreign nuns where she is often punished for speaking and writing 'Indian words' (30). Sam's introduction to the collection details the suppressed history of Indians in South Africa, one which Sam herself was relatively unaware of until the death of her grandfather. That event and the subsequent unearthing of a number of documents about indentured labour in South Africa spurred Sam to research her family's history in South Africa, which she traced to the arrival of her great-grandfather in Durban in 1860, along with the first wave of migrants from India. Sam historicises indenture as part of the continuum of slavery, since this system of trading in human lives replaced the outlawed slave trade throughout the British empire.

Another important literary contribution by a black woman during the 1980s was Ellen Kuzwayo's autobiography, *Call Me*

Woman (1985), published to great acclaim, and awarded the CNA Literary Prize. Focusing on her experiences as a teacher, social worker, and anti-apartheid activist, *Call Me Woman* constitutes a major contribution to the struggle against apartheid, one that Kuzwayo (2001, 49) herself believed 'intensified the awareness and immediate need for change in South Africa'. The autobiography also documents her struggles with an abusive husband, the eventual breakdown of her marriage, and the way in which apartheid warped her experience of motherhood. She explains that her youngest son was not allowed to live with her in Soweto because of apartheid's influx control policy:

> Think of it. A young child denied by the state his right to receive his mother's tender loving care – care which would help him grow and mature into a worthy citizen of the community. Very many mothers and children in Soweto, for a variety of reasons and under different circumstances, have at one time or another come face to face with this problem. In trying to solve it, some of them have met with some success; but the majority have knocked their heads against a hard granite wall. (18–19)

In this autobiography Kuzwayo demonstrates the way in which African identity is conceptualised as communal by elucidating the conditions of black women as a group under apartheid. She achieves this by relating, in Part One of the book, the stories of women she has encountered as a social worker. Only in Part Two of the volume does she relate her personal story, thus grounding her individual experience of apartheid within the collective experiences of oppressed women.

Emma Mashinini's *Strikes Have Followed Me All My Life*, published in 1989 by the Women's Press in London, is another important contribution to the canon of black women's writing. Like Kuzwayo's, Mashinini's autobiography offers a gendered labour perspective on African women's lived experience in South Africa under apartheid. Winnie Mandela's *Part of My Soul Went With Him* (1984) was also published during the turbulent 1980s. It is not, however, an autobiography in the conventional sense, as Mandela's experience is mediated by editor Anne Benjamin, who records her story and also interprets it. Benjamin (Mandela 1984, 7) describes this process as follows:

> The restrictions placed on her activities by the government and her daily involvement in the liberation movement make it difficult for Winnie Mandela to sit down and write a book ... Winnie Mandela granted me the privilege of conducting lengthy tape-recorded interviews with her over a considerable period of time. She also entrusted me with letters from her husband in jail and other documents for selection, editing and publication.

Davies (1991, 274) theorises Mandela's mode of narrativisation as paradigmatic of African women's (early) autobiography: what is related is 'a self linked to an identification with another; the self-and-husband paradigm. It is also linked to the community and – a third linkage – to revolutionary struggle'. For Davies, Sikakane's 1977 text, as well as those of Winnie Mandela and Ellen Kuzwayo in the 1980s, represent a mode of narration where 'the female self represents, in terms of narrative/textual space and time, only a small fraction of the entire text' (Davies 1991, 279). It would take some thirty years for black South African women to start writing autobiography on a more prolific scale – works that more strongly centre their own subjectivities, though their lives remain linked to struggle and the political experience of, for example, exile.

Gcina Mhlophe is another powerful black woman's voice that entered the literary scene during the 1980s. Today a world-renowned poet, playwright, director, actor and storyteller, Mhlophe took her first tentative steps as a writer at the age of 17 after hearing an imbongi for the first time. In *Love Child (2002)*, a collection of her earlier writings, Mhlophe describes how the moment completely transformed her: she decided immediately to become a praise poet, even though she knew of no women imbongi on which to model herself. After writing her first poem, she read it out aloud to herself and decided: 'I liked the sound of my own voice, and I liked hearing the poem' (8). Whereas she had thought herself physically ugly and unlovable before, writing a poem and then hearing her own voice recite the words powerfully transformed her relationship with herself: 'For the first time, I liked the texture of my hard curly hair and my face didn't feel so ugly ... My voice sounded like it was a special voice, made specially to recite poems with dignity ... That's the day I fell in love with myself; every thing about me was just perfect' (8). Here, Mhlophe attests to the liberatory and healing power of writing; how the practice of creativity and writing enabled her transformation from an 'ugly' woman condemned by apartheid to the lowest rung of humanity, to a self-loving subject producing works of beauty and dignity, uplifting both to herself and to those who would eventually hear them.

Mhlophe's public debut took the form of a play, *Have You Seen Zandile?*, which was co-authored by Maralyn van Reenen and Thembi Mtshali, and performed at the Market Theatre in Johannesburg in 1986. Written in English and isiXhosa, the play draws heavily on matrilineal oral traditions with its focus on the importance of storytelling not only in creating intergenerational relationships, but also in constructing the self. *Have You Seen Zandile?* tells the story of a young girl's relationship with a beloved paternal grandmother, and her kidnapping at the age of eight by her own mother. It draws on the life experience of Mhlophe, who herself was forcibly taken and separated from a beloved aunt during her childhood years. Both Dorothy Driver (1996) and Devarakshanam Govinden (2006) argue that, in focusing on the personal, everyday experiences of a child, Mhlophe's play maps out a psychic space for creative imagining and dreaming, a realm altogether different from that of protest literature and its demands in the 1980s. *Have You Seen Zandile?* was, consequently, panned by critics who found it too 'apolitical' (Govinden 2006). Mhlophe weathers such criticism by countering: 'If I can write about the masses, I can write about me. I'm one of the masses' (Perkins 1998, 81), thereby insisting upon opening up the space to chart the subjectivity of black women outside of the political discourses of Black Consciousness and black nationalism. It is telling that the central character, Zandile, writes letters in the sand for the birds to read to her grandmother. When her mother discovers the letters in the sand, she berates Zandile for being 'full of dreams' (Perkins 1998, 91), before promptly erasing them with her feet and urging Zandile to get on with the physically gruelling task of cutting grass. Yet Zandile insists on being a dreamer and writer, and like her creator, grows up to be an imbongi.

Mhlophe has also published several short stories, including 'My Dear Madam' (Mutloase 1981), 'Nokulunga's Wedding' (Brown et al. 1987), and 'The Toilet'. The latter gestures painfully to the material conditions of black women's literary production during the 1970s and 1980s; perhaps the best-known of Mhlophe's stories, it is analysed in the Introduction of this book.

'The Toilet' was anthologised in *Sometimes When it Rains: Writings by South African Women* (1987), and published in London by Pandora. This volume was one of two published during the 1980s that highlighted the poetry and short fiction of black South African women. Even though *Sometimes When it Rains* contains work by white women writers such as Nadine Gordimer and Elsa Joubert, the volume showcases a number of creative works by – at the time – relatively unknown black writers such as Maud Motanyane, Gladys Thomas, Lizeka Mda and Fatima Meer. Also included in this collection is Miriam Tlali, who contributed a short story and an interview with Albertina Sisulu.

A second anthology devoted entirely to black women's short stories appeared in 1989. *One Never Knows: An Anthology of Black South African Women Writers in Exile* Mabuza 1989 features the work of Baleka Kgositsile, Ponkie Khazamula, Rebecca Matlou, Mavis Nhlapho, Susan Lamu, and, significantly, two short stories by Dulcie September, the ANC representative who was murdered in Paris in 1988. Both volumes were important avenues of publication in a climate of severe censorship that also targeted black women's creative writing.

Literary organisations and black writing during apartheid

Writers' organisations were critical in the production and publication of black literature during the 1970s and 1980s. Ndebele (1989) documents the proliferation of literary organisations – both multiracial and black – during this period, the most influential and longstanding being the Congress of South African Writers (Cosaw). Established in 1987 from the remnants of the Writers' Forum founded two years earlier, Cosaw sought to 'protect the interests of writers and artists against the interference of the State or censorship' (Ndebele 1989, 413); though non-racial in membership, Cosaw was deeply grounded in the ideology of the Black Consciousness Movement. The organisation aligned itself with the goals of the United Democratic Front and the Congress of South African Trade Unions and pledged its 'total creative resources to advance the struggle for the creation of a non-racial, united and democratic South Africa' (Ndebele 1989, 416). An important vehicle for black writing as resistance to apartheid was the literary journal, *Staffrider*. Founded by Cosaw in 1978, with Miriam Tlali one of its founder members, the journal aimed to 'provide a forum for the literary and art-istic work from the oppressed communities in South Africa' (Oliphant and Vladislavic 1988, 1). Deeply invested in Black Consciousness ideology, the journal aimed to disseminate BC ideals through literature, and was named for black Johannesburg commuters who 'rode staff' illegally on overcrowded trains travelling from Soweto to downtown Johannesburg (Gqola 2001). However, (Gqola 2001, 146) contends that the literature published in *Staffrider* reproduced some of the sexism of Black Consciousness ideology: 'Two tropes operate in the representa-tion of women in *Staffrider*: supportive mothers ... and sexually transgressive women who are inscribed consequently with the trope of rape by *Staffrider* narrators and writers'. Nevertheless, *Staffrider* published creative and journalistic writing by a number of black women, including Carol Mathiane, Alice Ntsongo, Dudezile Ndelu, Jumaimah Motuang and Susan Lamu. Miriam Tlali wrote a regular column, 'Soweto Speaking', and in 1979 the magazine introduced 'Women Writers Speak', a column providing contributors with a platform for articulating their commitment as black women writers (Gqola 2001). Yet these gestures were not enough to redress the journal's male bias in terms of content matter and contributors. The 1989 ten-year anniversary edition containing the 'finest' work of *Staffrider* included no contributions by women, resulting in regular con-tributor Boitumelo Mofokeng's (1989, 41) lament:

[I]t is a sad history, at least for me, because it suggests that women's contribution in that period was a very small, almost non-existent one. But the truth is that women did write for *Staffrider* and almost all of them have been excluded from this anthology … The international world has been denied the opportunity of knowing and understanding the role of women writers, especially Black women writers, in South Africa.

Staffrider's omission of women from its commemorative issue is representative of the larger exclusion of black women from the South African literary canon during the apartheid period. As Davies (1986, 31) has noted:

> The writings of South African women writers have so far been relegated to the literary [critical] bushes. White male and female writers have for years maintained privilege in literature as they do in life: the literary establishment knows Athol Fugard and Alan Paton, for example, and has some degree of familiarity with Nadine Gordimer and Doris Lessing. Within the African literary tradition, South African male writers like Es'kia Mphahlele, Alex la Guma, Peter Abrahams and Dennis Brutus have visibility. Few have ever heard of Noni Jabavu, Lauretta Ngcobo or Miriam Tlali.

As with their exclusion from political life and citizenship rights, black women's creative expression was severely restricted during the years of apartheid. Where black women did write and publish, their works remained unexamined, generally considered without artistic merit and unworthy of analysis, as the literary criticism of both white and black male critics demonstrates.

The end of legislated apartheid: 1990 and beyond

By the late 1980s, it had become apparent that the apartheid regime would no longer be able to cling to white minority governance and would have to capitulate to international and internal pressure to transfer political power to the majority. Spurred on by examples of other African postcolonial nations where women had been deployed in liberation struggles only to have their demands for gender equality deferred post-liberation, women aligned with the anti-apartheid struggle, had, by the early 1980s, started to strategically insert demands for gender equality within the ANC. Hassim (2004) has documented a number of interventions, staged by women activists in exile throughout the 1980s, placing gender equality firmly on the liberation movement's agenda; this was in anticipation of a democratic South Africa, with the result that '[b]y the end of the decade, the ANC had come to accept that not only could the liberation of women not be separated from national liberation, but that it was an integral part of how liberation itself was defined' (Hassim 2004, 433). This push to include women's concerns for gender equality in the movement's vision for a democratic South Africa culminated in the Malibongwe Conference, held in the Netherlands in 1990, as a means of placing gender concerns and the position of women on the agenda. Themed 'Women United for a Unitary, Non-racial, Democratic South Africa', the Malibongwe Conference for the first time brought together activist women within South Africa and those exiled by the apartheid regime. The aim of the gathering was overtly political: it sought to outline a position on women's emancipation, so that women's demands would not be forgotten once national liberation had been achieved.

At the conference, Frene Ginwala called for the inclusion of a gender equality clause in a new, post-apartheid constitution. In addition, she demanded that such a constitution should protect women from discriminatory customary law, and protect their reproductive rights (Hassim 2002). With prescience, the conference resolved, inter alia, to 'ensure that the issue of women's liberation receives priority on the agendas of the ANC and all progressive organisations and that there is an ongoing discussion about the relationship between national liberation, women's liberation and working class victory in these formations'. The conference also noted that 'there is an urgent need for united action towards the formation of a national women's structure', the creation of which would enable the women 'to place firmly on the agenda of the National Liberation Movement, the Mass Democratic Movement and all our organisations, the process of integrating women's emancipation into the national liberation struggle' (Malibongwe Conference Programme of Action 1990).

Thus, if national liberation was a prerequisite for women's emancipation, the women's movement would make sure that the corollary would also hold true: that national liberation would not take place without the emancipation of women. The Malibongwe Conference paved the way, too, for the formation of the Women's National Coalition in 1992.

Mere weeks after the conference, the National Party government unbanned the ANC and other prohibited political parties, released from prison key anti-apartheid activists, the most prominent being Nelson Mandela, and began the process of negotiating a peaceful transfer of power from the white minority to the majority of South Africans. South Africa, in 1990, was in a unique position: an oppressive political regime was being dismantled through a gradual process of negotiated settlement, and the liberation movement, branded 'terrorists' by the apartheid regime, became a legitimate political party, charged with negotiating the transition to democracy on behalf of the majority of disenfranchised black South Africans. The women's movement had, by then, been decimated by the continued bannings and detentions of the 1980s. And, as Hassim (2002) has demonstrated, the unbanning of the ANC saw a variety of women's organisations subsumed by the ANC Women's League, which weakened the power of autonomous women's organisations to insert their demands into the national discourse of transformation. Political parties, including the ANC, came to the negotiating table in 1992 at the Convention for a Democratic South Africa (Codesa) with not a single woman delegate present – provoking the outrage of women's movements across the political spectrum, and causing the ANC Women's League to threaten to mobilise women for a mass boycott of the first democratic election.

The political parties' exclusion of women from the Codesa negotiating forum, as well as the resolution at the Malibongwe Conference to work towards a national women's organisation that would foreground women's emancipation, led women from all political parties to form the Women's National Coalition (WNC) in 1992. The coalition resulted from a 1991 meeting of women across the political spectrum. The WNC was a pioneer: for the first time, women were not seeking to build an organisation affiliated with the anti-apartheid movement, but were organising explicitly around their gender, across political divides.

The coalition marked a key moment in the liberation movement's history: black women within the movement, for the first time, broke ranks with African nationalist and aligned movements to form an alliance, based on gender, with women political opponents in parties such as the National Party. The WNC, strongly driven by the ANC Women's League, was a direct signal to the liberation movement (and the incumbent government) that the issues of women's emancipation and gender equality would not be ignored. With 'the single purpose of drafting a Women's Charter of Equality, which would gather the demands of individual women as well as women's organizations' (Hassim 2002, 700), the message from the women's movement was unequivocal: women's emancipation would no longer be pushed onto the back burner in the interests of national liberation.

The WNC, at its inception, gave itself a life span of one year, from April 1992 to April 1993. Its strategy, according to Hassim (2005), was to seize the opportunities for inclusivity made available by the national negotiation process – a strategy which proved highly successful once the WNC was allowed to participate in the Codesa negotiations. Having secured many political and legal gains for women during South Africa's transition to democracy, the WNC seized the opportunity, insisting that gender equality and women's issues be inserted into the discourse of inclusivity arising from the transfer of political power. These gains include the entrenchment of the right to sexual equality within the Bill of Rights enshrined in South Africa's new constitution. Another important political gain was the institutionalisation of a quota system, whereby political parties would only be allowed to contest an election if at least 30 per cent of their candidates were women.

The WNC did not survive as a political force after the first democratic election in 1994. Racial and ideological tensions within the coalition were difficult to quell. The ANC Women's League withdrew from the coalition almost immediately after the ANC was elected to govern, leaving the coalition without a sizeable, mass-based constituency. Key women leaders, having abandoned the WNC, fell back into the fold of the ANC, and were given leadership positions in the legislature, the cabinet, and the new state bureaucracy, leaving a vacuum of leadership within the already weakened women's movements (Hassim 2005).

Another important gain of the WNC was, nevertheless, the creation of gender machinery within government. In 1993, the year before the general election, the WNC organised an international conference to strategise around mechanisms that would guarantee post-liberation equality for women. The result was an impressive gender machinery consisting of a number of institutions, implemented after 1994, and aimed at achieving gender equality within society. Chief among these were the Commission on Gender Equality; the Office on the Status of Women, located within the office of the South African president; the parliamentary Joint Monitoring Committee on the Improvement of Quality of Life and Status of Women; and the Parliamentary Women's Caucus. These structures, however, became a double-edged sword, with women's emancipation becoming part of 'official' government discourse, and the government claiming to be the only real authority when it came to effecting change in women's lives (Goetz and Hassim 2003).

Gender analysts such as Gwendolyn Mikell (1995), Florence Wakoko and Linda Lobao (1996), Hassim (2002), and Goetz and Hassim (2003) suggest that periods of political flux and uncertainty, such as the transition from apartheid to democracy in South Africa, open up strategic space for women to insert gender-specific demands within the national framework. The examples of the Malibongwe Conference and the Women's National Coalition bear out this assertion. The transition to democracy also opened up a new, strategic discursive space for black women and their writing. Whereas black women's writing under apartheid focused largely on the injustices of apartheid and the political disavowal of black people, the end of apartheid signified the potential exploration of new literary terrain in which to grapple with topics not directly related to apartheid. And while the dominant national narrative prior to 1994 was the ideology of apartheid, a post-apartheid narrative arose of a unitary African nationalism, which was deployed to foster a united new South Africa and inaugurate the project of nation building. The ways in which black South African women writers fracture this dominant narrative, with many choosing to explore heretofore unexplored issues of minority ethnicity as well as black women's subjectivity and sexuality, are explored here (see Chapters Four, Five and Six). The women's literary excavations have engendered a multitude of narratives that run counter to the construct of a unitary nation.

2

Rewriting the Apartheid Nation: Miriam Tlali and Lauretta Ngcobo

Writing turns space into place.

Margaret Daymond et al.
— *Women Writing Africa: The Southern Region*

*Black women's histories, lives, and spaces must be understood
as enmeshing with traditional geographic arrangements in
order to identify a different way of knowing and writing
the social world and to expand how the production of
space is achieved across terrains of domination.*

Katherine McKittrick — *Demonic Grounds:
Black Women and the Cartographies of Struggle*

A poignant scene opens Lauretta Ngcobo's debut novel, *Cross of Gold* (1981). Sindisiwe Zikode, a mother, an anti-apartheid freedom fighter, and a former domestic worker, is on the run from the South African Police. When the reader first encounters her, Sindisiwe is stalking the border between Botswana and South Africa. Exiled in Botswana, Sindisiwe tries to facilitate the safe passage of her young sons from South Africa. The novel's opening pages make palpable the danger the family faces in its bid for freedom from a politically oppressive regime.

Early in the first chapter of the novel, Sindisiwe is shot by police from the South African side of the border. She secures a safe crossing for her sons, but unable to get to a hospital, dies an excruciating death under a searing southern African sky. Sindisiwe is buried in a shallow grave by strangers as her sons try to process the loss of a mother they hardly knew. She has, however, left some sort of legacy, one that her sons discover in a suitcase after her death: a long, lyrical letter, describing the change in her subjectivity from apolitical domestic worker to militant anti-apartheid activist. The letter describes, in great detail, Sindisiwe's transformation into a political subject. Its pages bear witness to the Sharpeville Massacre of 1960, which killed 69 peaceful black protestors in a township on the outskirts of Johannesburg. Determined to frame the political event from her own perspective as a black woman, Sindisiwe makes her standpoint clear in the opening sentences of her letter. 'Whatever you know, it is not from me you got it' (*Cross of Gold*, 20), she writes, providing a rationale for her letter writing. Making clear the urgency of rendering her own version of an event which changed the South African political landscape and marked the beginning of the armed struggle against the apartheid regime, Sindisiwe emphasises her intention to 'recount to you here events as I saw them, and as they have affected me and brought me here'. In this way, Sindisiwe produces for her sons a counter-narrative of the political uprising and massacre which differs from the official, apartheid discourse on the event. In doing so, she renders an account 'from below', as one who had actually experienced the massacre. Though she is a witness to this monumental event in South Africa's history, Sindisiwe is doomed to die early in the novel, while her son, Mandla, carries on the political activism she has started.

Sindisiwe's fate can be read as allegorical, reflecting the state of black South African women's literary writing at the time of publication of Ngcobo's novel in 1981. By that political moment, only three black women had published novels in English: Bessie Head, South Africa's most prolific published black woman novelist at the time, who would prematurely die in exile in Botswana the very year *Cross of Gold* was published; Miriam Tlali, who became the first black woman to publish a novel, *Muriel at Metropolitan* (1975), within the borders of apartheid South Africa; and Ngcobo herself, who had written and published *Cross of Gold* from the relative safety and solitude of exile in England.

The similarities between these authors and Ngcobo's protagonist, Sindisiwe, are striking. Like Head and Ngcobo, Sindisiwe is immediately marked in the text as an exile, situated outside the boundary of the nation. Her words come to her children, and to her readers, from beyond 'those few strands of barbed wire fence [standing] between her and her children, her home, her husband and her country' (*Cross of Gold*, 1). As a writer and black woman, Ngcobo is spatially and discursively displaced from the country about which she is writing. She is an outsider, trying to enter national political discourse, but succeeding only minimally because of constraints placed upon her by the apartheid state.

Like Sindisiwe's letter, which is smuggled back into the country by her son and furtively disseminated there, these writers' literary output was forced underground almost immediately upon publication by an apartheid government which deemed it politically incendiary, and censored their writings. The novels of Tlali and Ngcobo were stealthily read and circulated at high personal risk, much as Sindisiwe's letter was.

Sindisiwe's tragic and premature death at the hands of the security police comes to signify the predicament of the black woman author in apartheid South Africa. Through censorship, banning, imprisonment, harassment by the security police, exile, and disenfranchisement, black women writers were effectively given a death sentence in that their creative expression was threatened with extinguishment. Yet, like Sindisiwe, these writers insisted upon rendering creative accounts of people's lives, political events, human relations and whatever else they chose to depict.

Through an examination of space in Tlali's *Muriel at Metropolitan* (1975) and Ngcobo's *And They Didn't Die* (1990), I argue that black women writing fiction during this period wrote as an act of resistance against a system that denied them creative agency and what Mamphela Ramphele calls 'intellectual space' (Ramphele 1993). In so doing, they critiqued dominant ideologies of Afrikaner nationalism and white supremacy. Read together, their novels construct a narrative of nationlessness and dispossession that functions as a counter-narrative to the ideology of apartheid, and the apartheid state's attempted justification of its policy of 'separate but equal' development.

My analysis of these writers' works is situated within the pertinent literary debate of the 1980s about the state of black South African writing during that period. This discussion among critics of black South African literature – many of them creative writers – centred around the aesthetic, or rather, lack of aesthetic, in black South African writing during apartheid. Critics such as Njabulo Ndebele, Lewis Nkosi and Es'kia Mphahlele bemoaned the perceived lack of any literary aesthetic beyond the banality of the political spectacle that was apartheid. They indicted apartheid literature, particularly black protest literature, as overdetermined in its desire to represent the grim reality of apartheid; their arguments emphasised, in particular, the hyperrealistic portrayals of the dismal materiality of black lives under apartheid. Ndebele (1986) referred to this mode of production as the literary culture of the spectacular. The obscenity of apartheid hinged, in part, on the spectacular public exhibitionism which was part of the display and the enforcement of white might. And since the maintenance of apartheid depended on the continued spectacle of public humiliation, degradation and obliteration of black subjects, Ndebele argued (1986, 143), the black South African writer could hardly be faulted for having 'his imagination almost totally engaged by the spectacle before him'. Ndebele (1986, 149–150) describes the literary culture of the spectacular as follows:

> [It] documents; it indicts implicitly; it is demonstrative, preferring exteriority to interiority, it keeps the larger issues of society in our minds, obliterating the details … it establishes a vast sense of presence without offering intimate knowledge; it confirms without necessarily offering a challenge. It is the literature of the powerless identifying the key factor responsible for their powerlessness.

Ndebele posits the need for the 'rediscovery of the ordinary' as a way of refining black literature and dealing with the complex problems of apartheid South Africa.

In similar vein, Nkosi writes of the 'naïve realism' of writers like Lauretta Ngcobo and Miriam Tlali, reducing their fiction to 'journalistic fact parading outrageously as imaginative literature' (in Barnard 2007, 124–125). Mphahlele refers to 'the tyranny of place' in black South African literature: the black writer's obsession with mimetic depictions of the black township – the locus around which apartheid processes played out in all their brutality. For Mphahlele, the black writer 'tends to document minute-to-minute experience. There is a specifically African drama in the ghettoes that the writer cannot ignore ... He must have place, because his writing depends on his commitment to territory' (cited in Barnard 2007, 125). In a summation of this debate, literary historiographer Louise Bethlehem (2001), names this purported (anti)aesthetic the 'rhetoric of urgency' in black South African writing.

More recent feminist rereadings of Head, Tlali and Ngcobo's work expose this debate about the 'realist', anti-aesthetic mode of black literary production during apartheid as androcentric. Critics such as Wisker, Daymond and Barnard have demonstrated how, by using gender as an analytical lens, a rereading of women's writing during the apartheid era makes room for new interpretations of these works, allowing the critical space for discovering a more meaningful aesthetic. This gendered aesthetic often pioneered new literary forms, rendering more nuanced, richly textured accounts of life under apartheid.

For example, in a comparative analysis of the short stories of Head and Tlali, Daymond repudiates Ndebele's claim of a black literary aesthetic governed by the impulse to document the spectacular, arguing that in his neglect of these women's oeuvres, he dismisses an important site of literary production which does, in fact, return to the 'ordinary', as he exhorts. Daymond makes the case that gendered reflection, both in writing and criticism, represents one pathway to 'the ordinary'. She asserts that in drawing on communal experiences as source material for their short stories, Head and Tlali pioneered an 'inclusive aesthetic for Southern African writing' (Daymond 1996, 225) as their stories constitute a hybridised, new form dependent on interrelated modes of speech, storytelling and writing. In doing so, both writers 'have begun to invent a new tradition which re-establishes the weight and dignity, as a subject matter for writing, of women's view on gendered experience' (Daymond 1996, 226).

Gina Wisker, too, argues convincingly that South African women's writing during the apartheid era negotiates a paradox: though such literature may well have documented in the realist mode, it simultaneously creatively envisioned alternative worlds. For Wisker (2001, 143), the works of Tlali, Head, Ingrid de Kok, Gcina Mhlophe and Zoë Wicomb are instructive in their offering of 'an imaginative rebellion, a creative alternative or set of alternative envisionings of life and its values'. Wisker posits that, through their literary investigations of female subjectivity in relation to location or place, these works open up a creative space to re-envision and reimagine the self, and by extension, the place of the (black) female subject in the given social order of apartheid South Africa. Furthermore, Wisker (2001, 144) demonstrates how, in these writers' works 'imagery which enables an exploration of the ideas of identity and hope for creative change in the future recurs as that of geography, of the house and home space, and of journeying'. She goes on to argue (2001, 146) that, for these women writers, a sense of place is an aid to develop and improve the imagination, [engendering] a place from which to plan and build, create and project forward positive developments and alternatives … Bound up with space, place and people is the security of identity from which to project a positive future.' While this analysis of space seems prematurely celebratory, given the conditions of black women's literary production during apartheid, it is nevertheless worth remembering that in writing the nation – rendering their accounts of what it was like to be a black gendered woman during apartheid – black women writers were creating an intellectual space for examining black women's experience of the nation in the conditions imposed by apartheid.

If conceptualising the nation as narration allows for a recognition of its ambivalence, making visible 'those easily obscured, but highly significant, recesses of the national culture from which alternative constituencies of people and oppositional analytic capacities may emerge' (Bhabha 1990, 3), reading the nation from the standpoint of those most disavowed by its ideologies offers a fruitful site from which to re-examine South Africa as it is discursively constructed as a nation. And if writing turns space into place, as asserted by the editors of the comprehensive anthology, *Women Writing Africa*, black South African women's acts of writing the apartheid nation-space effectively created a place deserving of analytical excavation.

I therefore examine the ways in which Miriam Tlali and Lauretta Ngcobo use space in their respective novels, *Muriel at Metropolitan* and *And They Didn't Die,* by way of depicting and reimagining the South African nation. After briefly contextualising the novels, I analyse the authors' use of space and location as literary strategies. In this, I am indebted to Katherine McKittrick and Clyde Woods, who advanced the concept of oppositional black geographies as a set of theories for understanding both the spatiality of race – the way blackness is implicated in the production of geographic space – and the ways in which black subjects respond to, and resist, the oppressive geographies produced through racialisation. Black human geographies can thus be read as a means to determine the ways in which 'the lives of these [black] subjects demonstrate how "common sense" workings of modernity and citizenships are worked out, and normalised, through geographies of exclusion, the "literal mappings" of power relations and rejections' (McKittrick and Woods 2007, 4). I then argue that both Tlali and Ngcobo, in rendering visible the fissures within the seemingly naturalised apartheid sites they construct in their fiction, are engaged in situated knowledge production and a reconfiguration of apartheid space into a more socially just place. I demonstrate that in revealing the inherent contradictions and injustices of apartheid spatiality, 'their contributions to both real and imagined human geographies are significant political acts and expressions' which make visible and geographically available the 'erasure, segregation, marginalization, and the mysterious disappearances' inherent in apartheid spatiality (McKittrick and Woods 2007, 4).

Caught between two worlds: Miriam Tlali

Miriam Tlali's pioneering 1975 novel, *Muriel at Metropolitan,* provides a record of Tlali's work as an administrative assistant and debt collector for a furniture store in Johannesburg; for her, this was a way of 'fighting the system with my pen – the only way I could' (Tlali 2004, 7). Tlali started writing the novel at a time of great personal and political frustration: unable to cope with the humiliation of spending day after day in a racist work environment, she had left her job at the furniture store that is fictionalised in her novel. She had also quit, in part, to care for her ailing in-laws. In an interview I conducted with her, Tlali laments her situation:

> I would be sitting here and my mother-in-law would be moaning, groaning from pain in the bedroom, the little bedroom, and then the only way to keep sane [was writing]. I was aware that my studies had been interrupted, and the feeling that I had disappointed my mother, that I had disappointed myself – all those things, and what was happening [under the apartheid system]. The system was so very cruel to us, and especially women, African women. We were nothing … All these things, they were revolting inside of me. Had I not written it, really I would have gone crazy. (Tlali interview, 2006)

If finding the physical and intellectual space for writing was hard, getting the manuscript published was even more difficult. *Muriel at Metropolitan* was rejected by several publishers, and lay 'at the back of the dressing-table, gathering dust' (Tlali 2004, 8). Ravan Press in Johannesburg finally agreed to publish it, on condition that Tlali cut substantial portions from the manuscript. Tlali recalls (2004, 8): 'Some months later, they handed me the expurgated version. After I had read it, I was devastated and I sighed: "What have they done to you?" I looked at the pages of this baby I had given birth to, now reduced to shreds.' At first, Tlali refused to have the edited version of her novel published, but with her mother's approaching death, she relented. Forced to accept the compromise so that her mother could see the work in print, Tlali told me (2006) that she was further incensed by the title the publisher chose for the work. 'The title was ridiculous, because they wanted to call it "Miriam at Metropolitan". I even said, "I don't want my name on it," so they said, "Okay, we shall call it Muriel." So I thought it was really very debasing.' Tlali remembers (2004, 10) the despondency she felt when the book was released with the publisher's chosen title:

> It was a far cry from 'Between Two Worlds' – one of the tentative titles I had preferred. And I returned to my matchbox house in

Soweto, locked myself in my little bedroom and cried ... Five whole chapters had been removed; also paragraphs, phrases, and sentences. It was devastating, to say the least.

To deal with her disappointment and avoid harassment by police, Tlali fled to Lesotho, the country of her mother's birth, to escape attention. Notwithstanding the publisher's intervention, the novel was summarily banned.

Muriel at Metropolitan is aimed largely at exposing the inhumanity of apartheid and the exploitative labour conditions experienced by black South Africans. The novel is set within the extreme confines of the Metropolitan Furniture Store in downtown Johannesburg, where the title character, Muriel, works. The store, which sells radio and electronic equipment, functions as a simulacrum for apartheid South Africa, with the latter's separatist rituals distilled and re-enacted within the microcosm of the shop floor. Tlali begins by sketching a bleak picture of the nation within which she situates the store:

The Republic of South Africa is a country divided into two worlds. The one, a white world – rich, comfortable, for all practical purposes, organised – a world in fear, armed to the teeth. The other, a black world; poor, pathetically neglected and disorganised – voiceless, oppressed, restless, confused and unarmed ... (11)

Daily, Muriel traverses these two worlds as she journeys from the township to her place of employment. As an African woman in the metropolis, Muriel inhabits a liminal space – she is that which is not wanted within the space of the city, and is actively prohibited from moving freely within it. She embodies abjection. Yet, like countless other black bodies, her labour is needed for the smooth functioning of the largest South African city – the economic powerhouse of apartheid South Africa. Like the other black bodies inhabiting the apartheid city, Muriel needs the despised pass book in order to enter and exit its bounds. She inhabits Johannesburg conditionally, contingent on her ability to labour, and dependent on the whims of the white officials who have the power to facilitate or prohibit her entry into the space. Her very presence in the city, which simultaneously needs and abjects her, points to Tlali's production of an oppositional black geography – and this, in the words of McKittrick and Woods (2007, 4), accounts for her making visible the 'unknowable' and figuring these unknowable bodies into the 'production of space'.

Muriel's liminality extends to the store, which is spatially arranged to maintain apartheid through the separation of racialised bodies, together with the omnipresent surveillance of these bodies. Metropolitan, from Muriel's perspective, is labyrinthine in structure; its myriad 'L-shaped' passages (8, 35) are clogged with bodies – 'too many people moving or sitting in too small a space, and there was too much brushing against and bumping into one another' (24). Within this space, the owner, Mr Bloch, occupies a 'strategic point' next to the till, facing the door, from where he can 'see almost every point in the large shop except the workshop above' (67).

The reader encounters and negotiates the space of the store through the movements as well as the confinement of Muriel, the only black woman staff member. On her first day at Metropolitan, Muriel receives a taste of what is to come when the owner removes the cushion from her seat before she is allowed to sit down. Because she is not allowed to inhabit the same physical space as the white women who work as clerks, Muriel is initially given a workspace in the attic above the store, which she shares with three radio mechanics, all men. Muriel grows to like this space, since it allows for an unobstructed view of the store below, and knowledge of the boss's movement within the space. Her only complaint is a steep set of stairs she must negotiate every time a customer needs her assistance. Muriel's movements between the attic and the store eventually become too cumbersome and time-consuming, however, forcing her downstairs to share the white women's space.

Here, she encounters bureaucratic separateness from the white women that mirrors the country's laws. In a store which so rigidly enforces apartheid that even the coat rack is labelled 'Whites Only' (106), Muriel's presence causes a dilemma. Like the city she serves, Metropolitan needs her labour; yet her physical presence is undesirable. Consequently, the space within the store is completely reconfigured in order to 'accommodate'

Muriel downstairs while maintaining apartheid between her and the white women workers:

> Old furniture standing behind filing cabinets was moved; a more or less convenient place was created for me just below the stairs. I was separated from the rest of the white staff by the cabinets and steel mesh wires. (15)

Tlali's description of the store's interior, segregated by means of cabinets and mesh wire, resonates with the grim description of the nation as 'a country divided into two worlds'. Even Muriel's bodily functions need to be regulated in accordance with apartheid laws. After the white women complain because she uses their restroom, Muriel is forced to use an outside latrine, one of her most debasing experiences at Metropolitan:

> It was filthy. It was open to anybody from the street. I had forgotten that I had resolved never to use it again. Being in there was like being in hell. As you sat (if you had the courage to do so) holding your breath, drunken men of all races kept pushing the door open and peering in at you. (34)

The liminality that is invoked by Muriel's placement within the space of the store becomes a trope for her state of mind: she negotiates the psychological space between her reality as a black disenfranchised woman, and her co-opted position as a functionary of white oppression. She is literally 'between two worlds' as she becomes the interlocutor between her white employer and the African customers he is exploiting. As the only clerical worker in the store who speaks an African language, Miriam translates and fills out hire-purchase agreements for the customers, becoming an accomplice in their economic exploitation as they become mired in debt. She also asks for their pass books in order to fill out their payment agreements, thus acting as an unwilling agent of apartheid surveillance, and struggling with the guilt of feeling like 'the white-master's-well-fed-dog' (91).

Muriel is confined to her side of the 'colour line', where she goes about her duties first as a clerk, and later as credit control manager. Tlali sets up this situation to demonstrate, through a series of vignettes which unfold against the backdrop of the store, how the arbitrariness of racial classification and its resultant racial hierarchy undercuts the productive functioning of the store, and, by extension, the nation. The absurdity of Muriel's separation from the white women becomes apparent soon after her move from the attic, when Mr Bloch requires her to put payment statements into customers' ledger cards. Muriel is not allowed into the white side of the store to do this task because she is black, but the cards are the only record of customers' payments, and are too important to be allowed into Muriel's 'black' space. The boss is forced to temporarily co-opt Muriel into the 'white' side of the store, a prospect Muriel does not relish, given the chaotic state of that space:

> I looked at the little space I was going to share with the unfriendly white staff. There was no proper office with convenient, modern, labour-saving, systematic methods of record-keeping. There were just piles and piles of papers, books, catalogues, stacks of folders and files containing invoices, statements, delivery-notes, hire purchase agreements, approved and pending approval, old and recent, lay about. In fact, everything you can think of. Things were just jumbled around on tables and desks ... There were radio spare parts, tape recorders, irons, electric kettles, and so on. (24)

Despite being rigidly policed by apartheid laws and Mr Bloch, the state of disorder in the store and its constant crowdedness gives it a shambolic air, the antithesis of the racial ordering and separateness that is apartheid's preoccupation. Thus, while the store is set up to maintain the separation of races, it is impossible for it to function smoothly without the integration of Muriel's black body within its bounds. The constant abjection of Muriel is an integral aspect of the space, as is its reluctant reintegration of her body into its white confines, which demonstrates the illogical nature of apartheid. The clutter and chaos prefigure disintegration and decay, and, ultimately, apartheid's demise.

While Metropolitan's primary function is presumably to make as much money as possible for its owner within the framework of apartheid capitalism, Tlali demonstrates, through her rendering of Metropolitan's spatiality, the manner in which the maintenance of apartheid undercuts this capitalist function. While the store must make a profit, its secondary function is the constant maintenance of apartheid within its confines, an objective which consistently subverts the store's money-making capacity. The owner is constantly engaged in 'clearing' the store of black customers, whom he paradoxically needs for the maintenance of his business. In the novel's opening sequence, several black customers and prospective employees are lined up in the store's aisles, waiting for Mr Bloch. He immediately orders the black foreman to 'just get rid of these boys, man; they've been here too long, man' (9). In a later exchange, when two black men are found lingering, Mr Bloch exhorts the store manager: 'Get rid of them quickly, Pont, they're smelling the shop out!' (26).

Mr Bloch's anxiety with 'clearing the shop' (9) becomes a recurring theme, a fixation which extends to the black workers. Throughout, they line up to see him, take orders, or receive their pay, causing Mr Bloch to constantly reconfigure the space by moving their bodies around. He constantly bellows: 'Stand there!' (45). In policing the store in this way, Mr Bloch is also engaged in the project of maintaining whiteness, ensuring that it is not contaminated. As geographer Perry L Carter points out (2006, 241–242), configuring and reconfiguring human geographic spaces can be read as a racialised act aimed at preserving white privilege:

> 'Race' at its basic level has to do with bodies and the spaces between them. Whiteness, or any other racial identity, cannot exist without the concurrent existence of exclusive racial spaces. These exclusionary spaces can range in scale from the home to the nation-state. White privilege is largely the prerogative of not having to share spaces with non-Whites. White privilege requires the power to keep certain bodies within certain places.

Yet the maintenance of apartheid and, by extension, Mr Bloch's maintenance of uncontaminated whiteness within the store, works at cross-purposes with the store's capitalist aims. The customers are, after all, the lifeblood of the business; their presence and money are necessary for its continued survival. Yet Mr Bloch's obsession with purging the store of black bodies and maintaining its whiteness, along with the spatial layout of the place, paradoxically abjects those most needed for its survival, in the same way that the apartheid state abjects those black subjects upon whose labour its functioning hinges. Again, in using the recurring trope of clearing the space, Tlali articulates a subaltern, black geography, which points to the structural contradiction within the system of apartheid – one that prefigures apartheid's eventual demise.

Tlali makes visible a similar flaw in apartheid-capitalist logic in her depiction of endless rounds of waiting in the store. A recurring motif in *Muriel at Metropolitan*, related to the allocation of space, is the image of queues of black customers and workers, standing around, idly waiting for Mr Bloch. Apartheid is encountered even in the difficulties imposed on black bodies trying to move through the space of the store. White customers are never expected to queue – they are served immediately upon entering the store, regardless of the number of black customers, or how long these customers have been waiting. As the white owner of the store, Mr Bloch is unwilling to delegate responsibility for the store's functioning to a black employee. As part of the maintenance of apartheid in the store, he must oversee or approve any significant transaction or interaction. As a result, the workers spend hours of unproductive, idle time, merely waiting for him. When Muriel is granted special permission to cross over to the white side of the store in order to do the job of reconciling the statements with the ledger cards, she has to wait on Mr Bloch to prepare the space for her by reorganising the chaotic desk. 'I just had to wait,' Muriel says (24). 'No one else was allowed to touch those piles of paper. He alone could do it.' Frustrated yet resigned, she continues:

And so I waited. For hours I had nothing to do. Later in the afternoon, I grew more and more restless, so I went and asked him if there was nothing I could do while waiting for the clearing to be done.

'Just wait, Muriel,' he said calmly. (24)

Many other vignettes centre around the black salesmen waiting. Such lining up and waiting directly undermines Mr Bloch's constant clearing of the space, since it paradoxically leads to black bodies spending longer periods of time in the space he wishes to purge of blackness. Yet he seems unable to reconcile his methodology of making black people wait with the constant congestion of the store. His two anxieties, constant surveillance of the store, and repeated, almost ritualistic, clearing of the space of black people, thus work against each other to further chaos in the space. In addition, the waiting subverts the primary capitalist function of the store: when workers wait, they are unproductive, and are unable to make money for the business. Mr Bloch seems oblivious to these contradictions inherent in his systems of surveillance and cleansing, and the larger contradiction between apartheid, productivity and wealth-creation.

The impossibility of maintaining a pure form of apartheid through the ritualistic cleansing of space becomes a larger theme within the novel, one that haunts the perimeters of Metropolitan Furniture Store. While the self-perpetuating drama of surveillance and unproductive clearing of the store repeatedly occurs, another type of 'contamination' takes place just beyond its doors. Metropolitan is housed on the ground floor of a block of flats occupied by white tenants. And yet these flats are also the sites of 'location[s] in the sky' (16) – cramped quarters at the top of apartment blocks which by night house the black domestic workers who tend to the occupants of the flats by day. Again, the black body is abjected from the space that cannot function without its labour into the liminal space of the location in the sky. The black body and its necessary labour are thus present within the city and the white domestic space, but the location in the sky marks an attempt to erase all traces of the black body. These traces can, however, never be completely erased.

Tlali shows how the liminal space of the location in the sky, used by whites to abject black bodies, works to subvert the apartheid system. During her visit to the outdoor toilet, Muriel becomes acquainted with Ben, a caretaker at a block of flats, and the occupant of a tiny room that is part of the location in the sky. Ben has considerable disposable income, and when Muriel enquires about its source, he reveals that, at night, he rents out the room for purposes of illicit sex. Ben's best-paying customers are white men wishing to have sexual intercourse with African or coloured women, an act prohibited by South Africa's Immorality Act of 1950.

'Do you have many such mixed cases?'

'Oh yes!' Ben exclaimed. 'This Saturday night, for instance, the Marshall Square Police sergeant is coming with Hazel ... He is always coming with her, and he gives me a lot of money. Ten rands per night. I don't mind. I give them the room and squeeze myself into the boiler room or the toilet.' (34)

On another occasion, Ben defends Muriel from white children who are throwing stones at her. When Muriel cautions him that he might be jailed for harming white children. Ben replies:

'Not when their fathers are some of my best customers. They are my brothers-in-law at night when the lights are out.' (111)

Again, a space that is created to preserve the purity of white South Africa becomes the site of 'contamination' by means of inter-racial sex. The structures meant to maintain the pristine nature of whiteness, policemen and the patriarchy, become the very agents of white contamination by black bodies. Again, Tlali shows how apartheid works against itself, its contradictions ultimately becoming the source of its demise.

The ultimate commentary on apartheid's unviability occurs towards the end of the novel in a climactic confrontation between Muriel and the white women workers, shortly before Muriel resigns. The women are discussing the world's first successful heart transplant in South Africa, notably the fact that a coloured person's heart was transplanted into the body of a white man. The conversation centres around the permissibility of putting a coloured heart into a white body, and how the authorities could have allowed the transplant, given the apartheid laws. Mrs Stein, one of the most racist of the women, argues that 'the heart is merely a muscle. It merely pumps blood' (176).

To this, Muriel retorts: 'Surely the Coloured's heart was not cleaned out or sterilised first to make sure that none of his blood would be introduced into the white man's veins' (176). This, says Muriel, is proof that human beings are human beings, since blood cannot be black or white. 'Blood is blood,' she insists, to the dismay of the whites in the store. The ultimate 'contamination' of white space – implanting a non-white heart into a white body – points to the constructedness of race, extending the trope of deconstructing pristine, uncontaminated white space to the arena of the body, thereby deconstructing racial physicality and boundaries. The transplant demonstrates the hypocrisy of apartheid's foundational lie: that differentially marked, racialised bodies are materially different, and may therefore be treated unequally. Tlali shows the interdependence of these differently categorised bodies, demonstrating again how black bodies are literally the lifeblood of white bodies and the white nation which abjects as it exploits black subjects. In thus focusing on the socially constructed nature of both the body and of space, Tlali denaturalises white hegemonic ideology relating to the racialised body and racialised space – the idea, as McKittrick (2006, xi) puts it, that space 'just is' – demonstrating instead the manner in which apartheid's use of racialised bodies and space co-construct each other.

Lauretta Ngcobo: stirring up the nation to create a feminist space

In contrast to *Muriel at Metropolitan*, Ngcobo's *And They Didn't Die* (1990) is set against the sweeping backdrop of a vast rural landscape, with the main character's migrations between this and various urban settings. Stung by feminist criticism that the only woman in *Cross of Gold*, Sindisiwe, dies too soon, Ngcobo uses her second novel, *And They Didn't Die*, to bring to life a host of strong, resilient black women characters. Chief among them is Jezile, who is engaged in countless acts of resistance against the apartheid state. Like many other black writers, Ngcobo had found within the physical space of South Africa little room for creative expression: it took time and the development of a feminist consciousness for her to conceive of a strong, agentic black woman character. In 2006, years after *Cross of Gold* was published, Ngcobo reflected in an interview that Sindisiwe's premature death was a product of her socialisation within a deeply patriarchal and racist society:

> I had learned earlier that women didn't count much. They hadn't got an independent life of their own. When Sindisiwe dies, only her sons can live and go into the cities. Women remained in the rural areas. They didn't go out, they didn't make things happen … Sindisiwe herself dies because what else can she do?

The title of her second novel is a direct response to criticism concerning Sindisiwe's premature death in *Cross of Gold*. Set in the small rural reserve of Sigageni in what was at the time the province of Natal, *And They Didn't Die* elucidates the effects of apartheid on the most dispossessed group in South Africa: black rural women confined to the bantustans through apartheid law. The main character, Jezile, is just such a woman: separated from her husband, a migrant worker in Durban, by pass laws which prohibit her from entering the city or joining him there, Jezile is forced to live with her mother-in-law in abject poverty. Prohibited from working, she ekes out a living as a subsistence farmer. However, prolonged drought, exacerbated by oppressive apartheid laws, make life unbearably difficult for Jezile. At first, she is plagued by childlessness – and this in a deeply patriarchal society where a woman's worth is measured by her ability to produce children. Later, however, she suffers the misery of watching her children slowly starve in harsh conditions spawned by apartheid segregation and the confinement she is forced to endure. The novel shows the impact of the apartheid government's exploitative migrant labour system, which saw strong, fit men torn from their families to work in the cites as cheap labour, with devastating consequences for black family life.

Like Tlali's novel, *And They Didn't Die* is path-breaking in its portrayal of the experiences of a black woman from her own perspective, thereby giving its main character a subjective life, interiority and a voice heretofore not encountered in South African literature. While the primary source of oppression in the lives of Jezile and the other women in her community is apartheid law, Ngcobo makes visible the ways in which African women are positioned between two competing forces of oppression: apartheid and patriarchal African customary law. Apartheid denies the women the right to own property, thus condemning them to unrelenting poverty, and delimits where the women may live, how often they see their husbands, and their freedom of movement. While Sigageni is gendered as a female space owing to the forced absence of men conscripted into the migrant labour workforce, customary law nevertheless renders it a deeply patriarchal space. Customary law considers all married women minors and prescribes rigid behavioural codes which, in the absence of men, are enforced by mothers-in-law. The women of Sigageni defy these codes at the risk of being ostracised from their community. In grappling with these intersecting forms of oppression, Jezile shows a keen understanding of the ways in which these two oppositional forces operate upon her and constrict opportunities to create a fulfilling life for herself and her three children. Jezile expresses feelings of being 'trapped between the impositions of customary law, state law and migratory practices' (40), but once able to identify the sources of her oppression, she is able to act strategically in order to resist and mitigate them.

Ngcobo introduces Sigageni as a space that is gendered female, with a community of women who act collectively to resist apartheid and to transform the space where they are forced to live. The novel has an omniscient narrator, and while the reader identifies with Jezile, its main character, it is not as intimate an identification as with Muriel, the first-person narrator of Tlali's novel. This is a deliberate strategy, since Ngcobo attempts in her second novel to demonstrate the mechanics and value of communal women's resistance, as well as the strength of the women's movement in a rural location. *And They Didn't Die* opens with a fictionalised scene of the 1959 protests against the extension of pass laws to African women, showing a rebellion by the women of Sigageni. That year, in rural Natal, women had started destroying government-owned dipping tanks used to eradicate parasite infestations in white farmers' cattle, eventually demolishing up to three quarters of all such tanks. Because of these protests, hundreds of rural Natal women were arrested in 1959. Though no official figures exist on the number of women arrested for destroying dipping tanks, one rural prison built for 115 people held 482 women during the time of the dipping tank revolt (Sambureni 1995).

Ngcobo's novel opens with a white government official surveying a destroyed dipping tank as he condemns the women and their behaviour:

> [T]these women, this strange breed of womanhood, thin and ragged and not like women at all – they think they rule the world, they spill men's beers, they herd cattle, they plough fields, they run this community. That's what it is; that's why this defiance – they've lost respect for manhood, for all authority, but they haven't got the sense to do it properly. (2)

In contrast with Muriel's initial silence and acquiescence to the system in which she works and lives, the characters in *And They Didn't Die* are from the outset portrayed as rebellious, resistant women who refuse to be co-opted into implementing and per-petuating the apartheid system. Their illicit middle-of-the-night forays to the dipping tanks on the outskirts of their village marks them as women who are not afraid to transgress the spatial restrictions placed upon them by apartheid law. The reader is introduced to Jezile through these acts of resistance: though one of the younger women in the community, Jezile is a ringleader, the initiator within the group.

Jezile's transgressive movement through space, despite the restrictions placed upon her by apartheid and patriarchal culture, becomes an enduring theme throughout the novel. When, as a newly-wed, she does not become pregnant because of the infre-quency of her husband Siyalo's visits, Jezile takes matters into her own hands and resolves to travel to Durban without her mother-in-law or husband's consent in order to spend time with Siyalo. She makes the decision to leave Sigageni by herself, resolving to 'wait no longer for other people to do things to make decisions about her life' (10). Having written to Siyalo to inform him of her imminent visit, she reflects as follows:

> Her letter had a decisiveness about it that thrilled her. It felt wonderful to be taking charge of her own destiny, she had never done it before. She stopped for a moment as an encroaching doubt about Siyalo reared to intimidate her. She dismissed it as instantly as it had come – he would have to live with a changed wife just as she was coping with a fast-changing husband. (11)

Radicalised by the communal activism of the women of Sigageni, Jezile is emboldened to act in her personal life and to decide for herself what is needed to improve her life. This sense of agency plays out mostly through migration: she leaves the village and travels on her own to the unknown city of Durban in order to be with Siyalo and conceive a child. Through a developing sense of personal agency, she is able to act decisively and embark on a journey from a familiar place into the unknown. And migration, in turn, further radicalises Jezile, with increasing levels of agency following the political protests she encounters and participates in once she arrives in Durban.

Jezile's first encounter with the space of the city is overwhelming, invoking contradictory feelings. Durban, with its 'hotch-potch of human experience, that patchwork of human endeavour' is 'at once elevating and shattering; vast yet constricting' (22). Ngcobo sketches a detailed picture of the hostels where African men work, conveying Jezile's shock at the living conditions where she finds Siyalo. The hostel, 'honeycombed with a thousand windows', proves an unpleasant surprise as she goes on to describe its effect on her:

> Except for the free flow of the people, in and out of the gate, the place was so austere and grim it could have been a prison. It gave the feeling of prohibition, and a feeling of trespassing that made Jezile's heart beat faster. (24)

The inside of the hostel is even more grim. The description of the space Siyalo occupies makes clear the intention of apartheid spatial design of such hostels: to dehumanise those who live there by affording them no personal space or privacy. Beds are crammed into long passages, indicating the transience of the bodies meant to occupy these spaces. A passage is not a space which shelters and contains; rather, one passes through it in order to move from one location to another. The migrant workers who occupy this space are clearly temporary cogs in the wheel of apartheid capitalism, easily disposed of and interchangeable with other black male bodies.

In an attempt to secure some privacy, the occupants of the hostel have created small cubicles by curtaining off a space around each bed. Registering Jezile's shock at his living conditions, Siyalo creeps 'with stooped shoulders' towards his cubicle where he disappears behind the curtain 'as though they were back in childhood, playing hide-and-seek' (24). The space seems to reduce those who live in it to the status of children, making them appear and feel smaller than what they are. Siyalo's stooped shoulders signify a shrinking of dignity; a constriction of the self in order to fit within a designated space. As Jezile inspects the tiny cubicle, Siyalo is filled with embarrassment and shame as he finds 'the Durban of their dreams, and his life in it, under scrutiny' (25). As Siyalo becomes smaller before her eyes, Jezile finds herself resenting both Siyalo and Durban, the place that has turned him into less of a man. When he takes her, the following day, to the township of KwaMashu, he also becomes associated with the 'matchbox houses' of the squalid township – that 'human reservoir of Durban' (30) with its 'little houses stuck on the green hills like scabs' (28).

> Everything he said shattered her illusions and she resented it. She turned her head and fixed her gaze in the distance in an effort to cut out Siyalo and the city. Nothing seemed right about this place. She was not sure whether it was the place or Siyalo. (28)

In this way Siyalo's identity becomes entangled with that of the space that delimits the bounds of his person, and, ultimately, reduces him in his wife's eyes. Here, Ngcobo demonstrates how 'practices of domination, sustained by [white hegemony's] unitary vantage point, naturalize both identity and place, repetitively spatializing where non-dominant groups "naturally" belong' (McKittrick 2006, xv). However, Jezile's oppositional vantage point, her questioning of her husband's 'place' within the space that dehumanises him, serves to interrogate the natural order of apartheid hostels, questioning the idea that space 'just is' (McKittrick 2006, xi), and that Siyalo belongs in that space. In this way, Ngcobo succeeds in separating Siyalo's identity from the oppressive space in which he finds himself, denaturalising both the space of the hostel and the racialised construct of Siyalo as a black man shaped through place.

As Margaret Daymond (1990) points out, *And They Didn't Die* functions as a treatise on the effects of the Natives Land Act of 1913 on black South African women, in particular. This Act severely curtailed black ownership of agricultural land. Its extension in 1936, the Native Trust and Land Act, saw black ownership of rural farm land restricted to 13 per cent of all available land. While its effects had been documented by black male writers, for example, in Sol Plaatje's *Mhudi* (1930), Ngcobo's is the first novel to depict the consequences of this abrupt severance from the land from the standpoint of a black woman. Ngcobo uses motherhood as a theme to convey the devastating psychic disruption that results from being torn from one's ancestral land. In traditional African culture, an individual's connection to the land of his or her ancestors is an integral part of identity. Dispossession therefore has far-reaching consequences on the self. As Wisker (2001, 146) has shown, in black women's literature 'space, place and the people in that social context enable self-definition, the establishment and maintenance of an identity, a sense of belonging, and a place from which to grow'. Upon the birth of her first daughter, Jezile is viscerally confronted by the destabilisation of identity stemming from dispossession from the land. Alarmed at the death of her friend Zenzile during childbirth, Jezile takes the unusual precaution of birthing her baby at a hospital. Her mother-in-law, MaBiyela, resents this because it severs the new-born from her place of birth. Visiting Jezile and the baby in hospital, MaBiyela feels 'something constricting about the place ... They were dealing with Jezile and herself and the baby as though they owned them' (73). MaBiyela berates Jezile for handing over the placenta to the nurses:

> The placenta is the bond between you and the baby and the earth. It will always draw you together. It should be buried in a secret spot, known only to the members of the family. Otherwise, it leaves you and the child vulnerable ... And for the baby, it is the tie that binds her firmly to her place of birth. It will always draw her back to her home, no matter how far she travels. (74)

Jezile does not know what has happened to the placenta – it has probably been incinerated, leaving her daughter forever disconnected from the place of her birth. With this realisation, she is filled with remorse:

> Jezile shuddered visibly. It was her turn now to look disturbed. It was as though the hospital had deprived her of a prized possession; a bequest to her child; an affinity so abstract, yet so binding to her and to the land – the place of her birth. (74)

MaBiyela agonises over the future that awaits the baby, who has started off 'a waif', just as 'our whole nation is that of waifs and strays now' (74). The poverty that indirectly unhomes the baby is a direct result of apartheid policy. This disconnection from her place of birth echoes that of millions of other babies born in apartheid South Africa, forever dispossessed from the soil of their country, and thus from a fully actualised identity.

Ngcobo's most valuable contribution by far to South African literature is the feminist reconfiguring of space in *And They Didn't Die*. The women in her novel constantly disrupt the spaces they occupy, transforming space into protective feminist enclaves or political tools with which to resist apartheid. Several scenes in the novel attest to this spatial reshaping. The first space transformed by women's activism is the prayer meeting every Thursday afternoon. Here, the women are aware that 'they were keeping a tryst with a large number of other women from the length and breadth of the country. Few things could bring together so many women at one time of day throughout the country, every week of every year' (40–41). Nosizwe Morena, a local physician, leads the prayer meeting, which is ostensibly a religious gathering. While these meetings are partly aimed at prayer and worship, 'in some parts, prayer had assumed a much wider meaning over and above the strictly religious intention. They still sang and prayed and cried, but they also talked and discussed the causes behind their beset lives' (41). After prayer, Nosizwe leads the women in a consciousness-raising session, expounding on the causes of their hardship. She explains:

'There are times I feel that many of us suffer and fight back without the full understanding of what is going on, why it is going on, and where it is taking us to. We, the women in the rural areas, need to know why we are here when our husbands are there; why we starve when South Africa is such a large and wealthy country, and what might happen to us if we keep on asking these questions.' (42)

Nosizwe further explains the reserves and their function as providing 'a source of cheap labour for white people's agriculture, mining and industry' (42), with the women being the producers of migrant labour, forced into starvation by their husbands' absences. She links the women's grinding poverty to their lack of access to land, and their struggle to wider, pan-African anti-colonial struggles led by Patrice Lumumba in the Congo and Kwame Nkrumah in Ghana, urging the women to 'rise and demand our own freedom in response to the call of that spirit of freedom that is raging through our continent' (48). Though ten policemen are monitoring the prayer meeting, they are impotent in the face of the form the gathering takes. To break up a meeting in a church would be obscene; 'their purpose foiled', the policemen 'stood there watching people praying to their God' before leaving the women's space (49).

This meeting is a key event in the novel, which radicalises the women of Sigageni and charges the atmosphere of the entire village. After the meeting, it is as if 'a fuse had been lit and the moment of detonation was not far off' (50). In this way, the women use the seemingly benign space of the prayer meeting, transforming it before the very eyes of the oppressors into a tool for fighting their political oppression. So, the women come to inhabit two parallel spaces in their day-to-day living. The surface activities of daily subsistence obscure the subversive space within which they are constantly strategising against, and resisting, the enforcers of apartheid:

> To the casual observer the women of Sabelweni (the larger district) were at home looking after their livestock. But beneath the surface, within the community, they formed a network of messengers relaying messages from one group to another. And whenever the police or soldiers came round, the women gave warning cries as signals to others in hiding. (180)

In this way, they continuously reconfigure apartheid space and geography, and, in their resistance, succeed in transforming the space into one that works for the benefit of black women. The women similarly subvert space so as to use it as a protective mechanism when they are being persecuted. While protesting the extension of the pass laws to African women, the women deliberately defy the officials who have arrived in the village to issue passes. The women collectively move away from the area where official tents have been erected, prompting police to follow them. Sitting down around Jezile, the women draw a protective circle around her with their bodies as they drop their pass books at her feet:

> Jezile, facing away from the assembly of policemen, stealthily set the pile of books alight. The police watched unable to observe exactly what was happening at first. Then there was a sudden cry of triumph from the women who were mingling and dancing, some ululating and others shouting slogans. The police were thrown into total confusion, and it was quite some time before they realised that the women were burning their passes. Although they had seen the women forming a ring around Jezile, they could not say exactly who had done what. (79)

When they are arrested a few days later for protesting against the extension of the pass laws, the women are sentenced to six months of hard labour. Once imprisoned, they spend their days crushing enormous quarry rocks into small stones, 'an exercise in futility, a waste of physical strength ...' as they pitch themselves 'against the might of the earth, against nature, in conflict with the bedrock of life' (96). At the quarry, they protect their leader, Nosizwe, a doctor who is unaccustomed to hard physical labour, using the same tactic as when they protected Jezile:

> The women around Nosizwe drew closer, so close that from a distance the watchful guard could not count her flagging strokes. In quick, deft movements Jezile dragged mounds of broken pieces in front of Nosizwe, a pile larger than any in front of the others. That evening, the women went back to prison happy that they had shielded her from the prison guard. (97)

In using their bodies to protect Jezile and Nosizwe, the women demonstrate the effectiveness of communal political action. When the women are acting together, it is difficult for police to single out a scapegoat: their collective shielding forms a community poised to act against apartheid's enforcers. Ngcobo, through the reconfiguring of space via black female bodies, here provides a model for effective feminist political action.

Both Tlali and Ngcobo use space in their novels as a means to 'write' the nation and its geography from a subaltern standpoint. Tlali's *Muriel at Metropolitan* uses the compressed space of a capitalist enterprise to show the structural contradictions of apartheid, foretelling the eventual demise of the system. Ngcobo's novel uses a larger, migratory space which is constantly reconfigured and reordered by the women inhabitants for the express political aim of gaining their liberation. Both iterations of the nation-space offer readers a novel way of reading and understanding the nation as a space which is not only raced, but also gendered in specific ways. Written from the subjective viewpoint of black women, these texts offer ways of understanding the nation that had not previously existed.

While both writers engage creatively with apartheid space, with Ngcobo, in particular, offering an alternative way for black women subjects to inhabit space, both novels end on a sombre note, seemingly offering little in the way of an alternative vision of a liberated South Africa in the immediate future. Ngcobo's protagonist, Jezile, eventually becomes a fugitive from the law after killing a white soldier who attempts to rape her daughter. She explains the death to her estranged husband: 'I had to kill him. They've destroyed us, Siyalo. They broke our marriage, they broke our life here at Sabelweni, and they've broken all our children's lives and killed many. He was raping our daughter. I had to defend her. We have to defend ourselves' (245). This conclusion represents an unapologetic justification for the armed struggle against the apartheid state.

While Jezile is able to exert a certain amount of agency as a black rural woman through her and other women's creative use of space, apartheid structures ultimately come crashing down on her, quashing what little agency and resilience she has left. All the relationships that make meaning in of her life are destroyed; she has to abandon her home and become a fugitive after killing a white man, and all she escapes with is her life.

Tlali's Muriel, having had enough of the racism in the store, quits her job at Metropolitan for a better-paying one at a motorcycle repair workshop. While the new position offers the hope of better conditions, the offer of employment is ultimately withdrawn, as the owner of the workshop does not have a separate restroom for Muriel. Her hopes for a better life are crushed – no matter where she moves, she cannot escape the rigid confines of apartheid. At the end of the novel, she is unemployed, and reflects on her desperate situation:

> Those damnable laws which dictate to you where, and next to whom, you shall walk, sit, stand and lie ... This whole abominable nauseating business of toilets and 'separate but equal facilities' ... What is one to do anyway? One is forever in a trap from which there is no way of escape ... except suicide. (189–190)

The novels analysed in this chapter represent an insertion of black women's experiences into a realm from which they have been deliberately 'written out' by apartheid law, structures and ideology. Given the brutality of the apartheid state, these writers are preoccupied with highlighting the adverse conditions black people, and especially black women, face; the harshness with which apartheid laws are implemented, and the consequences of apartheid in black people's lives. These works were produced with the express political aim of toppling apartheid. As such, these novels should be read as highly subversive acts of writing: writing which countered a brutal metanarrative of white supremacy and segregation. In a very concrete way, these writers, in inscribing their versions of reality on South African history, were risking their lives. For all their preoccupation with the mechanics of apartheid and its effect on the nation and the subjectivity of black women in particular, a close reading of their work reveals that it can hardly be termed anti-aesthetic, as characterised by critics such as Ndebele and Nkosi. In narrating from the standpoint of black women, and in creatively engaging the spatiality of apartheid, Tlali and Ngcobo offer new ways of reading the nation; these are valuable for elucidating the ways in which the national space genders black women, and how black women, in turn, shape and reshape that space.

3

Dissenting Daughters: Girlhood and Nation in the Fiction of Farida Karodia and Agnes Sam

South African women of Indian descent form a category of South African writers until recently almost completely absent both in South African literary criticism and critical consideration within the field of South African English Studies. Until the publication of Devarakshanam Govinden's *Sister Outsiders: The Representation of Identity and Difference in Selected Writings by South African Indian Women* (2008), South African Indian women's writing fell between the literary cracks of black South African writing, and 'Indian' writing, with both areas of study dominated by the analysis of men's writing. Training a critical lens on the writing of women of Indian descent in South Africa, Govinden (2008, 2) argues that such writers' pervasive concerns are 'those of colonial and neo-colonial domination (and in South Africa, rampant racial oppression), dispossession and cultural fragmentation, finding and defining "home", crises of identity, and living with differences'. Attentive to the critical 'disappearance' of Indian women's literary production in South Africa, Govinden (2008, 3) seeks to draw attention to 'a neglected corpus of writing in South African literary criticism'. As Govinden (2–3) cogently argues:

> With some effort, one may discover that Indian women's writing in South Africa also provides a useful lens with which to read and reread the important issues of our time. As with those of other black women writers in South Africa who were largely excluded and 'othered', autobiographical, fictional and discursive writing produced by Indian women in South

Africa constitutes a way of 'talking back', and it demands to be recognised as such.

Departing from Govinden's premise that Indian women's subjectivity, as portrayed in their fiction, provides a singular lens through which to examine significant moments in the construct of the nation, this chapter examines South African Indian girlhood and female subjectivity during the apartheid era as portrayed in Farida Karodia's *Daughters of the Twilight* (1986) and Agnes Sam's short story, 'Jesus is Indian' (1989). Particular attention is paid to the ways in which contact with coloniality and the apartheid system positions the young protagonists of both texts in a liminal space between their 'Indianness' and colonial culture, and examines the ways in which the girls negotiate their identities within the racial tumult of the apartheid years. As two of the first works of fiction by South African Indian women which examine the coming of age of Indian girls during apartheid, these texts produce a vantage point from which to observe hybrid female subjectivity, as shaped by the discursive and legal imperatives of apartheid, as well as patriarchal tradition. The emphasis on girlhood in this chapter draws strongly from the work of Miki Flockemann (1992), which examines processes of coming into womanhood in postcolonial women's literature. Citing Toni Cade Bambara's critical observation that 'not enough attention is paid to the initiation or rites of passage of the young girl' (in Flockemann 1992, 37), Flockemann argues that the process of becoming a woman for the racially 'othered' girl in postcolonial fiction often stands as analogous to the postcolonial nation's processes of coming into independence.

Both Karodia and Sam aim to make visible the histories of 'Indians' in South Africa as well as the obscured, gendered history of the indentured labour system. A related concern is the relationships both girls have with other girls, as well as their own mothers, who figure prominently in the girls' negotiation of their identities. These maternal figures, which can be read as standing for the nation, complicate both protagonists' development into young women as they straddle two cultural worlds, caught between their 'Indianness' and hegemonic apartheid culture.

Indian women in South Africa and the history of indenture

The lineage of the category of South Africans known as 'Indian', and referred to locally as 'Indians', can be traced to the colonial practice of indenture. This practice came into being in the wake of the anti-slavery legislation of 1807 and 1833, which abolished slavery throughout the British empire, thereby creating a demand for cheap alternatives to enslaved labour. The first indentured Indians, mainly Hindus (and later Christians and Muslims) from Madras, were requisitioned to arrive in South Africa in 1860 to work as labourers on the sugar cane plantations of the British colony of Natal (Ebrahim-Vally 2001). Agnes Sam, writing on her family's history in South Africa, describes indentureship as follows:

> In colonial times an indenture was an official requisition for stores or goods from abroad. It was also a document binding a person to a master. The indentured labourer was therefore the equivalent of inanimate goods requisitioned by a colonial person through the Colonial Office, and was also in bondage to a master until the period of indenture was over. (Sam 1989, 3–4)

Initially indentured for a period of three years, the indentureship period was soon prolonged to five years because of the scarcity of labour to work the sugar plantations. If indentured labourers agreed to work for ten years, they were entitled either to a free passage back to India or a patch of Crown land (Sam 1989). It may be argued that the practice of indenture existed on a continuum with the practice of slavery, as indentured Indians were rarely allowed to leave the estates on which they worked, and were routinely forced to work longer hours than those stipulated in their contracts (Frenkel 2010). Fatima Meer (1987) has argued that 'indenture was cheaper than slavery for plantation owners as the average life span of a slave was ten years, and the first few years were of low productivity, as the slave had to recover from the arduous journey' (cited in Frenkel 2010, 10). Sam corroborates this formulation of indentureship as a continuation of slavery, showing through her research on her family's history how Indians were often kidnapped into indentured labour, or lured by touts with promises of inflated earnings. Stranded in Natal upon their arrival, they had no means of returning to India, and were forced to labour under harsh conditions, including non-payment of wages and separation from their families. Many Indians remained in South Africa, and continued to form an ethnic and cultural group after 1911, when indenture finally ended. Before this, in 1865, indentureship from India to Natal was temporarily halted by India as a result of the ill-treatment of indentured labourers. By 1874, a new agreement was reached between the colonial authorities in Natal and the Indian administration, introducing longer, five-year contracts for indentured labourers (Ebrahim-Vally 2001). Labourers who left their employment after five years did not have the right to leave Natal for another five years, effectively locking these indentured labourers into ten-year contracts. This amended labour agreement had the effect of consolidating Indian immigrants to Natal as a small but permanent population:

> The ten-year clause was created by the Natal government to have a cheap and available workforce at its disposal for the construction of harbours, railways and public buildings. More importantly, from the perspective of the development of an 'Indian' community in Natal, the government also asked that for each 100 men 40 women be imported. (Ebrahim-Vally 2001, 81)

Another wave of Indians, mostly traders, arrived in Natal around 1875. Because of the renewed agreement with India, the Natal colony could not prevent these traders – who were British Indian subjects – from entering, along with indentured labourers. The Natal government needed cheap indentured labour, but soon found the traders to be unwanted competition in the commercial domain (Ebrahim-Vally 2001).

With the formation of the Union of South Africa in 1910, the movements of Indians were restricted to Natal, if they had not left there by 1895. Treated with suspicion and often disdain by the nascent apartheid state – these Indians were an abject group no longer wanted once their labour had been exhausted. Because of their status as British subjects, the Union of South Africa could not directly discriminate against them. They were, however, seen as a threat to emerging Afrikaner capitalism, a threat which spawned a number of economic regulations against them to prevent direct competition with white commerce (Ebrahim-Vally 2001).

Sam (1989, 8) notes that 'between 1914 and 1919 there were moves to repatriate South African Indians to India; in 1927 there were plans for assisted emigration from South Africa; in 1930 there were plans to resettle Indian South Africans in other parts of the British empire'. In 1925, DF Malan, then Minister of Home Affairs for the Union of South Africa, tabled the Asiatic Bill, the aim of which was to 'ruin "Indian" traders and farmers by declaring them aliens and by segregating them on grounds of unsanitary premises and unfair competition' (Ebrahim-Vally 2001, 84). Indians, along with other South Africans, strenuously resisted apartheid. The Natal Indian Congress and African National Congress founded in 1894 and 1912 respectively, were key opponents to British imperialism in the first half of the twentieth century, and often fought segregationist laws together (Raman 2003). Many Indians belonged to both organisations, and several key leadership positions in the African National Congress were filled by Indians.

Indians were only given conditional citizenship in apartheid South Africa in 1961, a century after they had first arrived. Ebrahim-Vally (2001) notes that this was not a move motivated by magnanimity, but rather, a manoeuvre by the South African state to avoid interference in its affairs by India after that country gained independence in 1947. Until 1961, South African Indians lived 'under constant threat of repatriation' (Frenkel 2010, 11); yet apartheid laws continued to discriminate against them, consolidating them into the racial group 'Indian' with the passing of the Population Registration Act in 1950. As with other races, apartheid legislation structured the very materiality of their lives, determining where they could work, live and study, as well as whom they could marry or enter into relationships with. Apartheid law harshly discriminated against 'Indians', politically disenfranchising them and seeking, inter alia, to curtail their economic ventures while also restricting free movement.

Frenkel notes that the discriminatory labour policies refined during and after indentureship became the blueprint for later discriminatory legislation against Africans by the apartheid state – a type of pilot scheme for influx control laws that would later decimate African social and familial ties. Likewise, Sam (1989, 9), too, notes that the rights of settlement and land purchase denied Indians in the nineteenth century recurred in the twentieth century when Africans were denied the same rights and confined to bantustans: 'Indentured labour replaced slavery. Migrant labour replaced indentured labour' – thus powerfully articulating the economic and legal progression from slavery, through indentureship, to apartheid. In other words, the indentureship of Indian labourers could be seen as the often invisibilised link between the economic practices of slavery and apartheid's devastating migrant labour policy, which brutally rent the fabric of African communal and family life.

Indians became full citizens of democratic South Africa after the 1994 election, counted, in the census of 1996, as comprising 2.6 per cent of the South African population –just over one million people (Ebrahim-Vally 2001).

Indian women writers in the South African literary canon

Before the publication of two relatively recent works of scholarship on South African Indian literature, Ronit Frenkel's *Reconsiderations: South African Indian Fiction and the Making of Race in Postcolonial Culture* (2010), and Devarakshanam Govinden's *Sister Outsiders: The Representation of Identity and Difference in Selected Writings by South African Indian Women* (2008), literary criticism on South African Indian writing was scant. Govinden locates the genesis of South African Indian cultural production in their Natal arrival, citing early literature, both oral and written forms, often expressed through religious practices. Meer (1969) has shown that art forms were brought from India, including storytelling and dance, with men being the main practitioners and performers and women mainly audience members. Govinden (2008) cites as one of the first examples of South African Indian women's writing the response by the Indian Women's Association to oppressive indenture laws, which was published in a newspaper, the *African*

Chronicle, in 1908. Other forms of cultural production took place under the ambit of the Women's Cultural Group, formed in 1954 in Durban, and included the production of musicals, poetry recitals and plays. The director of the Women's Cultural Group, Zuleikha Mayat, also wrote plays – her first, *Be Ghadi Moj*, may be translated as 'a few moments of fun' (Govinden 2008). The Cultural Group also wrote and published recipe books.

Govinden's (2008, 104) historiography of South African Indian women's literary production names Ansuyah Singh as a significant Indian writer, 'generally seen as the first Indian writer, male or female, in South Africa'. Singh, who was also a medical doctor, wrote across a number of genres, including the novel, plays and poetry. Her novel, *Behold the Earth Mourns* (1960) was the first novel published by a South African Indian, presenting a 'highly racialized topography through which Indians move in concert, and sometimes in collision, with Black South Africans' (Burton 2010, 1). Another significant South African Indian woman literary figure was poet Sanna Naidoo, who was also a member of Cosaw in the 1970s and 1980s. Muthal Naidoo, too, was prolific during the 1980s, writing and staging plays, including 'We 3 Kings' (1982), 'Of No Account' (1981), 'Coming Home' (1982), 'The Masterplan' (1983) and 'Nobody's Hero' (1987) (Govinden 2008). Other significant South African Indian women poets who emerged during the 1980s include Roshila Nair and Deela Khan, both known for their anti-apartheid poetry, as well as topics that dealt specifically with gender and gender-based violence. It is from this tradition that Agnes Sam's and Farida Karodia's first works of fiction emerge.

Dissenting daughters: 'Jesus is Indian' and *Daughters of the Twilight*

There are only three Indian women who had book-length writings published in the 1980s. Fictional works by Farida Karodia and Agnes Sam appeared in 1986 and 1989 respectively, while short story writer Jayapraga Reddy's 1987 collection, *On the Fringe of Dreamtime and Other Stories*, predates Karodia's collection, *Coming Home and Other Stories* (1988) by a year, and that of Sam by two years.

What makes Sam's and Karodia's works of fiction singular is their focus on South African Indian gender identity as shaped by structures of colonialism, apartheid and patriarchy. Additionally, both works subvert the genre of the bildungsroman, whose traditional subject is a male coming of age through a journey involving a quest, rewriting it from the perspective of a postcolonial girl, whose identity-affirming 'quest' is often located in the treacherous terrain of home. Home is often the site of danger for the young female postcolonial subject, a location where she is 'unhomed' (Bhabha 1992, 141) as a result of the intersection of her race, gender and burgeoning sexuality, with the latter two forming the basis of her oppression.

Tracing tropes of representation of girls in postcolonial, proto-feminist fiction, Flockemann (1992, 38) notes the prevalence of a literary strategy she terms the 'dual focus' of the writers. This involves a young woman protagonist, coming of age, who is mirrored by another young woman – a slightly older sister, cousin or friend – so that 'these relationships become indicative of the choices available to young women in different post-colonial societies' (Flockemann 1992, 37). In addition to showing the multiplicity of these young women's experience through making visible the range of choices or constraints structuring their lives, the 'dual focus' also acts as a strategy for 'bridging the uncomfortable and problematic relationship between insider/outsider, self/other in writing by Black women in the post-colonial context, where women have been traditionally positioned as the object (or native/other)' (Flockemann 1992, 38). Offering at least two perspectives on experiences, choices, as well as structures of opportunity and oppression, thus undercuts the binary opposition of insider/outsider in the subjective viewpoints represented in such novels.

I position both Sam and Karodia's works of fiction as characterised by this dual focus strategy in depicting South African Indian girlhood and coming of age in apartheid South Africa. Both works present young protagonists whose subjectivities are strongly shaped by and enmeshed with an older sister. In the first of these, Sam's 'Jesus is Indian', Angelina narrates not only her own, but also her sister Honey's experiences growing up in a South African Indian home in an unspecified time period, and in

Karodia's *Daughters of the Twilight*, Meena stands as witness to her older sister Yasmin's tragic fate, while simultaneously narrating her own social and political coming of age.

'Jesus is Indian', from the collection *Jesus is Indian and Other Stories* (1989), reflects the experience of an Indian girl as she enters adolescence while at the same time narrating multiple stories relating to her older sister's imminent arranged marriage, her father's alcoholism, and her interaction with colonialist ideology at school through the figure of her strict English teacher, a nun called Sister Bonaventura. Sam's collection was published in 1989, a year before the apartheid state bowed to international and internal political pressure and announced its dissolution in favour of a multi-party, non-racial democracy. For Flockemann (1998), the date of publication in the late-apartheid era is significant, as Sam's fictive world foreshadows pertinent issues around the transition to democracy, as well as the new regime about to unfold. Flockemann (1998, 77) suggests that 'the fact that the first two stories in *Jesus is Indian* are told from the perspective of a child seems significant in terms of the way "new" South African writing uses recollections of childhood to explore South African subjectivities from a variety of perspectives, informed in interesting ways by the writers' own race/class/gender positions.' Flockemann (1992, 46) contends that, although many of Sam's stories were authored during the 1980s, they prefigure the 'new' democratic South Africa, and point to important ways in which the society might develop, with a feminine subject positioned near the bottom of the social and political hierarchy, showing the way. Positing that familial relations often stand for the colonial subject's relationship with the coloniser in postcolonial fiction, Flockemann goes on to argue that as a developing nation, South Africa would need to go through processes of 'development' similar to those of Angelina in interrogating both colonial and 'traditional' discursive formations and cultures, and casting off oppressive aspects of both in order to forge a new, inclusive and hybrid national identity. While this may seem like an iteration of Fredric Jameson's theory of third world literature standing as national allegory, Flockemann (1998) views the subaltern positionalities of postcolonial girls more as 'historic witnesses to their changing society, as well as their changing selves'.

In Angelina we have a questioning young girl capable of critical thinking as a narrator; she takes nothing for granted when it comes to the logic and structure that underpin her received culture. She exposes the underlying hypocrisy and absurdity in the assumptions of adults through incessant questioning of the social order, displaying agency and a critical consciousness with which she interrogates and negotiates the world around her. While Flockemann reads 'Jesus is Indian' as a collection of discrete short stories, Govinden (2008) argues that the collection also works as a loosely connected series of short stories, which ultimately functions as a bildungsroman. For Govinden, 'Jesus is Indian' thus consolidates the subjectivity of the various female narrators in the volume, anchoring it within the childhood experiences of Angelina. Similarly, Frenkel (2010, 137) notes a coherency across the collection in the ideological work the short stories perform: 'Each story in this collection can then be read as an intervention in opposition to apartheid discourse in terms of its anti-apartheid themes, while also theorising an alternative Left ideology to that of the anti-apartheid movement, resulting in a strong conception of the inseparability of (or complicitous relationship between) racial and gendered experience.'

As the narrative progresses, Angelina displays a growing consciousness of her position within the society, along with a burgeoning realisation of how her own agency lies in negotiating different aspects of her two cultural worlds. The reader is introduced to Angelina as she sits writing an essay at a mission school, under the tutelage of Sister Bonaventura. Sam gives Angelina three narrative registers in which to convey overlapping stories. The three voices in which the story is written are 1) her thoughts, narrated as interior monologue, which are bracketed in the text; 2) her actual dialogue as she interacts with various characters, set in quotation marks as direct speech; and 3) the story she is writing in a notebook about her sister, Honey, and her family, set in italics. The polyphonic narrative structure offers the reader multiple perspectives on Angelina's point of view through access to her thoughts, her speech, and her writing. We are privy to her private musings, as opposed to her – sometimes contradictory – public utterances and writing, as she negotiates her way through school and familial relationships. All three narrative strands are rendered in South African Indian

English, a dialect that developed as indentured Indian labourers learned English upon arrival in South Africa:

> The vast majority of Indians learned English on South African soil, developing a distinct dialect, which was initially used for outgroup communication with English speakers, and which soon developed into an 'internal' *lingua franca* among subsequent generations of Indians. Thereafter, in the 1960s and 1970s, it turned into a first language. SAIE [South African Indian English] is today a covert badge of Indian identity and unity in South Africa. (Mesthrie 2005, 305)

Given the three narrative registers of the story, the author had several choices regarding how to present the narrative linguistically. She could have chosen to produce only Angelina's writing or direct speech in South African Indian English. The choice of conveying all processes of Angelina's articulation, including thought, which is where her critical consciousness originates, in South African Indian English, signals a decolonial intent on the part of the author, who, like her protagonist, refuses the hegemony of standard South African English in her mode of relating the tale. Form and diction correspond, thereby becoming an act of resistance against the colonial language order.

The story opens with Angelina's stream-of-consciousness description of the scene in the classroom as she attempts to write her essay on Honey, her sister. From the outset of Sam's short story, Angelina characterises herself as 'not a good girl' (14), signalling a self-conscious refusal to assimilate into the dominant culture, which the mission school seeks to achieve through obedience and adherence to the ideology of feminine respectability. Sonnyboy, a fellow student, mocks Sister Bonaventura as she writes on the blackboard, making 'monkey' faces behind her back, while Angelina stifles the urge to laugh out loud at his antics. Subverting the colonial logic that presents the coloniser as a knowledgeable, civilising force whose duty it is to teach ignorant, uneducated natives, Angelina astutely sums up the foreign nun's ignorance and inability to discern and interpret events around her: 'It's Sister's veil and skirt and things. It makes so Sister can't see what's going on right behind her' (4). Though she is very young, Angelina's perspective on the colonial educator subverts the power dynamic that structures the interaction between the colonised subject and the coloniser – here, Sister Bonaventura, whose clothing signals her colonising mission and status, and the one who is in fact at a disadvantage, and who lacks knowledge of what is happening plainly in sight of her students, right behind her back. Her colonial garb, the nun's habit and skirt, instead of marking her as intellectually and morally superior, have the opposite effect of weighing her down and blunting her interpretive skills, putting her at a disadvantage that impedes her ability to perceive and interpret the local culture.

This critical consciousness, which continually assesses and subverts Sister Bonaventura's supposedly superior position, is apparent in Angelina throughout the story. After Sister Bonaventura instructs the students not to copy the words she has written on the board, Angelina cannot contain herself, and questions the teacher's logic in issuing such an instruction:

> 'Sister, why lately Sister keep saying, No copying from the blackboard today?'
> (Sister says she wants we must write from up here – she's tapping her head.)
> 'Then why sister keep on changing every word we write?'
> (Sister says she wants we must write like she writes.)
> 'But why?'
> (Sister don't want me must ask so many questions.) (24)

These lines, in addition to challenging the teacher's logic, also function as an interrogation of what counts as knowledge, or what is worthy of being written down and recorded for posterity. While the nun ostensibly wants the students to use their own critical thinking skills in writing their stories, she also wants her young charges to write like her, but without directly copying the words she has written on the blackboard. Here, Angelina demonstrates the colonised subject's practice of mimicry (Bhabha 1984) – in postcolonial theory, the act of mimicking the culture and language of the coloniser, but in ambiguous ways that can be read as mockery. What Sister Bonaventura seeks to produce is obedient colonial subjects who represent the 'reformed, recognizable Other, as a subject of difference which is almost the same but not quite' (Bhabha 1984, 126). Yet Angelina's critical conscious-ness produces a colonial subjectivity steeped in ambiguity, whose mimetic articulation produces an excess that veers into mockery, disrupting colonial discourse and posing an 'immanent threat to both "normalized" knowledges and disciplinary powers' (Bhabha 1984, 126).

In deploying mimicry, Angelina privileges the hybridity (Bhabha 1994) of South African Indian English; her written and verbal articulation signal a refusal to fully assimilate into the dominant colonial culture, resisting both the standard English her teacher insists upon, and the instruction to purge Hindu phrases from her writing. When Angelina questions why she may not use words that are not English, the teacher replies that she does not understand Hindi. Angelina audaciously offers to teach her the language, subverting the power structure of the colonial class-room, only to be met with a haughty reply that Sister Bonaventura came to South Africa to teach, not to be taught. Sam here exposes the colonial ideology of superiority through the questioning of a seemingly naïve child.

As the story progresses, Angelina ignores Sister Bonaventura's repeated attempts to substitute the word 'Mother' for the Hindi 'Hama' in her essay, arguing openly with the nun: 'Sister can say mother for Sister's mother. I say Hama for my Hama' (33). After this, the teacher concedes defeat. This discursive victory for Angelina comes after a protracted battle with the teacher around her mother's Christian name. Angelina is sent home from school for insisting that her mother's Christian name is Kamatchee, after the nun declares that Angelina's mother cannot possibly be a Christian with a name like Kamatchee, and mocking the name by translating its meaning as 'Little Cabbage'. Language, its articu-lation and its signification become a battlefront where Angelina wages war against colonial dominance. Having questioned her mother about her name and telling her about the nun's suggestion that she will go to hell because she does not have a Christian name, Angelina confronts the nun: 'Hama says if she is a Christian and

her name is Kamatchee then Kamatchee is a Christian name'
(33). Angelina's mother had, indeed, expanded this argument by
questioning the authority of Sister Bonaventura:

> 'What that sister know? Hey? Don't Jesus wear a dhoti like
> Ghandi? Don't Hama talk to Jesus in our language? Don't Jesus
> answer all Hama's prayers? ... You so clever, what you think that
> means? Hey? You electric light children and you don't know?
> Jesus is Indian. You go to school and tell that Sister.' (33)

Through the syntax of her writing and her speech, her refusal
to purge Hindi from her English articulation, and her insistence
on using the hybrid cultural construct of South African Indian
English, Angelina produces discourse from the 'Third Space of
enunciation' (Bhabha 1994, 54); the space that hybridises colonial
and indigenous culture; the space which is 'interruptive, interrogative and enunciative' (Bhabha 1994, 55), and which ultimately opens up new possibilities of articulation for the colonial
subject that enable a strategic and provisional untethering from
the binaries of colonial/indigenous.

Frenkel (2010) reads Sam's short stories as focusing on
women and adaptation, creating gendered accounts of history
that foreground the gendering of hybridity. For Frenkel (2010,
131), Sam's work is significant because it 'redefines history and
identity in South Africa as heterogeneous and multivocal, and
shows that women undergird these processes because they syn-
thesise cultural experiences in difficult circumstances through
reconsidering positionalities'. This articulation from a subaltern
feminine point of view extends to Hama's voicing, as a Hindu
woman, of her Christian world view. Where Bragard (2008) reads
Hama's declaration that Jesus is Indian as her retreat into 'trad-
itionalism', and thus as a kind of antithesis to mimicry, my own
reading of Hama's articulation shows her consciousness to be characteristic of hybridity. In 'Indianising' the figure of Jesus Christ,
Hama constructs a cultural figure that embodies both Christian,
colonial norms and Indian culture: this figure operates through
both sets of logic by wearing a dhoti, thus conforming also to the
image of a benevolent monotheistic, patriarchal God-figure who

answers prayers. Such hybridity allows Hama to fit Jesus within a framework that accommodates her two formative cultures and their seemingly incompatible belief systems.

Angelina's linguistic hybridity extends to her cultural milieu. She is adept at negotiating between her 'Indianness', which, like Kamatchee's, would probably confine her to the kitchen, and the English-speaking Catholicism that seeks to erase all traces of her Indian heritage. In traversing the two constructs of colonial culture and 'Indian' culture, she performs a hybridised melding of the two that relies on her selecting the best from both worlds. In so doing, Angelina is able to use each to gain insight into the other, so that 'each system, oppressive alone, became interrogative and subversive in the matrix of multiculturalism' (Lim 1993, 246).

Though she dislikes school, being there provides her with the necessary tools to transcend the narrow confines of her illiterate mother's life. Angelina knows that in order to write her essay on her own terms, she needs to be able to author her own story. Because her mother cannot read, Angelina is aware of the need to go to school. This is evident from an essay she writes:

> On Sunday when Hama's washing the rice and I'm stamping garlic and ginger I ask Hama, 'Why didn't we stay in India, Hama? Why Hama want us to speak our language, but Sister Bonaventura want I must leave out Indian words?' Now Hama say she don't want us to go to school anymore. Hama thought Sister Bonaventura is teaching us our language. (30)

Hama's stance alarms Angelina, despite her hatred of school. She tells herself: 'I don't like Sister Bonaventura, but I rather go to school than stay home and do cooking and housework with Hama. Now I'm sorry I told Hama about Sister teaching us English in school' (30). When she realises her mistake in telling Kamatchee about the incident, Angelina quickly rectifies the situation, insisting that no one will understand her if she does not learn English at school.

That Angelina succeeds in completing the essay, describing her sister's marriage negotiations in South African Indian English, is testimony to her successful negotiation of both cultures, interrogating both, and rejecting what does not allow for her actualisation as a thinking, knowledge-producing subject. The very act of writing is transgressive in the case of a young sub-altern girl firmly under the control of a colonial regime that sees her as an empty vessel waiting to be filled with knowledge. That she succeeds in rendering her articulation in the creole of South African Indian English makes this doubly transgressive: not only does Angelina refuse to conform to the demands of the colonial education system, but the dialect is not often encountered in its written form. In vocalising from the third space of articulation (Bhabha 1990), she crafts a language of her own that is suitable for expressing and interrogating her gendered experiences at the matrix of colonial and apartheid power. Her voice, even in mim-icry, is her own – a not insignificant achievement for a girl located close to the bottom of the social and political hierarchy of the society in which she lives.

Despondency in *Daughters of the Twilight*

Farida Karodia's *Daughters of the Twilight* represents a much more sombre coming-of-age narrative of a South African Indian girl at the height of apartheid repression. Published by the Women's Press in England in 1986, the novel was banned in South Africa because of its attack on apartheid, resulting in the novel initially being ignored by critics, particularly in South Africa. As with Angelina's story, the plot unfolds in the form of a first-person narrative. Fourteen-year-old Meena also witnesses and narrates the – very different – experiences of an older sister, Yasmin, whose life takes a disastrous turn when she is raped by a white farmer's son and becomes pregnant. The novel's title gestures to the location of Meena and Yasmin in apartheid society: their lives are circumscribed and severely curtailed by apartheid law, most notably the 1950 Population Registration Act and Group Areas Act. As the progeny of a mixed-race couple – their father a South African of Indian descent, while their mother belongs to 'that nebulous group generally referred to as Coloured' (11) – the young women inhabit a liminal, twilight world as a conse-quence of their mixed-race origins. This racialisation, with the resultant liminality, becomes important to the plot of the novel when apartheid's rigid racial classificatory system forces Meena to 'choose' one race over the other in order to attend the high school of her choice.

The liminality of the women's identities and their social position is perhaps an iteration of the author's own. Karodia's debut novel was written while in exile in Canada, where she had fled after the government withdrew her passport in 1968 (Pirbhai 2009). Referring to Karodia's identity as forged by her membership of a 'twice displaced' group of people, Pirbhai (2009) notes that, for politically exiled South African Indian writers, displacement had deeper, historical roots going back to the system of indentured labour and forced migration to other British colonies in the 1800s. For Pirbhai, this doubled exilic consciousness, though casting writers as almost perpetual outsiders, holds intriguing political and creative potential, making Karodia one of the

> unique voices in African literature . . . [that does] not fully belong to a small minority of writers of European origin who speak from the historical centre of institutionalized power, nor do they belong to the vast majority of indigenous African writers who speak from the cultural and political centre of the post-colonial condition ... What the in-between, or to use Karodia's titular phrase, 'twilight' atmosphere of these texts undermines is the diasporic community's sense of volatility in Africa as a twice-displaced people; that is, both in their historical displacement from the Indian subcontinent and in their status as a political and rival minority in the new land. (Pirbhai 2009, 79)

Govinden (2008) argues that historicising South African Indian identity and culture in literature expands the scope of the South African literary canon. The title *Daughters of the Twilight* could also be read as a commentary on the fractured and often traumatic history of South African Indian women in the country of their birth.

Jo Beal's study of women indentured labourers reveals that those who were brought to South Africa had often been kidnapped or misled by touts in order to make up the quota of women required by the 1874 agreement between India and Natal (Beal 1990). Though the quota system was a prerequisite for the trade of labourers, insisted upon by India, women were not wanted by planters who grew sugar and tea in Natal. Estate owners preferred males as labourers, since men were seen as stronger and able to endure the more gruelling physical labour demanded for culti-vating plantations. Indian women indentures were consequently regarded as 'dead stock' (Beal 1990, 151). As a result, women were often subjected to extreme physical and economic abuse, by both planters and Indian men. Indian women in Natal often suffered sexual abuse, and Beal has uncovered evidence of their being bought and sold by both Indian men and white landowners.

The sombre tone of *Daughters of the Twilight* could be read as a product of its time in the mid-1980s, when the promise of freedom from apartheid was anything but certain. The novel opens with an ominous foreshadowing: Karodia's setting of the scene in 1950s Sterkstroom, a small rural village in the eastern Cape, is littered with references to death. Meena refers to a wind that 'brought sickness and death, an observation substantiated by the pealing of funeral bells', and describes her bed as 'oppressive as a coffin' (1). A beautiful doll given to Meena as a birthday gift is stolen and mangled by the white farmer's son, Cobus – pre-figuring the destruction of Yasmin's life after Cobus rapes her several years later. From the outset, then, the terrain of home is permeated by an air of danger and death, with white masculine violence looming as a perpetual threat to the lives and well-being of the young Indian protagonists. Both daughters, but especially the older Yasmin, who is exuberant and ambitious, find Sterkstroom dull and stifling, and their actions throughout the novel pivot on plotting an escape from the village.

Meena's parents have been married for several years, despite the fact that, under apartheid law, they are classified as belonging to different races – Indian and coloured. The Immorality Act of 1927 was amended in 1950 to outlaw sexual relations not only between white people and black people, but between white people and anyone classified as non-white; this law functions as a constant disciplining structure and threat to freedom in the novel. Early in the narrative, Meena and Yasmin's grandmother, Nana, catches Yasmin and the white farmer's son, Cobus, engaging with each other as they sit on a park bench. When Nana warns Yasmin not to 'cheapen' herself (34), her admonition performs a discursive abjection of the black feminine body. Writing of the nascent sexuality of both Yasmin and Meena, Wendy Woodward (1993, 84) notes the following:

> [T]he apartheid cultural formation actually has the body of the subaltern woman as its abject. If the fiction of the purity of the 'white' race has to be upheld, then the body of the black woman must be represented as pollutive and defiling in order to counter any potential desire felt by the 'white' male.

The burgeoning sexuality of these young black/Indian girls is thus perceived as a threat in colonial, patriarchal logic, a dangerous force that needs to be rigidly controlled and contained. Nana cautions Yasmin: '[Y]ou'd better watch out, my girl, or you'll be spending the rest of your life behind bars' (34). Cobus, on the other hand, receives no such warning. This pathological attempt at the maintenance of racial purity by forbidding sexual relations between people of different races, yet laying the responsibility for cross-racial desire upon the body of the black/Indian young woman, ironically does not protect this abject figure from rape by the same white man with whom she shares the bench.

When Yasmin's parents eventually find out about the rape, they do not take any legal action against Cobus, and nor do they tell the doctor attending to her how Yasmin became pregnant, out of 'fear for a system of justice which punished the victim and not the offender' (134). Such fear is not unfounded: Pumla Gqola (2015), in her pathbreaking inquiry into rape in South Africa, documents how, during apartheid, even though the legal system allowed for the death penalty, no man, white or black, was ever sentenced to death for raping a black woman; by the same token, the only black men who were hanged for committing rape were those found guilty of raping white women. Yasmin inhabits the category of the seemingly 'unrapable' black female body, a colonial trope functioning in concert with the stereotype of the black male rapist to produce ideologies of black deficiency in response to black and indigenous resistance against colonial rule (Gqola 2015).

Yasmin is even blamed by members of her family for the rape, with her grandmother, Nana, intimating that she had invited the rape because she held ideas that were above her station in life: 'Because of all her fancy ideas, I feared for her. Lord how I feared for her ... I hoped that she would accomplish something special in her life ... Deep down I knew that some day she'd get into trouble, but Dear Lord, I never expected anything like this' (135). The blame for the rape and the resultant pregnancy is placed squarely on the victim, whose abjected body absorbs the culpability and shame of the violation. Addressing the connection between rape, race and shame, Gqola (2015) posits that shame is a function of oppression, in that the shame which should reside with the oppressor is often transferred onto the victim of such oppression. Shame points to who in society is valued, and who is not: 'Although logically, it would seem to follow that those who have something to be ashamed of, that those who behave badly should feel ashamed of themselves, the opposite is true. Shame is the product of dehumanisation, and all systems of violent oppressive power produce shame in those they brutalise' (Gqola 2015, 38). Cobus's shame is transposed onto the body and psyche of Yasmin, who is ultimately psychologically destroyed by the dehumanising act of rape.

The rigidity of the racial classificatory system, and the extent to which it structures the life choices of the protagonists, becomes more apparent as the novel progresses, with Meena having to disavow her Indianness and, with it, her father, in order to attend the school of her choice, which is designated coloured. Meena chooses to be reclassified as coloured in order to attend this school. The process of racial reclassification centres around an interview at the Department of Coloured Affairs in Johannesburg as Meena's mother lies to the official, stating that she is no longer married to her daughter's father: 'We don't associate with Indians. She's Coloured. All our friends are Coloured' (77). Her complicity with the deception leaves Meena feeling 'debased and degraded by what had happened in that office' (78). As with Yasmin's rape, the shame of the oppressor is transposed to the psyche of the victim. For Meena to advance through education, she is forced to disavow an essential part of her identity, and the father who bequeaths her this identity. In this way, the social construction of rigid racial categories, through law and ideology, fractures Meena's sense of self as she is forced to choose one aspect of her identity over others. Furthermore, her complicity in her mother's betrayal of her father results in Meena experiencing a profound sense of guilt.

Another apartheid law that circumscribes, and ultimately destroys, the lives of these characters is the Group Areas Act; it is used by the state not only to forcibly remove the family from their home in Sterkstroom, but also as a mechanism to placate white anxiety about Indian entrepreneurship. The Indian family's livelihood comes from a general supply store that serves the farm community. As the segregationist laws tighten, white farmers drive their workers into town, at the same time forcing them to shop at white-owned grocery stores, resulting in a loss of business for Mohammed's General Store. There is talk among the community that Indian traders will soon be moved out of small towns to reduce competition against white-owned small businesses. When the Mohammed family visits East London, Meena and Yasmin's father, Abdul, is chastised by his friends there: they tell him that he 'should have moved to the city … It won't be too long before all the Indians are moved out of the dorps. The white-owned stores can't take the competition' (56).

The discourse around forced removals eventually manifests in the removal of the family from Sterkstroom to a rudimentary settlement called McBain, where they have to adapt to life without running water, sanitation or electricity. When Abdul receives a letter informing the family that they are to be evicted and relocated under the Group Areas Act, he retreats into denial and does not inform the family. The women are, thus, surprised when men from the Group Areas Board arrive to evict the family while Abdul is away on business in East London. Meena, her mother and grandmother Nana are thus forced to deal with the violent and traumatic move on their own. Furniture and other possessions are dumped on the pavement by police, and the kitchen, together with priceless family heirlooms, is destroyed during the eviction. In this way, not only is a home destroyed, but also the objects linking the family to its history and collective memory.

Woodward notes that the destruction of the family home also undoes the female body. Through the eyes of Meena, we witness her mother's bodily trauma: 'Her bun had come undone; her large anguished eyes were turned on Sergeant Klein, pleading. Her hands dropped to her sides in a gesture of helplessness. This was the image of my mother I took with me as I hurried away to phone Papa'. At the same time, Nana has a slight stroke: she 'slid to the floor ... roughly pushed aside' by one of the men, then 'staggered' (87) as she reached the door.

Both women's bodies enact the dissolution and destruction of the home, threatening to collapse. Woodward (1993, 86) reads this destruction of the domestic space as one which deprives the women of their identities 'with rights to their own domestic space'. The destruction of the home, with its multiple histories and its memories, thus registers in the buckling of the two women's bodies. This imagery of women's bodies flailing, on the brink of coming undone, and the destruction of bodily coherence, prefigures Yasmin's experience, both bodily and psychological, as a result of the rape. From her younger sister's perspective, Yasmin seems destroyed: 'Would anything ever be the same again? Could she ever put the shattered pieces of her life together, I wondered' (124).

The life Yasmin had before the rape, like the family's home in Sterkstroom, is irretrievably lost – both destroyed by the ideology of white supremacy and of patriarchy. The novel ends with Yasmin running away and never returning to her family home in McBain, leaving the rest of her family uncertain as to whether she is dead or alive. The impossibility of a return to the wholeness of what went before leaves everyone in the family trapped in nostalgic longing for the past, unable to focus on a future that seems oppressively grim. For Meena, after the Group Areas Act removal, 'our future did not exist' (70).

The voices of Meena and Angelina provide important registers for reading the changing narrative of South Africa as a nation, Angelina's even more so as a precursor to its transition to democracy. Both texts offer portraits of the growing political and cultural consciousness of South African Indian girls, one poised to become an adolescent, and the other on the brink of womanhood.

Though both narrators are Indian girls, there are differences in their narration of their lives and the nation which gesture to the heterogeneity of South African Indian identity. While Angelina dislikes and does not always see the value of attending school, she is clear that school is advantageous to her, and insists on attending when her Hama threatens to withdraw her. For Angelina, school offers a counter-narrative to traditional Indian life, one that enables her to interrogate aspects of South African Indian culture, and to actively choose whether to disavow or embrace these. In contrast, for Meena, school is a much harsher terrain. School is where she first encounters racism and is othered as an Indian; on the first day, she opens her textbook to find the inscription: 'Coolie, coolie, ring the bell; coolie coolie, go to hell' (20). This racial slur causes her to tear out the front page of the reader, resulting in a harsh beating for Yasmin, who has volunteered to take the punishment in place of Meena.

In *Daughters of the Twilight*, school is a site of reproducing the power relations of apartheid. Even when Yasmin is accepted into an expensive private school for Indian and coloured girls in East London, it is made clear to her family that, although she will receive the most expensive education money can buy a young Indian woman, Yasmin will only ever have the opportunity to become a nurse or teacher. These were the only professions available to 'Non-European' women during apartheid. And while school, for Angelina, also structures her social position within South Africa, she is able to resist and rewrite the story pre-scripted for her by her colonial education.

The difference in the consciousnesses of these two protagonists may be ascribed to the time of writing and publication of each text. In 1986, when Karodia's novel first appeared, South Africa was mired in the brutality of the regime's attempts to crush the anti-apartheid struggle, and to quell popular resistance. The tone of hopelessness in the novel, with repeated references to death, reflects the political mood in the country. It is little wonder that part of Meena's coming of age is her engagement with members of the liberation movement in Johannesburg when applying to her new school. While in the city, she visits a group of young men – one of whom is a love interest – and participates in a political discussion about ways to overthrow the regime. She is shocked to learn, a week later, that one of the young men she had met that evening has been murdered by the apartheid police. Meena's consciousness seems here to be developing politically, gesturing towards her later role as a political activist. However, by the end of the novel, Meena feels completely hopeless and unsure of the future – or the fate of Yasmin. However, in *Other Secrets* (2002), the sequel to *Daughters of the Twilight*, it becomes clear that Yasmin has not been crushed by apartheid, despite Karodia's first novel offering the reader little hope of Yasmin's or the family's survival.

While Angelina's consciousness might also be described as political, this does not relate to a role as an activist. In contrast, her critical consciousness interrogates power and its operations in the classroom and at home, as a means of charting a strategy between oppressive systems that have the potential to harm her. A narrative of late apartheid, Angelina's growing consciousness seems, as Flockemann (1992) suggests, intent on charting a liberatory discourse into the future, within a rapidly changing political system where apartheid would soon be vanquished. Furthermore, what is called for is a careful, critical treading into the future, as a young Indian girl, displaced by traces of otherness produced by indenture, the gender system and apartheid, leads the way.

In her critique of *Daughters of the Twilight* and another African postcolonial feminist bildungsroman, Tsitsi Dangarembga's *Nervous Conditions* (1988), Woodward (1993, 88) notes that 'neither novel looks forward to a new identity for women after the demise of colonial legislation; future narratives written about the present moment in history will have to take cognisance of political changes in their representation of women's subjectivity.' Even so, foregrounding the experiences and perspectives of two subaltern girls in societies where colonial/apartheid powers are being challenged by nationalist movements, and giving these subjects a voice with which to narrate the changes in their respective societies, is itself a subversive act on the part of Karodia and Sam.

Colonialism and apartheid constantly enact and inscribe their dominant ideologies of racial hierarchy and segregation on society, which black nationalism counters with its own set of discourses. Several feminist analyses of the nation have shown that discourses of nationalism often deploy women strategically for specific political aims in anti-imperialist struggles and the creation of 'nation-states' (Boehmer 1991, 3). Similarly, McClintock (1994, 353) argues that nationalism positions male subjects in the same relation to the nation as they stand to women, so that that 'nations have historically amounted to the institutionalisation of gender difference'; nationalisms are always gendered, and 'all are dangerous'. Boehmer (1991, 7) correspondingly points to the dangerous correlations between nationalism and patriarchy:

> Nationalism, like patriarchy, favours singleness – one identity, one growth pattern, one birth and blood for all. Though this interpretation relies a little uncomfortably on ideas of immanence, the claim is therefore that nationalism, like patriarchy, will promote specifically unitary or 'one-eyed' forms of consciousness.

In other words, nationalism attempts to replace the dominant narrative of imperialism with a new, hegemonic narrative of the nation. This new, ascendant narrative of the nation often elides women's experiences – together with other vectors of difference that interrupt its seamlessness – in order to put forward the idea of a unified, unitary nation. By offering stories from the points of view of Meena and Angelina, who represent the most marginalised sectors of society because of their gender, race and diasporic 'otherness', Karodia and Sam construct counternarratives that interrogate not only colonial but also emerging masculinist nationalist discourses. In privileging diasporic Indian female experience, Karodia and Sam give voice to a heterogeneous group of subjects hitherto grossly underrepresented in South African literary canons, both as subjects and as authors.

4

Interrogating 'Truth' in the Post-Apartheid Nation: Zoë Wicomb and Sindiwe Magona

The South African Truth and Reconciliation Commission (TRC) has, arguably, been this country's most ambitious post-apartheid nation-building project. As a nationalist apparatus in an emerging democracy, the Commission was conceived of to unify a fractured people and construct the 'Rainbow Nation' conceived of by Archbishop Desmond Tutu, the anti-apartheid cleric who eventually came to serve as TRC chairperson. In an attempt to uncover the 'truth' of the gross human rights abuses committed during apartheid, it started to hear testimony in 1997, soon after the birth of democracy in 1994. It also strove to foster national reconciliation and forge unity after decades of division and violence. But how did the practices of, and the discourses generated by, the TRC as a nation-building project situate women in this new nation?

Feminist theorists have long noted the contested relationship between nationalisms and women. In seeking to forge the united 'imagined political communities' (Anderson 1991, 6) that constitute national formations, nationalisms gender women as always different to male subjects in relation to the state (Yuval-Davis and Anthias 1989; Boehmer 1991; McClintock 1995; Kaplan, Alarcon and Moallem 1999; Layoun 2001). In nation-building processes, the concept 'woman' is often deployed as a sign of the nation (Ray 2000), allowing male subjects to position themselves in relation to their country in the same way as they stand in relation to women (McClintock 1995). Thus, male critics figure the nation as feminine, often in need of protection, or in the case of war, open to invasion in the same way women's bodies are protected or invaded. Feminist critics (Boehmer 1991; Jayawardena 1986; McClintock 1995) have likewise theorised nationalism as inherently patriarchal and dangerous, especially in the ways it positions women as different to men by institutionalising gender difference. Thus, while key nation-building moments such as those produced by the staging of the TRC may hold liberatory potential for women, they may also be perilous in the ways that they discursively produce women citizens.

Zoë Wicomb's *David's Story* (2000) and Sindiwe Magona's *Mother to Mother* (1998) exemplify a black literary feminism which interrupts and interrogates a number of nation-building discourses that position women in precarious ways in relation to the new South African nation. Set during the interregnum between the 1990 unbanning of the liberation movement and the first democratic election in 1994, both novels register a sustained critique of an emerging nationalism that threatened to deny women unqualified citizenship rights by refusing to acknowledge the full range of abuses black women experienced under apartheid.

Given the political investments of the two novels, this chapter examines the ways in which *David's Story* and *Mother to Mother* intervene in the unitary, masculinist discourses of nationalism produced by the TRC during South Africa's transition to democracy.

Women and the TRC

The Promotion of National Unity and Reconciliation Act of 1995 established the TRC the year after the first democratic election secured political victory for the ANC. The TRC aimed to uncover the 'truth' of human rights abuses under apartheid; provide amnesty to perpetrators of gross human rights violations on condition they fully disclosed their roles as perpetrators; provide redress to the victims of gross human rights abuses; and build national unity in a severely fractured nation. The Act clearly states that

> gross violations of human rights means the violation of human rights through –
> a) the killing, abduction, torture or severe ill-treatment of any person; or
> (b) any attempt, conspiracy, incitement, instigation, command or procurement to commit an act referred to in paragraph (a).

'Gross' human rights violations thus exclude acts of violence such as rape, sexual assault, sexual harassment or other forms of gender-based violence, an omission that would have serious repercussions for women's testimony at the TRC. Motsemme and Ratele (2000) argue that the gender discourses produced by the TRC were patriarchal in that they privileged heroic male accounts of abuse and resistance, accounts which became the discursive bedrock for forging a new South African national identity. Consequently, many women's stories, couched mostly as narratives of loss, were subsumed by dominant, masculinist nationalist discourses.

In her study of the TRC, social anthropologist Fiona Ross (2003) asserts that the Act reified the binaries 'victim' and 'perpetrator' in relation to gross human rights violations, so that people testifying before the Commission inevitably had to categorise themselves as one or the other, not both. The constructs 'victim' and 'perpetrator' elided notions of agency, especially women's agency. Women who had experienced abuse or violation and had recast themselves as survivors, instead of victims, would necessarily have been excluded from either of these categories.

Women's tendency to testify about gross human rights abuses committed against men prompted the Centre for Applied Legal Studies to convene a workshop focusing on the early exclusion of women-centred narratives at the TRC. Subsequently, gender scholars Sheila Meintjes and Beth Goldblatt (1996) presented a submission titled 'Gender and the Truth and Reconciliation Commission' at the TRC in May 1996. Noting that most women described the experiences of men while testifying at the hearings, the submission proposed that women 'should also be encouraged to speak about their own experiences', and that the TRC 'should empower these women so that they are able to locate themselves not just in the private realm as supporters of men but in the public realm as resisters to oppression' (Meintjes and Goldblatt 1996).

A number of actions stemmed from this submission: the TRC held two workshops with the media and women's organisations to encourage women's participation; it subsequently held three special women's hearings aimed at eliciting women's accounts of gross violations of human rights abuses in Cape Town, Johannesburg and Durban; and in 1997 it inserted the following statement on forms used to record testimony: 'IMPORTANT: Some women testify about violations of human rights that happened to family members or friends, but they have also suffered abuses. Don't forget to tell us what happened to you yourself if you were the victim of a gross human rights abuse' (TRC 2001a vol. 4, 283). These interventions were somewhat successful in encouraging women to testify more fully about their own experiences: after the submission on gender, women more often testified about their own experiences of human rights abuses, including sexual assault by apartheid police. At the first special hearing in Cape Town, '[w]omen spoke about giving birth in prison in front of laughing warders, being detained while still breast-feeding, being threatened with rape and being given drugged food which warders said might result in a detainee's foetus being aborted' (Meintjes and Goldblatt 1997, 8). At the Durban hearing, women testified behind screens before a panel of all-women commissioners.

Despite these interventions, women's experience of rape and torture at the hands of their comrades within the liberation movement remained shrouded in silence. While a study of ANC women in exile during the 1980s shows that violence against women was a 'significant and widespread problem' for exiled women (Hassim 2004, 438), no excavation of actual experiences of such violence has taken place and nor has the ANC attempted to redress these. This silence was perhaps not surprising, given the fact that, if women involved in the liberation movement claimed that they were raped, according to senior ANC official Jessie Duarte, 'they were regarded as having sold out to the system in one way or another' (Meintjes and Goldblatt 1997, 5). The Commission notes in its final report that 'where sexual abuse was perpetrated by men within the liberation movements, there were further pressures not to speak' (2001a Vol 4, 295).

Truth, narrative and gender in *David's Story*

Zoë Wicomb's novel represents a counter-narrative to the three dominant nation-building narratives produced by the TRC: discourses of truth as a fixed phenomenon; grand narratives of unifying nationalism; and the elision of women's experiences of rape and torture within the ranks of the liberation movement. *David's Story* pivots around the interactions of four central characters: David, a 35-year-old commander in the military wing of the ANC; Dulcie, another high-ranking soldier within the same army; an amanuensis, an unnamed woman writer to whom David relates his story in an attempt to record his history and, by extension, the history of the liberation struggle; and David's wife, Sally, a decommissioned MK soldier. While the title's 'story' ostensibly belongs to David, it is just as much the stories of these women, whose stories often confound and contradict the narrative he tries to spin. David relates his story to an unnamed female writer because he is 'unwilling or unable to flesh out the narrative' himself (1). Though the novel does not directly deal with the subject of the TRC, it does portray the experiences and subjectivities of women soldiers within the movement through characters with whom David has relationships.

David's Story represents an important intervention into the way in which the TRC constructed women who testified before it as 'secondary', indirect victims of apartheid (Jolly 2004; Ross 2003; Motsemme and Ratele 2000), and elided women MK combatants' experiences of rape and sexual violence. The novel challenges discursive constructions of women as secondary victims of human rights abuses by means of a narrative structure that destabilises the identity of the main character, thus undercutting and de-authorising the story he tells and highlighting the perspectives and experiences of his fellow combatants, Dulcie and Sally. In doing so, Wicomb disrupts the notion of a coherent self, capable of producing and laying claim to a cohesive 'truth'.

Mirroring the language of the TRC, which promised amnesty to human rights abusers with the proviso that they made 'full disclosure', Wicomb's amanuensis narrator opens the narrative with a meditation that 'David was simply unable/unwilling to disclose all' (2). He 'believed it possible to negotiate a path between the necessary secrecy and a need to tell' (2) while the amanuensis detailing his story finds herself 'unequal to the task … not understanding such a notion of telling or for that matter of truth' (2). The notion of truth is thus contested from the outset.

Wicomb also inverts the gendered confessional structure of the TRC, where women related their stories to a commission consisting of mostly men, who then interpreted their stories and presented them in the TRC report. These gendered power relations of representation are inverted by Wicomb's deployment of several seemingly peripheral women characters who comment on, contradict and add texture to David's story. Many of these women, such as his wife, Sally, and his mother-in-law, Ouma Sarie, provide counter-narratives more nuanced and insightful than David's own story, which is characterised by a severely reductionist view not only of the mechanisms of the liberation movement, but also of his own role and that of women within the struggle. Thus, it becomes evident that David's story is not merely David's: he is surrounded by women, and the reader furthermore has access to their perspectives and interior worlds. These women's interpretations of events are often contradictory to David's, in keeping with the novel's postmodern decentring of truth. In frustration, David says to the narrator: 'You have turned it into a story of women; it is full of old women, for God's sake ... Who would want to read a story like that? It is not a proper history at all' (199).

The most intriguing and elusive woman character in the novel, and also the most frustrating textual subject, is Dulcie, David's love interest and fellow soldier in the struggle against apartheid. Dulcie is depicted as a shadow haunting David and his story, a character that cannot be fleshed out because she cannot be adequately represented. Her story – equally compelling, but in the text, untellable – represents a ghostly parallel to that of David. He initially refuses to speak about Dulcie, but by his own admission, David's story cannot exist without hers. She is, in David's words, 'a kind of scream echoing through my story' (115). David must tell Dulcie's story in order to relate his own: he betrays a belief 'that some trace of hers is needed for his to make sense', but also reveals a desire 'to lose her story within his own' (78). Dulcie is thus conceptualised by the narrator as a 'protean subject that slithers hither and thither; out of reach, repeating, replacing, transforming itself ...' (35).

With Dulcie, Wicomb undercuts the binary between perpetrator and victim produced by the TRC. The reader's first encounter with Dulcie comes as she is washing a 'sticky red' substance from her hands before rubbing oil on them (18). But this oil 'will never be enough as the skin, washed over and over, laps greedily at the oil', implying Dulcie's guilt as a perpetrator of human rights abuses, the memory of which can never be erased. The reader later learns that 'her legendary marksmanship does not fail' and that 'on such days her hands are raw with washing' (18).

Despite these glimpses into her character, Dulcie remains a shadowy outline throughout the novel, an unknowable figure located within no discernible temporal space; neither amanuensis nor reader is able to get a hold on the character, who remains ephemeral – as if she were merely 'a page torn out of a novel – a story re-remembered as belonging to another' (181). Dulcie is the 'scream echoing through' David's story (115), and her narrative becomes the palimpsest underwriting David's. It is a narrative David needs in order to tell his story, yet he repeatedly attempts to erase it, even as it continues to bleed through his story.

Dulcie is thus the unspeakable in the text – alluded to, imagined by the amenuensis, a product of conjecture: all but a fully rounded character, Dulcie can never be circumscribed as within the confines of the novel. In her story there is 'no progression in time, no beginning and no end. Only a middle that is infinitely repeated, that remains in an eternal, inescapable present' (151). David 'wants her traced into his story as a recurring imprint in order to outwit her fixedness in time' (151). Dulcie is thus a 'recursion' (184), representing a kind of inverted, endless looping of David's story, which haunts his insistence on inscribing an androcentric 'proper history that excludes women' (199).

Frustrated by his unwillingness to address Dulcie's experiences, the narrator prods and probes, often infuriating David:

> I ask about the conditions of female guerrillas. Irrelevant, he barks. In the Movement these kinds of differences are wiped out by our common goal. Dulcie certainly would make no distinction between the men and women with whom she works. (78)

David's insistence on a gendered experience of war as 'irrelevant' echoes the silence of the ANC concerning gender and human rights violations within the underground liberation movement, in its submission to the TRC. In this regard, the report states: 'In presenting the ANC report to the Commission, Deputy President Thabo Mbeki acknowledged that men had committed "gender-specific offences" against their women comrades. He said that the perpetrators had been punished, but *did not describe either the offences or the punishment in any detail*' (TRC 2001a vol.4, 295) (emphasis mine). The gendered experience of violence at the hands of the ANC is completely effaced by this 'acknowledgement', causing Commissioner Hlengiwe Mkhize to remark that the ANC submission had 'fail(ed) women' (TRC 2001a vol. 4, 295). However, the TRC report perpetuates this elision of women's experiences in ANC camps in its findings, which contain only three paragraphs on women in general under apartheid, and only one sentence about the experiences of women within the ANC's military wing.

Only one woman testified before the Commission about being tortured and raped by her comrades within the liberation movement, which had dire consequences for her. Dulcie holds uncanny parallels with this woman, for, as both victim and per-petrator, Dulcie represents that which cannot be spoken about or adequately represented. Lita (alternately named 'Lita' and 'Rita' in the TRC report) Nombango Mazibuko was responsible for helping combatants enter South Africa from Swaziland but was suspected of being an apartheid informant after nine of her charges were killed in two separate ambushes, on 8 and 12 June 1988, by members of the notorious Vlakplaas counter-insurgency unit. Though she denied her involvement as a police spy, Mazibuko was subsequently found by the TRC to have been a police informer and a co-perpetrator of police human rights abuses and to have gained financially from the murders of the anti-apartheid soldiers entrusted to her care (TRC 2001b). At the same time, she is also listed as a victim of gross human rights abuses in the Commission's final report. Testifying before the TRC, Mazibuko described being kidnapped in Swaziland and tortured by her comrades after nine of them had been murdered. She was then transported across the border to Mozambique, where she was left in a hole in the ground for three days without food or water. Furthermore, she was then detained for several months in Zambia, in a hole that was regularly filled with water, and was raped at a prison in Sunset Camp multiple times by at least three different ANC soldiers.

The TRC report states: 'She was kidnapped, tortured and interrogated. Torture included hitting and kicking, as well as being forced to stay in holes for long periods' (TRC 2001a vol. 4, 307). The report goes on to record her testimony before the Commission, that is, 'being raped by at least three comrades, one of whom "cut through my genitals … he tied my hands, my legs, they were apart, he also tied my neck and he would also pour Dettol over my genitals. The pain that I experienced I have never spoken about this, I have never even told my children about this. It is the very first time I speak about this"' (TRC 2001a vol. 4, 307–308).

Mazibuko claimed she was also raped repeatedly at gunpoint by a senior ANC figure, whom she named as Mdu, after her return from exile in 1993. She had approached him at the ANC's Johannesburg headquarters, at the time known as Shell House, in order to help her re-establish her life.

Mazibuko's testimony unleashed a great deal of controversy after she testified that a senior ANC official, then-premier of Mpumalanga province, Matthews Phosa, had tried to intimidate her to prevent her from implicating senior MK members in her rape. Phosa threatened to institute defamation charges against Mazibuko, who subsequently publicly apologised to him. In response to her apology, the ANC issued a public statement expressing support for Phosa:

> The ANC has never been in doubt about the bona fides of Premier Matthews Phosa in this regard. We expressed our conviction that Premier Phosa gives his unswerving support to the current process as led by the Truth and Reconciliation process. In this context, Premier Phosa would not engage in activities aimed at undermining the integrity of the TRC process. As a member of the ANC NEC [National Executive Committee] sub-committee on Truth and Reconciliation, Phosa is guided in his actions by the views of the movement to add impetus to the process of peace, reconciliation and nation building among all South Africans. The ANC accepts the apology tendered by Mazibuko. (ANC 1997)

The statement goes on to warn: 'We however, express our convic-
tion that the TRC will ensure that in future no unsubstantiated
allegations are allowed to be made against the integrity of individuals without allowing those affected an opportunity to respond.'

The allegation made against Phosa was serious and warranted
his swift attention. However, the party's closing ranks around a
senior male figure, while sending out the message to those within
and outside of the ranks of the ANC that dissent would not be
tolerated, obscured the more important issue: the alleged rapes of
Mazibuko. The media spectacle created by Phosa's legal threats,
in particular a comment by an ANC spokesperson that '[s]he
[Mazibuko] must bear the consequences of her loose utterances'
would have made any woman think twice about testimony that
could implicate senior ANC officials. It is telling that the ANC
conflates Phosa with the organisation itself in its statement: 'The
ANC accepts the apology tendered by Mazibuko'. The apology
had been made to Phosa, but it was accepted by the ANC. Implicit
in the ANC's statement is the notion that an attack against a
senior male member is an attack against the party. This patriarchal attitude would have discouraged any dissenting daughters
within the ANC.

Furthermore, the veiled warning to the TRC to ensure
that no future 'unsubstantiated allegations' were made, would
have further enabled a culture of silence around human rights
abuses within the former liberation movement. The task of the
TRC was to investigate allegations of gross violations of human
rights. How, then, could it establish the veracity of allegations if
it suppressed testimony? The debacle drew strong criticism from
freedom of expression organisations, much of which was aimed at
the Commission for not ensuring that testifiers' comments would
enjoy a privileged status. Thus, the only woman to testify about
sexual abuse and torture at the hands of members of the liberation
movement had her testimony of the actual rapes effaced by the
ensuing fray about Phosa's involvement in attempts to silence her.
The Commission report (TRC 2001a vol. 5, 2) refers very briefly
to her testimony, and names her as a victim of gross human rights
violations. It includes just one sentence on the experience of human
rights abuses of women in exile: 'Women in exile, particularly

those in camps, were subjected to various forms of sexual abuse and harassment, including rape' (TRC 2001a vol. 5, 6).

It is in Wicomb's character Dulcie that the reader hears echoes of the treatment meted out to women like Mazibuko. The novel contains many surreal scenes where Dulcie is tortured. Though Dulcie does not know the identities of her torturers, whether they are 'friend or foe' (184), she does know that the torture intersects with her love for David and the possibility of their having a romantic relationship:

> She does not know why or how, but notes nevertheless: that this pretence of relationship coincides with the visits by night; that the coincidence of it carries a meaning that she has not yet fathomed; that one is a recursion, a variant of the other: the silence, the torture, the ambiguity; and that in such recursions – for if on the edge of a new era, freedom should announce itself as a variant of the old – lies the thought of madness ... (184)

Thus Dulcie's torture, and her love for David, the male guerrilla, are intimately bound, suggesting again the inextricability of the woman soldier's interests from the strivings of the male nationalist figure. Her love for David and the movement keeps her in the ambiguous position of enduring the pain and torture, while entering an era of freedom in the 'new' South Africa. Indeed, this entry into a free future is predicated upon her torture, her body in pain.

David's reluctance to talk about Dulcie exacerbates the tension between the amanuensis and himself. Unable to extract from David answers to her questions about 'facts: age, occupation, marital status, what she [Dulcie] wears, where she was born and raised – necessary details from which to patch together a character' (78), the narrator invokes Sethe in Toni Morrison's *Beloved* in order to construct Dulcie's subjectivity and corporeality. Similar to Sethe, Dulcie bears the imprints of torture upon her physical body:

> Her back is strong, broad, almost a square depending on where one considers the back to end. This square is marked with four

cent-sized circles forming the corners of a smaller inner square, meticulously staked out with blue ballpoint pen before the insertion of a red-hot poker between the bones ... Each circle is a liverish red crinkled surface of flesh, healed in the darkness under garments that would not let go of the blood. One day, a nice man of her own age will idly circle the dark cents with his own thumb and sigh, and with her bear it in silence, in the deepened colour of his eyes. (19)

This conjecture sees Dulcie fantasising about a man, 'perhaps a man called David, who will say nothing and who will frown when she speaks of a woman in *Beloved* whose back is scarred and who nevertheless is able to turn it into a tree' (19). But unlike Morrison's (1987, 287) Paul D, who is able to support Sethe and embrace the physical and psychological remnants of her torture, a man who 'wants to put his story next to hers', David is unable to weave the strands of his and Dulcie's stories together into a coherent whole, thus foreclosing the possibility of healing for both himself and Dulcie. It is no coincidence that the novel ends in David's suicide when he drives his car off the same Chapman's Peak cliff where Dulcie had previously considered ending her life. For David, the inability to put his story alongside Dulcie's, to weave the strands of their stories together, ultimately results in his psychic as well as his physical death – the end of his story.

Sally, David's wife, is also central to the unfolding of David's story and, significantly, is a former MK soldier; yet her corporeality is particularly weighted when compared with Dulcie's. Wicomb does not shy away from visual representations of Sally – the reader learns that after the birth of her first child, Sally becomes an 'emaciated scarecrow of a woman', with hair in 'uneven, vegetal tufts and liverish spots on her brown skin' (14).

More realistically rendered than that of Dulcie, Sally's corporeality resides in another act of textual elision that Wicomb performs toward the end of the novel in order to comment on the treatment by the ANC of women who had been raped in MK training camps. An important silence within the novel's structure, a silence that reproduces that of both the ANC and the TRC, is Wicomb's treatment of the rape of MK guerrillas by fellow soldiers. Wicomb uses the Sally character to show how this rape functions. The author raises the issue of rape within the guerrilla movement in an ambiguous way that challenges the structure of the silencing nationalist discourse around rape by replicating and subverting it. Consider the scene where Sally undergoes military training in Mozambique, and an impatient MK soldier is teaching her how to swim:

> Sally had not known that she was afraid of water. She loved paddling and took some pleasure in feeling the resistance of water, but required to swim at one of the training camps, she found it impossible to put her face in it. In the thick Mozambican heat the water felt like oil, and the comrade with his hand under her belly barked his instructions, Up, draw up your legs, and out, kick, flap the ankle, hands forward, round and again. And how poorly she performed, unable to confess her terror.
>
> He said, as they made their way gingerly across the burning sand, A fuck, that's what you need, and she saw his bulging shorts and knew that her time had come, as she had known it would come sooner or later, this unspoken part of a girl's training. And because she would not let him force her, lord it over her, she forced herself and said, Okay, if you want. It did not take long, and she had no trouble pushing him off as soon as he had done, and since she had long forgotten the fantasy of the virginal white veil, it did not matter, no point in being fastidious, there were more important things to think of, there was freedom on which to fix her thoughts. Then, cleaning herself in seawater, over and over, she lost her fear, found her body dissolving, changing its solid state in the water through which she moved effortlessly. Which was, of course, just as the comrade had said. (123)

While Sally's use of the word 'okay' implies consent, this consent is given under coercion and duress, which renders the intercourse an act of rape. Here, the entire reference to and description of the rape takes up one paragraph of the 213-page novel, seemingly replicating the way in which the TRC and the liberation movement leadership elided such occurrences. At no point is the word 'rape' used in naming the experience.

'Unable to confess her terror', Sally mirrors the silence of those who did not come forward to testify of rape or sexual abuse. The narrative is structured to replicate the effacement of women's experience by dominant nationalist discourses, yet in its very silence about the act of rape it functions to show *how* such discourses silence women. By portraying rape as a de facto part of a woman's training within the liberation movement, the inevitability of which is made explicit through the phrase 'her time had come, as she had known it would come sooner or later', Wicomb inscribes sexual violation onto the experience of being a woman and guerrilla; in this way she, as author, retrieves sexual abuse from the silence surrounding it at different levels of discourse within the liberation movement and at the TRC.

When one considers the testimony of General Andrew Masondo (TRC 2001a vol 4, 307), the attitude around rape in the setting of the camps becomes clear: 'In Angola there are at one time twenty-two women in a group of more than 1000 people ... there was an allegation that ... Commanders were misusing women ... *the law of supply and demand must have created some problems*' (emphasis mine).

What is striking about Wicomb's description of the rape is Sally's inability and refusal to see herself as a 'victim' of rape. While the experience is certainly dreadful, the naturalisation of rape makes Sally view herself not as someone who has been violated, that is, a victim of gross human rights violations, but as someone who perseveres throughout the ordeal. Sally's seeming compliance with her rapist helps her to assert some measure of control over her body and psyche while being raped. Perhaps paradoxically, the act of acquiescence is also an act of resistance, enabling Sally to conceptualise herself outside of the framework of victimhood.

In its report, the Commission (TRC 2001a vol. 1, 59) acknowledges some of the difficulties surrounding the construction of the victim/perpetrator binary:

However, when dealing with gross human rights violations committed by perpetrators, the person against whom that violation is committed can only be described as a victim, regardless of whether he or she emerged a survivor. In this sense, the state of mind and survival of that person is irrelevant; it is the intention and action of the perpetrator that creates the condition of being a victim.

However, this definition of a victim robs those described as such of agency. Clearly, in light of the formulation above, Sally is no victim – her strategy is one that minimises the violence, perhaps, of the rape, and is geared at securing her continued psychological and physical survival. This does not mean that Sally has not been raped. She is, however, not a victim. The TRC's conceptualisation of victim is, in any case, at odds with the way in which South Africa's strong anti-rape lobby conceives of those who experience rape and then live as 'survivors'.

Caught in this binary victim/perpetrator discourse, neither Sally, nor women combatants who may have been raped, choose to be complicit in their further victimisation by identifying themselves as 'rape victims'. The dominant, nationalist discourse describes victims in a way that is completely at odds with the vociferous counter-narrative of anti-rape discourse, thus closing up a space in which rape may productively have been articulated. Couple this clash in discourses with the fact that rape was not identified as a gross human rights violation in the parliamentary Act that established the TRC, nor in the discourse of the TRC itself, and it becomes apparent why women who had been sexually abused may have been unwilling to testify at the TRC. Having had the experience of rape being effaced, firstly by the discourse of the liberation movement which naturalised rape, and secondly by the Promotion of National Unity and Reconciliation Act which did not define rape as a gross human rights violation, then thirdly by the TRC's discourse of victimhood possibly eliding rape survivors' experience, it is little wonder that only one woman, Lita Mazibuko, came forward with her tale of sexual abuse during guerrilla training (see Mazibuko 1997).

Throughout the rape, Sally chooses to keep her mind's eye fixed on the goal of collective freedom – a freedom that turns out to be constructed within the framework of the 'national unity' the TRC seeks to build, but cannot and will not acknowledge the violation of women's bodies as part of its price. It is unsurprising, therefore, that Sally feels her body 'dissolving' after the rape.

Taking this metaphoric 'disappearance' of her body into account, David's inability to 'speak' Dulcie, to represent her subjectivity or experiences in any meaningful way, together with the novel's inability to 'speak' the rape and torture of women combatants at the hands of their comrades, represents the silence around the ANC's treatment of women guerrillas within their ranks, and forecloses the possibility that wrongdoing against women combatants might be acknowledged or redressed. Wicomb thus points to nationalism's deferment of restorative justice for women: the emerging nation, in suspending the possibility of genuine gender reconciliation, effectively builds the new South Africa upon the injustice inflicted upon the bodies of black women anti-apartheid combatants.

Sindiwe Magona's ideology of motherhood and the nation

As with *David's Story*, Magona's 1998 novel, *Mother to Mother*, is set within the highly ambivalent, transitional space of South Africa between 1990 and 1994, a time of great political instability and uncertainty about the country's future. To paraphrase Antonio Gramsci (1971), the old South Africa had been left behind, but the new had not yet been born. Yet ideologies about an as yet unrealised 'new' South Africa, and the shape the nation would take, were in formation and circulation. Magona's tale enters the world of the men held responsible for killing Amy Biehl, the American Fulbright Scholar whose death threatened to disrupt the fragile peace that had been brokered between political parties during the run-up to the historic election of 27 April 1994. The four young men charged and found guilty of Biehl's murder, Mongezi Manqina, Mzikhona Nofemela, Vusumzi Ntamo and Ntobeko Peni, were members of the Pan Africanist Students' Organisation (PASO), the student wing of the Pan Africanist Congress, an organisation known at the time for its slogan 'one settler, one bullet'. The four were convicted of Biehl's murder and imprisoned, and later appeared before the TRC to apply for amnesty. Peni testified that PASO's executive had ordered its members to make Guguletu ungovernable, and to assist the PAC's armed wing, the Azanian People's Liberation Army, in winning back black people's land. He regarded this statement, he said, as an instruction to injure or kill white people, and he believed that killing Biehl would return the land to black South Africans. Biehl's murderers were granted amnesty by the TRC and freed from prison. Magona fictionalises events leading up to Biehl's death by consolidating the murderers into one central character, Mxolisi, whose mother, Mandisa, relates the story of the murder from her son's and her own point of view.

In structuring the novel as a lament narrated from Mandisa's perspective, and by addressing the mother of the murder victim, Magona employs a strategy similar to Wicomb's multivocality in *David's Story*. Just as David's story is not just his own, but also the story of a cast of women surrounding him, so, too, *Mother to Mother* seems at first glance to be a narrative of Mxolisi's life, but becomes Mandisa's story as well. Magona interweaves the story of the son with the life story of the mother, narrated in the first person from her unique subject position. This narration interrupts the seamless, masculine unitary narrative which the new, emerging nation seeks to build. In giving Mandisa's story equal, if not more, prominence to that of Mxolisi, Magona interrupts the nationalist TRC discourse that, as Motsemme (2004) argues, sought to celebrate the male freedom fighter as heroic agent of the history that birthed the new South Africa. Given that 79 per cent of women who testified before the TRC bore witness to the experiences of men (Ross 2003, 17), this narrative of a heroic past was decidedly masculinist. Magona fractures this production of nationalism that perpetuates itself through the construction of the heroic male revolutionary as sole agent within black nationalist history, and in so doing she reverses the figure of woman as secondary player, as depicted by the TRC.

Mother to Mother decentres the idea of the TRC retrieving a fixed truth to be packaged for national consumption; it presents a counter-narrative to that which reduces women to the status of secondary victims of apartheid, specifically in their roles as mothers of the (male) agents of the liberation struggle. As Schatteman (2008) and Samuelson (2007) have shown, reading the novel against static discourses of the mother as a sacrificial figure in the creation of the new nation, as generated at the TRC, disrupts the notion of women as passive spectators to the liberation struggle. Samuelson (2007, 159) reads women's interpellation by the TRC as reducing them to the status of 'mother witness' so that their voices were 'always already produced as that of the suffering mother' (2007, 161). She argues that this trope of mother-witness valorises women's suffering while obscuring the other roles women have played in the struggle against apartheid. Furthermore, *Mother to Mother* disrupts the 'victim/perpetrator' binary constructed by the TRC in similar ways to Wicomb's novel, by portraying Mxolisi as a person who simultaneously inhabits both positions. He is the murderer of the young white woman, and therefore the perpetrator of political violence, but Mandisa's account of her son's life shows how Mxolisi is also the victim of sustained structural violence committed by the apartheid state. Such violence, including the daily indignities visited upon black bodies by the apartheid system, is not accounted for as a human rights abuse in the TRC's logic of confession and forgiveness.

Magona uses the position of mother to speak against nationalist patriarchy. As with the ideology of 'woman' as sign for the nation, motherhood has often been deployed in particularly gendered ways to underwrite the construction of the nation. The symbol of the mother is a particularly important construct of nationalism, with mothers playing a significant biological and social role: producers of the subjects of the state; transmitters of national culture; and socialising children in the private sphere (Yuval-Davis and Anthias 1989). The figure of the mother thus powerfully signifies both the apartheid and post-apartheid South African nation, though in different ways for the various ethnic and political groups.

In apartheid South Africa, the trope of woman-as-nation gained particular salience through the ideological construct of the mother of the nation, strategically invoked by both the liberation movement and Afrikaner nationalism. Deborah Gaitskell and Elaine Unterhalter's (1989) analysis demonstrates how white supremacy and black liberation politics, the respective ideologies underpinning Afrikaner and African nationalism (the latter expressed by the ANC) inflected the way Afrikaners and the ANC conceived of the ideology of motherhood. Following on Gaitskell and Unterhalter, Anne McClintock has shown how both Afrikaner and African women have used the term 'mother of the nation' to mobilise politically and achieve their respective goals; however, the ways in which this sign of woman-as-nation are deployed differ vastly. McClintock argues that, for both groups, political agency resides in the esteemed position of motherhood: women use motherhood strategically to insert into public discourse political demands that might otherwise not be heard. But whereas Afrikaner nationalism after the Anglo-Boer war portrayed mothers as grieving figures devoid of militancy, African nationalism has 'embraced, transmuted and transformed the ideology [of motherhood] in a variety of ways, working strategically within traditional ideology to justify untraditional public militancy' (McClintock 1995, 381).

The latter is exactly the way in which Magona utilises the ideology of motherhood: first, she uses the identity 'mother' as a privileged platform from which to articulate a subaltern standpoint through the character Mandisa; but in using this platform, she subverts the heroic male-centred discourses that construct the new South African nation, rendering them more complex than the unitary forms of national consciousness sought during the transitional period.

Magona goes on to locate Mandisa's identity outside of the constraints of traditional, patriarchal discourses of motherhood; in order to re-envision the mother figure, she transcends the permissible national discourse on motherhood that authorises her to speak.

Magona's remapping of motherhood

With regard to the way postcolonial African women writers have grappled with and transformed the idea of motherhood in their fiction, Elleke Boehmer (1991, 10) contends that '[t]o write is not only to speak for one's place in the world. It is also to make one's own place or narrative, to tell the story of oneself, to create an identity. It is in effect to deploy what might be called a typically nationalist strategy'. Here, Boehmer is pointing to the territoriality of text. If, as explored in Chapter Three, writing turns space into place, then writing from, and about, a previously 'unwritten' subject position indeed charts new territory within the realm of cultural production and representation. Rendering such an 'unwritten' subjectivity into fiction at a time that coincides with the emergence of a new nation may be an especially important writerly strategy for women, since the discourses surrounding subjectivities thus constructed run parallel with emerging ideas of the nation, thereby serving to underpin or subvert nationalist narratives. Magona writes the character of Mandisa, the mother of the liberation hero and murderer, Mxolisi, at a time when the 'new' South Africa is transforming, reconstituting itself into a unitary nation after years of apartheid fracturing and disenfranchisement. In regard to this, nationalisms and patriarchy may be said to overlap and buttress each other, promoting 'specifically unitary or "one-eyed" forms of consciousness' (Boehmer (1991, 7).

Magona undermines any possibility of a reifying, patriarchal narrative of motherhood in the story Mandisa tells by creating a space of articulation that is distinctively feminine. As the novel's title suggests, the narrative consists in the telling of a story by one woman to another, as the mother of the killer relates the events to the victim's mother. The narrative is pointedly directed at one particular woman, interpellating the white American into Mandisa's world on the basis of an assumed shared identity: motherhood. By the end of the novel, the other mother has become Mandisa's 'Sister-Mother ... bound in this sorrow' (201). It may be argued that, through this discursive device, Magona sets up a proto-feminist space devoid of male intervention for the telling and reception of her story. The narrative form Magona thus employs turns away from emergent nationalist discourse in two ways. She creates a woman-centred space for the performance and reception of her story, circumventing male mediation of her narrative by directly addressing the victim's mother. Furthermore, in Mandisa's refusal to ask for the white mother's forgiveness for her son's crime, Magona disavows the prevailing narrative of the necessity of forgiveness in achieving reconciliation and national unity. She asks only that the white mother 'understand' her son

(1), and never asks for her forgiveness or absolution. The only plea for forgiveness is directed at God: 'God, please forgive my son. Forgive him this terrible, terrible sin' (4).

Deftly interweaving the story of the murder victim with her own and that of her son, Mandisa relates the tale in the first person, from a perspective that generates reader empathy not only for Mxolisi, but also for herself, as a mother. Counter to sacrificial narratives of motherhood, the son's story does not displace his mother's. His birth is not a joyous celebration, but a contested event that seems to pit his very being against his mother. Thus, Mandisa casts even his conception in negative terms: he has troubled her 'from before he was conceived; when he with total lack of consideration if not downright malice, seeded himself inside my womb' (1). Mandisa goes on to declare that his coming into being 'unreasonably and totally destroy[ed] the me I was ... the me I would have become' (1–2), a refrain she repeats throughout the novel.

As a fourteen-year-old girl who has not yet completed her education, Mandisa's opportunities and choices are severely curtailed by the pregnancy, and she is effectively doomed to the life of a domestic worker. Only too aware of this, Mandisa does not couch the pregnancy or birth in celebratory terms. Her narrative refuses to sublimate her own feelings, her experience of the self, in her telling of the story of her son. She thus inhabits a seemingly contradictory space of motherhood: at one moment the pain of childbirth 'told me that I hated this child ... hated him or her with a venom too fierce to ever die', yet at the very next she is overcome with 'joy, pure and simple' (127). Motherhood, then, is not an uncomplicated experience: she professes love for her child while at the same time clearly and shamelessly articulating the effacing of her subjectivity which his birth effects.

The reader identifies with Mandisa's point of view, which is foregrounded through her first-person narration of the murder as she recalls her own and her son's life within the twenty-four-hour period before and after the event. One day in the life of the murdered white student becomes the scaffold for investigating Mandisa's entire life, spanning her traumatic childhood, adolescence, entry into motherhood, and her marriage. In this way, Magona retrieves the actual event of the killing from the sensationalised international media narrative that focused solely on the white woman's life and death, and contextualises this story within the history of South Africa leading up to the death. Magona thus transforms the story from a sensational headline-grabber focusing on the victim, to a more nuanced portrayal of the effects of injustice and sustained structural violence. The story of Amy Biehl, in Magona's telling, really begins with Mandisa's childhood: apartheid laws result in Mandisa and her family being forcibly removed from the Blouvlei Settlement – for Mandisa, a place of '[g]ood things. Lovely things. Delicious things' (49).

The story, in fact, stretches even further back in time, to the injustices visited upon Mandisa's ancestors through their removal from ancestral land by white colonisers. Rather than being the pivot of the narrative, the white woman's death becomes the culmination of decades of oppression and trauma. It is a story within a larger story, spanning decades; even centuries. Mandisa also imparts a sense of collective responsibility for the woman's death by relating her murder to the systemic failures of other 'fathers and mothers' who denied Mxolisi the opportunity of becoming a fully actualised human being. This insistence upon politically contextualising the white woman's murder recasts the killing as the consequence of historical forces set in motion centuries ago, rather than a random, atemporal crime. In assigning collective blame for the woman's death, Mandisa once again undermines the nationalist discourse generated by the TRC that a perpetrator's full disclosure, followed by forgiveness, will lead to national reconciliation. In Magona's novel, culpability is presented as far more complex; where there is systemic oppression and violence, culpability is collective. Thus, approaches to reconciliation and the healing of a fractured nation would require far more than the performance of a penitence and forgiveness that might satisfy the 'one-eyed forms of consciousness' required by nationalism and patriarchy to sustain themselves (Boehmer 1991, 1).

Magona further develops the trope of collective culpability by presenting Mxolisi as a Christ figure in the narrative. Mandisa becomes pregnant with him at the age of fourteen, despite having chosen not to have penetrative sexual intercourse with her boyfriend, China, so as to avoid early pregnancy. Mandisa even submits to regular virginity testing at the hands of her mother, and insists that she and her partner have 'playsex ... never going higher than a little above mid-thigh' (97). Despite these precautions, Mandisa finds herself pregnant, despite technically being a virgin. The virgin birth motif is further expanded when Mandisa's much older aunt becomes pregnant at the same time, and her grandmother exclaims that it is '[b]iblical Elizabeth's story all over again' (103).

In her analysis of women's testimony before the TRC, Ross (2003, 154) shows how '[w]omen testifiers were thanked for the "sacrifice" of their dead or injured kin and testifiers were told that their sacrifices (of health, well-being, or the lives of those close to them) had redemptive power for the national body.' Meg Samuelson (2007, 165) argues that Magona uses the trope of the virgin birth to 'grapple with, rather than underwrite a discourse of sacrifice', thus subverting the narrative of sacrifice which was one of the few modes of articulation open to women who appeared before the TRC.

Yet, Mxolisi is a saviour figure – as is evident in the allusion to Christ, and in fragments pieced together as the narrative unfolds. We learn that Mxolisi would readily confess his own sin, but would never betray another, preferring to 'take the blame himself' (154). He is also a saviour figure in the community, rescuing a young woman from gang rape. He earns numerous accolades, as his mother's anecdote bears out:

> In spite of all his politics, two-three weeks ago I could hardly walk anywhere in the whole of Section 3 without being stopped by people whose mouths had no other words to say besides singing Mxolisi's praises. To everyone, he was a hero ... Young and old, they stopped me on the street to tell me: 'Mother of Mxolisi, your child is really a child to be proud of. In this day and age, when children do everything but what is decent. We really thank the Lord for you. Yes. We really thank Him because of the son He has given you!' This Mxolisi! He can make one so proud sometimes. (162)

Like Christ, Mxolisi, whose name means 'peace', is a redemptive figure. Ross (2003, 154) points out that at the TRC, 'suffering and sacrifice, heavily predicated on a Christian model, were depicted as constitutive of the foundational order of the "new South Africa". Accordingly, Mxolisi becomes a scapegoat whose life is ultimately sacrificed to the nation-building project. He pays the price for the historical 'sins' of his nation – the structural violence, injustice and brutality of apartheid – and becomes the sacrificial figure who is effectively made to atone for the centuries of wrongdoing that culminate in one violent episode. In figuring him as the sacrificial Christ, Magona again comments on the nation's collective culpability for the death of the white woman. Mxolisi takes on this displaced sin, which is confessed, punished and absolved so that the nation-building project can continue. The Christ device thus also complicates the victim/perpetrator binary set up in the TRC proceedings.

Having discussed Magona's conceptualisation of motherhood, I now turn to her iteration of motherhood in relation to other mothers, notably white mothers. The novel depicts Mandisa's relationship with two white mothers: the mother of the slain student, and Mandisa's employer, Mrs Nelson. While Mandisa hails the American mother as a 'sister-mother', forging a discursive connection with her through their shared experience of the unfolding tragedy, Mandisa shares no such relationship with Mrs Nelson. The reason for Mandisa's different treatment of the two women can be found in the nexus of gender, race and class in South African power relations, which makes 'sisterhood' between black and white women virtually impossible.

In her extensive study of domestic workers in the eastern Cape region of South Africa, Jacklyn Cock (1989) conveys the reality of black and white women in this country. With two out of three white households employing black women as domestic workers in the 1980s (Cock 1989, 122), it is fair to speculate that the primary forms of interaction between white and black women in South Africa during apartheid took place through the exploitative system of domestic work, with white women being the main overseers of black women who worked in their homes. After interviewing 225 black domestic workers, Cock (1989, 1) issues an important warning:

In this context feminist theory has to be sensitive to the complex inter-relation of race, gender and class. The intersection of these three lines of oppression in the situation of Black women in South Africa raises important questions regarding both the limits and the possibilities of feminist struggle.

Among her findings is that black women employed as domestic workers often perceived themselves as little more than slaves, given the conditions of their employment: no protection from the law; no laws stipulating minimum wages or reasonable working hours; no unemployment insurance, maternity leave or sick leave; and the constant threat of instant dismissal. Working under these conditions, black women found themselves in situations of 'ultra-exploitation' (Cock 1989, 4), which left them with little time for social or family life. Whereas the majority of white women employers interviewed for Cock's study conveyed the sense that they treated their domestic workers as 'one of the family' (Cock 1989, 67), none of the black domestic workers shared this belief. Domestic work also had implications for both black and white motherhood. Whereas white mothers felt that employing a domestic worker freed up time to devote to the intellectual and emotional development of their offspring, the opposite was true for the domestic workers who were mothers: 'Clearly, this is done at the expense of Black children' (Cock 1989, 44).

By contrasting the lives of the two women in her novel, Magona demonstrates how apartheid structures even their most basic experience – mothering. Of her daily life, Mandisa states: 'Monday to Saturday I got to work in the kitchen of my mlungu woman, Mrs Nelson; leaving the house before the children go to school and coming back long after the sun has gone to sleep. I am not home when they come back from school' (8). Unlike Mandisa, Mrs Nelson works neither inside nor outside of the home, and is available to greet her children each day when they return home from school. Her only work-related responsibility is overseeing Mandisa's labour in her home; in Mandisa's words, 'breathing down my neck every minute of the blessed day' (20). From this task she has a weekly day off, during which she goes to the gym, goes shopping, and has lunch with a friend. The needs of Mrs Nelson's white family always trump the needs of Mandisa's children, as Mandisa demonstrates in her complaint: 'Where was the government the day my son stole my neighbour's hen; wrung its neck and cooked it – feathers and all, because there was no food in the house and I was away, minding the children of the white family I worked for?' (3).

Mandisa's labour of surrogate mothering for a white woman disconnects her from her own children, making her feel that her parental authority is a 'mere formality, a charade, something nobody ever heeds' (8). Cock's study demonstrates that black South African domestic workers cultivate a powerful sense of deprivation through their constant exposure to their employers' higher standard of living. Furthermore, even though the majority of white employers view their domestic workers as part of the family, the paternalistic employer/employee relationship which results from the extremely skewed power relations between black and white women in this situation perpetuates racial discrimination against black women, since it models, to white children, inequitable power relations between whites and blacks. Through their domestic workers, white children are thus 'socialized into the dominant ideological order and learn the attributes and styles of racial domination from relationships with servants, especially "nannies"' (Cock 1989, 3). The corollary is also true: via the experience of their mothers' domestic work and inequitable treatment, black children are often enraged and politicised. Cock cites Steve Biko as an example of a black man who first became conscious of apartheid's injustice through his mother's domestic service to a white family.

Feminist theorists such as Zoë Wicomb and Desiree Lewis point to the ways in which black women's consciousness concerning motherhood differs significantly from that of white South African women. Wicomb notes that in harnessing the role of motherhood, and the political agency it enabled in their fight against apartheid, black women's domestic roles in apartheid South Africa were politicised; this was a marked departure 'from the Euro-feminist view of motherhood as a condition of passivity and confinement' (Wicomb 1996, 47). In similar vein, Lewis (1992) cites a number of studies that have shown how black and working-class women transcend conventional dependent roles associated with femininity as they take on political activist and breadwinner roles, effectively becoming household heads and figures of familial and community authority. Thus, while white feminists attach importance to the notion of freedom from family duties and the domestic realm, for many black women '"freedom" to enter the male domain [of work outside of the home] is frequently oppressive.'

This position on motherhood, as exemplified by Mandisa's self-concept as a mother, indicates the salience of racialised identity for black conceptions of motherhood. Walker (1995, 436) argues that foregrounding 'difference' in South African feminist conceptualisations of motherhood is insufficient as an analytical tool because 'the opposition set up between a white = western oppressive discourse of motherhood and a Black = non-western = emancipatory discourse, is overly simplistic and does not appear to be based on a serious engagement with the available literature or primary sources.' While the argument of a simplified discourse of white motherhood as oppressive and black motherhood as emancipatory may be valid, it is my contention that one cannot investigate the construction of the identity of motherhood without investigating the material differences in the mothering experiences of women differently racialised as black or white by apartheid ideology and law. Given that feminists of colour around the world have argued for feminist analyses which are cognisant of the intersectional or co-constructed nature of identity, an unpacking of the system of racial privilege and the ways in which power operates between black and white women in the South African context is central to investigating the self-concept of motherhood in both black and white women. I would argue that, contrary to Walker's de-emphasis of racial difference, racial difference is perhaps the most important constitutive component upon which black mothers, particularly those who are domestic workers, base their concept of motherhood. As Magona's text and Cock's research demonstrate, the exposure of black women domestic workers to the affluence of the white families they work for, and the exposure to the relative ease with which white women are able to practise mothering, at the expense of domestic workers' family lives, creates a profound sense of deprivation in these black women's lives. Black women's exposure to white domestic life exacerbates the sense of powerlessness black mothers feel in being unable to fulfil the emotional needs, or control the destinies, of their children, as Magona's *Mother to Mother* poignantly demonstrates.

Through Mandisa's interiority, Magona shows the multiple facets and overlapping components of a mother's identity: she is woman, working class, a sexual being, daughter, friend, scholar and wife; she is also black in a country that severely oppresses black subjects, and black women in particular. Her own image or idea of herself as a mother cannot but be constructed against the iteration of motherhood she is exposed to in the form of her employer, Mrs Nelson. In the performance of her white maternal identity, Mrs Nelson provides an inverted mirror through which Mandisa is able to quantify how apartheid systematically produces a deficit in the quality of mothering she is able to provide for her own offspring. Mandisa's sense of powerlessness in being able to provide for or guide her children is a significant aspect of her identity as a mother.

In setting up mechanisms for processing human rights abuses as a means of national reconciliation, the TRC placed great store on the notion of restorative justice. In its final report (TRC 2001a vol. 1, 36), the Commission explicates the meaning of the concept as follows:

> Amnesty cannot be viewed as justice if we think of justice only as retributive or punitive in nature. We believe however, that there is another kind of justice – a restorative justice which is concerned not so much with punishment as with correcting imbalances, restoring broken relationships – with healing, harmony and reconciliation. Such justice focuses on the experience of victims; hence the importance of reparations.

Yet, in its inability to create the space for women to testify about their gendered, racialised experiences of apartheid and the human rights abuses inflicted on them as a consequence of their gender, the TRC forecloses healing not only for women combatants, as demonstrated by Wicomb in *David's Story*, but also for the daily abuses black mothers suffered during apartheid. Magona's emphasis in *Mother to Mother* on the difference between white and black motherhood, and the potential of the domestic worker/employer relationship for radicalising young black people, similarly interrupts the metanarrative of reconciliation, pointing to the impossibility of meaningful reconciliation between different classes of people when power relations between them remain fundamentally unjust and unequal, as is the case in post-apartheid South Africa. While the TRC as a nation-building mechanism focused on gross human rights violations such as the murder of Amy Biehl, it left little room for articulations of the corrosive effect of the millions of small, daily humiliations and acts of structural violence that degraded black South Africans, tearing apart the fabric of their lives. Mxolisi's loss of his mother's daily care, affection and guidance was of a kind never articulated before the TRC, and therefore never redressed. In fact, a deafening silence continues to surround such losses of parental guidance and love in the broader, reconciliatory nation-building discourses of the 'new' South Africa. They remain unacknowledged as South Africans are urged to 'move on'.

David's Story functions similarly as a crucial counter-narrative to the dominant discourse of national unity at all costs, most especially not acknowledging the abuses perpetrated by the ANC's armed wing against its own female guerrillas. This is Wicomb's greatest contribution with *David's Story*: in pointing to nationalism's deferment of restorative justice for women, she demonstrates how the emerging nation, in deferring such justice, forecloses the possibility of true reconciliation in the nascent South African nation. Both she and Magona demonstrate how nation-building discourses have, effectively, built the new South Africa on the injustices visited upon the bodies and psyches of black women.

5

Making Personhood: Remaking History in Yvette Christiansë and Rayda Jacobs's Neo-Slave Narratives

She struggled for years to unlock those doors,
to find the stories buried underneath those floors.
There she went all dressed in shame,
from there she returned without a name.

At night she tried to scale those walls,
to get a glimpse of figures in the halls.
She lay in her bed stiff and petrified
while trying to unravel who the ones were that lied.

Until she climbed the polished steps
and entered a place of many maps.
She found her fingerprints on the open doors,
Her footsteps mirrored on wooden floors.

She stepped into the dungeon and unearthed herself,
ever probing and learning where to delve.
She traced herself to bygone days,
to show how she existed in many different ways.

Diana Ferrus — from 'An Ode to the Slave Lodge'

It is not possible to fully understand enduring concepts
of race, sexuality and belonging in the country today, I
argue, without attending to the crucible of colonialism,
slavery, and Islam in which they were formed.

Gabeba Baderoon — *Regarding Muslims*

The neo-slave narrative is a relatively new literary form for black South African writers, especially for those traditionally excluded from circuits of publication by apartheid law. Originating in the United States, the form casts the practice of slavery from the perspective of the enslaved (Rushdy 1999), inviting the reader into a fictive world which not only portrays the horror of slavery, but also reimagines and recasts it through a lens of resistance. In this chapter, I examine how Yvette Christiansë's *Unconfessed* (2006) and Rayda Jacobs's *The Slave Book* (1998) – the first neo-slave narratives penned by black South African women – construct slavery at the Cape, in their transitional and post-transitional literature on the subject. While predecessors and contemporary companions to this genre have creatively imagined and explored the slave experience, notably André Brink, Trudie Bloem, Pamela Jooste and Claire Robertson, the novels of Christiansë and Jooste mark a turning point in the production of South African fiction about slavery: the slave experience was, for the first time, creatively imagined by black women who, quite likely, are descended from the enslaved peoples who built much of the infrastructure of early South African society.

Boswell (2016) has argued that contemporary post-transitional black South African women's poetry produces an ethic that seeks to restore both fragmented histories and fractured subjectivities that are the result of colonial and apartheid domination. The epigraph to this chapter, taken from a poem by self-described slave descendant Diana Ferrus, exemplifies this ethic. In the poem, an unnamed marginal subject of history struggles to unlock the doors of the Slave Lodge in Cape Town in order to 'find the stories buried underneath those floors' (Ferrus 2010). Once the subject of this poem succeeds in entering into the forbidden space of the Slave Lodge, a metaphorical entry into history, she is able to '[trace] herself to bygone days,/ to show how she existed in many different ways'. In grappling with her history of enslavement, neither hiding it away nor seeking to forget about it, the subject is able to trace her elided existence, bringing it into being, thereby restoring her place in history.

Rayda Jacobs and Yvette Christiansë, as black women writers who are members of the cultural group descended from slaves at the Cape, offer, from this positionality, insights not only into slave experience, but also resonances of what it means in the contemporary moment to be the descendant of slaves in a place that wilfully expunges from memory the fact of enslavement in establishing the South African nation (Bell 1994 and Wicomb 1998). In Christianse's acclaimed work, she reimagines the life and experiences of the historical figure, Sila van den Kaap, an enslaved woman imprisoned on Robben Island for infanticide in 1824; in this way, Christianse weaves a complex tale of captivity, loss and resistance. Jacobs's earlier novel similarly foregrounds the interior life of an enslaved young woman, Somiela van den Kaap, depicting numerous small acts of resistance against the system that holds her captive.

Both novels are examples of creative work that seeks to fill in gaps in narratives of the South African nation by restoring to history the centrality of slavery to the developing economy of the country. In doing so, these works also restore the erased subjectivities of those enslaved; women in particular. Christianse, especially, confers personhood on the figure of Sila van den Kaap in ways that illuminate the specifically gendered condition of slavery. Each of these novels illuminates the political economy of slavery in ways that make visible black women's reproductive labour, thereby critically engaging with the political economy of post-apartheid South Africa in the era of the Truth and Reconciliation Commission, which was aimed at building a unitary nation.

Both *Unconfessed* and *The Slave Book* depict slavery at the colonial Cape, in particular the gendered experience of enslavement and the political economy of slavery. The earlier of the two novels, Jacobs's *The Slave Book*, is set within a relatively short period, between 1832 and 1834. Christianse's *Unconfessed* follows the experiences of the historical character, Sila van den Kaap, who is on death row on Robben Island for murdering her son. Both novels are thus set in the interregnum between 1808 when the British oceanic slave trade was outlawed and 1838 when full emancipation came into effect at the Cape.

Slavery existed at the Cape from the time it was first colonised by the Dutch in 1652: the entire economy of the expanding settlement was dependent on slave labour, and the legal system introduced by the Dutch East India Company was based on slaveholding (Shell 1994). Nigel Worden (1985) argues that the practice of slavery shaped all social relationships in the Cape Colony, with enslaved people forming the majority of the population for significant periods before abolition at the Cape. As the settlement at the Cape grew, slaveholding practices changed to accommodate different categories of settlers and a growing economy. The Company, for example, owned slaves who lived at the Slave Lodge and were the first to benefit from the newly introduced 'Amelioration' laws. But slaves working for farmers closer to the frontier laboured under very different conditions, and were often at the mercy of individual slaveholders: 'Generally, the further from the port the family was, the more violence there was. The paternalistic-patriarchal spectrum stretched from the town to the country. In an expanding frontier-bound population, violence became more pronounced, and over time, easier to justify' (Shell 1994, xxix).

Various Amelioration laws were passed after 1806, when the British occupied the Cape for a second time, with a law abolishing the oceanic slave trade being passed in 1807. These laws gave enslaved people gradually increasing, but uneven, protection, such as the right to be baptised and the right to lodge complaints of ill-treatment with a Protector of Slaves. These protections did not, however, free complainants; they merely held slave owners accountable for certain abuses and the poor treatment of enslaved people. Slaves, however, remained chattel – objects that could be inherited, sold and bargained for. After the oceanic slave trade was outlawed in 1808, after the 1807 Act came into effect, a scarcity of slave labour followed in the British colonies, with slaves at the Cape becoming increasingly valuable. In this regard, Shell (1994, xxix) notes: 'The abolition of the slave trade ushered in a new era of paternalism, as slave owners realised that the slaves they owned in 1807 were going to be the only stock for the future.'

With anxieties about how to replenish slave populations that could no longer be traded along oceanic routes, enslaved women became very important within the political economy of slavery. Operating according to a system of matrilineal birth lines, the global practice of slavery began to rely more heavily on births by enslaved women to 'replenish' a declining slave stock. Children born through 'consensual' relationships with enslaved men, or who were the result of rape by either the slave owner or another slave, remained enslaved. Paternity was of no consequence – if a child was born to an enslaved woman, such a child was born into chattel slavery. Slavery thus reduced enslaved women's bodies to property, but also laid claim to their reproductive rights; in this way, slavery used enslaved women's bodies against women themselves, so that their bodies became instruments to create more slave labour, perpetuating the system. Baderoon (2014, 16) notes that women enslaved at the Slave Lodge were 'subjected to systemic sexual violence through the[ir] enforced prostitution'.

Enslaved women were therefore in the paradoxical position of reproducing slavery, a system which reduced them to owned objects. This reproductive co-option of enslaved women's bodies becomes important especially in reading *Unconfessed*, a novel that raises questions about why a mother who would do almost anything for her children, would resort to murdering a beloved son.

In analysing these two novels depicting slaves and slavery, which has been a feature of South African literary production since the 1830s (Johnson 2012), I employ the theoretical scaffolding of the neo-slave narrative. Early South African literature depicting slavery often represented enslaved people as props, a mere background to the unfolding drama of white slaveholders' lives. Early literature also portrayed slavery as relatively benign (Baderoon 2014; Keegan 1996), depictions which, David Johnson (2012) argues, may have contributed to the myth that Cape slavery was less brutal than in other parts of the world. In her pioneering work on Muslim identity in South Africa from slavery to the post-apartheid era, titled *Regarding Muslims*, Baderoon (2014) argues that this 'picturesque mode' of visual representation of Islam is a founding trope of South African culture, which acts to obscure the violence of slavery by rendering 'Malays' as visually pleasing, harmless and unharmed subjects. Baderoon (2014, 21) traces the critical neglect of slavery in South African historiography directly to such representations of Islam and slavery, arguing that the trivialising effect of the picturesque mode, [remains] an aesthetic tradition that has ensured that the brutal system of slavery at the Cape continues to be seen as 'mild' and to confer a benign beginning to colonial settlement in South Africa. Thanks to the prevalence of the image of the submissive 'Malay' slave in the visual tradition in South Africa, enslaved people have been envisioned as figures of exoticism or pathos, abstracted from history and functioning solely to add depth and distinctiveness to white subjectivity.

Johnson's (2012) tracing of slavery in various novels shows how this benign representation was a foundational trope in early colonial literature. In the 1830s, slaves were depicted as loyal servants in two colonial novels in English and in later fiction, consigned to the margins of the plots. Furthermore, early twentieth-century South African fiction contributed to the 'resilient myth that Cape slavery was relatively humane' (Johnson 2012, 550). Fictional slave narratives, written completely or partially from the perspective of the enslaved, became a feature of South African literature only in the 1980s with the publication of Wilma Stockenström's *The Expedition to the Baobab Tree* (1981) and André Brink's *A Chain of Voices* (1982), the latter a translation from Afrikaans. Written and published during the apartheid era, these novels, for Johnson, suggest the impossibility of successful black rebellion against white economic domination, so that 'the only consolation for slaves resides in in their achieving fragile moments of individual freedom' (Johnson 2012, 554).

What differentiates a neo-slave narrative from a historical novel? A foundational and often-cited definition of the neo-slave narrative originates in the United States, where the form emerged in the 1960s as part of, and in response to, the Civil Rights Movement. Ashraf Rushdy (1999, 5–6) defines the neo-slave narrative as 'contemporary novels that assume the form, adopt the conventions, and take on the first-person voice of the antebellum slave narrative.' Where the traditional slave narrative is a biographical or autobiographical narrativisation of enslaved experience, neo-slave narratives are fictive accounts in which the creative re-imagining of such experiences is rendered. Rushdy's definition, forged in the crucible of American literature and history, refers directly to the social and political history of the USA – a singular region in that modern slavery was ended through war, whereas throughout the British empire, it was ended by decree and shifts in ideological and legal codes. Rushdy's definition has been critiqued as being too rigid in its insistence on first-person narration as constitutive of neo-slave narratives – Toni Morrison's *Beloved* (1987), for example, is one of the USA's most acclaimed neo-slave narratives, and is partly effective as a novel because of the fragmentary nature of the omniscient narration. However, what is useful in Rushdy's conceptualisation of the form for the purposes of my argument, is the emphasis on narrative alignment with the perspective of the enslaved. Whether or not the narrative is rendered in the first person, the telling of the story from the point of view of the enslaved is an important literary strategy of the neo-slave narrative, as it subverts the traditional power dynamic between slave and master. The latter has, historically, held the discursive power that enables it to construct the slave – quite apart from having complete physical and legal control over enslaved persons. The neo-slave narrative, constructed as it is from the standpoint of the subaltern, restores subjectivity to human beings who have been rendered mere objects by slave owners and their practices. For Rushdy (1999, 6), the American neo-slave narrative has 'its origins in the social, intellectual and racial formations of the sixties and its cultural politics as these texts intervene in debates on the significance of race'. Rushdy refers to the resonances between the two periods – the historical setting of the slave narrative, and the contemporary moment in which racial and social relations are being remade – as a form of intertextuality, with the neo-slave narrative also commenting on contemporary political events.

This element of Rushdy's definition is useful for my argument that contemporary fictionalised rewritings of South African slave histories do the work not only of re-imagining history from the standpoint of the enslaved, but function also as commentary on contemporary political and cultural developments. Margaret Lenta (2010), in comparing *Unconfessed* with André Brink's slave novel, *A Chain of Voices* (1982), makes a similar argument, holding that Brink's novel draws direct comparisons between the brutal practices of the system of slavery and apartheid atrocities. Lenta sees *Unconfessed* as speaking less directly to the politics of its particular moment of publication, in 2006, a point with which I disagree. With regard to *Unconfessed*, I hope to show that it does indeed resonate with its political moment by highlighting the gendered political economy of slavery.

Rushdy's approach is shared by Pumla Dineo Gqola in her pathbreaking study of the deployment and utility of slave memory in contemporary South Africa, *What is Slavery to Me? Postcolonial/ Slave Memory in Post-apartheid South Africa* (2010). Analysing a wide range of cultural production, including poetry, fiction and television shows, Gqola traces the contours of slave memory in post-apartheid South Africa, arguing that the invocation of slavery at a moment that partially overlaps with the staging of the TRC reproduces slavery in particular ways that are often used in the construction and renegotiation of post-apartheid racial identities. Gqola argues that the transition to democracy, as well as its aftermath, has enabled an invocation of slavery previously taboo; the omission relates to the ways in which South Africa constructed its historiography – according to Zoë Wicomb (1998), partly because of the shame embedded in the 'miscegenation' that characterised the practice of slavery. Bodies racialised as 'coloured' retain traces of this shame, Wicomb contends, a shame that until recently precluded a reckoning of slave histories.

Gqola's (2010, 7) theorising of slave memory interrogates the eagerness, at a certain point in post-apartheid South African history, to (re)claim slavery and slave ancestry, by examining 'relationships of entanglement between the forms of memory found and the timing of their public rehearsal'. In Gqola's conceptualisation, post-apartheid cultural production that foregrounds slavery infuses contemporary discourse with the recursive effects of slavery, which is similar to the intertextuality Rushdy makes visible in his analysis of 1960s American neo-slave narratives.

The two novels examined here, besides filling the gaps in a historiography which has, until recently, denied the prominence of slavery as an economic and cultural force that has shaped the present, also speak to the contemporary moment in which each was written.

I will now examine how the two novels construct slave identity and South African slave history, and how they resonate with the South African nation today.

Gendered resistance in *The Slave Book*

Published in 1998, Rayda Jacobs's *The Slave Book* is the first neo-slave narrative to be published by a black South African woman. The novel centres around Somiela, a 16-year-old enslaved girl of mixed racial descent, and her stepfather, Sangora, both of whom are practising Muslims. Their religious practice is a key histor-ical corrective in this novel, as Islam is introduced in the Cape through slavery (Baderoon 2014), a fact often obscured in his-tory. The figure of Sangora also counters the 'benign mode' of representation of the docile, pliable 'Malay'/Muslim slave, which, as discussed earlier, contributes to the myth of the relative harm-lessness of the brand of slavery practised at the Cape (Baderoon 2014). The reader enters into Somiela's story on the day she is sold at the Slave Lodge to Andries de Villiers, a wealthy descendant of Dutch settlers, to work on his farm in Wynberg in the Cape. Andries buys Somiela and Sangora on a whim, but leaves the girl's mother on the auction block, thus destroying their nuclear family unit. After the purchase, there is a shift in the novel, with Andries's interiority giving insights into his decision-making pro-cess in buying Somiela:

> About the half-breed, Andries was not sure he'd done the right thing. Had his true motive for making the purchase been so that the girl could help in the kitchen, or to increase the slave popula-tion on his farm? There were no females at Zoetewater except for Rachel, a full-bred Ceylonese of fifty years. Andries was all too aware of the unrest amongst the males and the fact that soon all slave trading would be stopped. (22–23)

Somiela's entry into Andries's household is difficult and immedi-ately marked by conflict, sparked by the jealousy of Andries's wife and adult daughter, who both feel threatened by the girl's beauty. Upon arriving home with Somiela and her stepfather, Andries is met by his wife's displeasure because of the girl's youthfulness and attractiveness. She brands the girl a '*naaimandjie*' – a crude sexual slur which roughly translates in English to 'receptacle for fucking'. From the outset, Jacobs thus casts the experience of enslavement, for black women, as one of sexual exploitation, aggravated by the fact that sexual abuse and rape reproduce slavery. Through Andries's musings above, Jacobs crams in many markers signalling the conditions in which enslaved women labour. The slave trade is under threat with new laws being passed, and Andries is acutely aware of his dwindling stock. His only other woman slave, Rachel, is 50 years old and no longer of childbearing age; though he seemingly questions his own motives in buying the girl, sexual reproduction and thus the production of new slaves are clearly uppermost in his mind. This is an important mechanism to foreground: as Baderoon (2011) has noted, slave histories and historiography often obscure the gendered nature of slavery, which, for women, almost certainly meant rape and sexual abuse. This omission of sexual violence as constitutive of slavery is the result, for Baderoon (2011, 216), of the 'almost ontological shame' borne by the descendants of slaves. For them, the figure of the black enslaved woman comes to stand for

> both violation and culpability, or, as Wicomb (1998: 92) phrases it, 'the shame of having had our bodies stared at, but also the shame invested in those (females) who mated with the colonizer.' In a painful reversal, therefore, Black women's bodies have been made the bearers of the mark of sexual violence during slavery, rendering invisible the systemic violations of slavery.

Somiela is, in fact, sexually abused and almost raped by Andries, an event that leads to verbal and physical abuse from Andries's wife. By making the attempted rape a major turning point in the novel, having previously foregrounded Andries's calculations around Somiela's fertility, Jacobs brings to light this obscured part of an opaque history, demonstrating, through her fiction, the ways in which sexual violence is central to the practice of slavery. In this way, Jacobs exposes sexual exploitation, sexual abuse and rape as key aspects of the political economy of slavery – a fact wilfully forgotten and purposefully obscured on the part of those who would later claim racial purity and the protection thereof as grounds for constructing a white supremacist South African nation.

Somiela is a sympathetically drawn character, though the reader's identification with her is a complicated kind of complicity. Jacobs has been criticised for representing Somiela as a worthy subject of this fictional account because of her beauty, which is the first quality remarked upon by all who meet her, and is located in her proximity to whiteness. Her father, a white man, raped her mother, a dark-skinned slave, and Somiela has a fair complexion; Jacobs belabours the point that she looks white, and, indeed, passes for white when dressed in finery. Somiela, in this regard, is undoubtedly a troubling – yet troubled – character. The reader is interpellated into sympathy for her lot, not merely because she is abused, but because the abuse heaped upon her is constructed as all the more injurious because she is 'almost white'. Gqola (2001) has done a comprehensive analysis of the ideology of colourism in the novel, showing how negative character traits in slaves are associated with gradations of darkness in their skin colour, while fair skin is a signifier of good character.

The Somiela character is also problematic in the way she finds freedom – her liberation comes through whiteness: a man of mixed white and Sonqua descent, who easily passes for white, falls in love with her and works for two years as an overseer on Andries's farm in order to purchase her freedom and marry her. Whiteness, and visual proximity to it in terms of appearance, is thus central to her identity and her plight; as such, it eventually aids in her emancipation. Nevertheless, Somiela is still a singular and intriguing character – through her, the reader is afforded a glimpse into the longings and intelligence of an enslaved young woman, as well as her resistance to her slave masters. An aware subject, she resists her subjugation wherever she can, displaying in various ways an agency within the very system that so brutally confines her. She talks back to Andries's wife, for example, and changes the endings of fairytales she is tasked with reading to the children in her care. For Baderoon (2014, 52), the kitchen, in a slavocratic society, is a site of resistance, 'the "ambiguous" space in which familiar objects are subverted in ways not immediately apparent as resistance to dominant parts of society'. An example of this subversion comes early in the novel, when Rachel, the older slave who works in the kitchen, prepares a poultice for Sangora's shackle wounds, which she has made from kitchen ingredients. Significantly, Sangora remarks to Arend: 'It's a good thing your mother's in the kitchen to give us all these things' (Jacobs 1998, 56).

Given the potentially subversive nature of kitchen practices, Somiela's culinary creativity may be read as a form of resistance in instances where she is unable to speak, constituting a way for her to 'silently speak back' (Baderoon 2014, 53) to her masters. Her 'overspicing' of food with 'sadistic green chillies' (113) offends the palates of her masters, producing a complex mode of communication that refuses the straightforward co-option of her labour in the kitchen. However, the men in the household gradually come to enjoy her form of cooking, leading to conflict with the white women in the home. Andries insists, for example, that Somiela serves cabbage stew to guests, while his wife disapproves of the dish. Andries's insistence on the stew being served represents a small symbolic victory over his wife for Somiela; but the incident ultimately works against Somiela, as the mistress's resentment towards the slave girl hardens. Food and cooking practices thus become a way 'to marshal resources, presence and creativity under conditions of peril and poverty' (Baderoon 2014, 64) – a refusal of complete domination by slave owners, and a way of demonstrating agency, creativity and individuality.

The form of direct speech used most often by Somiela is the word 'no' – she refuses to surrender a prized dress, made by her mother, or to comply with the instruction to cut her hair. Her spoken resistance results in severe physical punishment, with the explicit aim of publicly humiliating Somiela while physically harming her. As the novel progresses, Somiela thus becomes less vocal, with her direct speech diminishing. Given the narrative strategy of the novel, Somiela's interior world is not as fully explored as that of the main character in *Unconfessed*.

The use of an omniscient narrator in *The Slave Book* provides insights into the thoughts and plans of many characters, detailing their motivations. In deploying this literary strategy, Jacobs sacrifices a black woman-centred point of view, but at the same time gives the reader insight into the anxieties of the slave owner as the date of emancipation approaches. Here, once again, is Andries's point of view as he considers the money he makes from renting out Kananga, his mandoor or overseer:

> His prize negro, Kananga, captured by a Portuguese slaver off the coast of Mozambique, was an excellent mandoor. Prize negroes were introduced into the Cape after British involvement in the slave trade ceased in 1808. Although not technically slaves according to official documents, prize negroes belonged to the category of 'slave' rather than 'free', and had to serve a fourteen-year apprenticeship. Seized as slaves by the British naval squadron from the ships of other nations, they were to be liberated and bound to prudent masters and mistresses to learn trades or handicrafts so that they could gain their livelihood when their apprenticeships expired ... Andries wished he had more like Kananga, but one prize negro was all he was allowed. (Jacobs 1998, 14–15)

Jacobs's style here is factual, almost stenographic. However, this is balanced by more poetic renderings of experiences and thoughts elsewhere in the narrative. The novel is crammed with passages conveying historical information, giving the reader insight into the ways in which history translates into the lived experience of enslaved peoples. It highlights, through the figure of Andries, the anxieties of white farmers, landowners and gentry at the Cape as the emancipation date for slaves nears – and demonstrates, through Andries's actions and motivations, the increased brutality meted out to slaves as their 'freedom' became more palpable.

The utility of a passage such as the one where Andries reflects on Kananga's role lies in its ability to convey a large amount of historical information which helps to fill in possible gaps in the reader's knowledge. It condenses another of the economic apparatuses by which the practice of slavery perpetuated itself after the oceanic slave trade was outlawed. Patrick Harries has written extensively about the system of so-called prize negroes, a population of enslaved men, women and children who were captured on French and Portuguese slave ships by British fleets patrolling the oceans in order to 'prevent' slave trading after it had been forbidden in 1808. Enslaved people who were on these vessels were, however, not freed: they were recaptured by the British and sold into indentureship at the Cape during a period that lasted 14 years. Historians such as Patrick Harries (1981) and Yvette Abrahams (1998) – and indeed, the novelist Yvette Christiansë – describe the practice of indentureship as a continuation of slavery under a new name. Harries (2013) shows that, although the oceanic slave trade was abolished in 1808, thereby prohibiting the importation of slaves to the Cape, many slave vessels continued to pass through the port of Cape Town en route to the Americas from Indian Ocean territories. A treaty between Britain and Portugal, signed in 1810, secured Portuguese slave traders' rights to transport slaves from Angola and Mozambique to Brazil. Slavers were, in fact, finally prohibited from docking at the Cape only in 1824, when the British parliament passed the Slave Trade Consolidation Act (Harries 2013). Harries (2000) estimates that around 25 000 Mozambicans were forced to migrate to the Cape between 1780 and 1880, first as slaves, and later as prize negroes. The latter were an important source of labour after 1807 when it became clear the slave trade would be outlawed: more than 2 000 were 'liberated' at the Cape to work in 14-year indentureships between 1807 and 1816 (Harries 2000). They did all manner of menial work, from farm labour to day labour: 'Such was their inferior status in the post-emancipation period that the term "Mozbieker" [Mozambican] required a distinctly pejorative meaning' (Harries 2000, 33). These 'rootless' (Harries 2000, 32) individuals were further exploited when their indentureships ran out, and many were shocked to discover that their children would be required to continue labouring as indentures until the age of eighteen.

Through the figure of Kananga, who is reviled not only by his master but also by the other slaves, the realities of indentureship are animated. When he becomes an inconvenience to Andries, Kananga is discarded and sold – an act that disrupts the slave community he was part of. Through Kananga, Jacobs shows the insatiable settler hunger for free or cheap labour, one which is almost impossible to satisfy, requiring an ever-evolving strategy of retaining labour in the face of the enslaved labourer embarking on a life of 'freedom'.

The theme of freedom and its meanings recurs throughout the novel, notably in the conclusion: Somiela leaves the farm a free woman, though this freedom is bought by a seemingly white man, with whom she enters into marriage. A freedom that sees her move from ownership by Andries to the patriarchal stewardship of her husband, Harman Kloot, is a questionable freedom; yet Somiela's marriage to Harman, whom she loves, is of her own choosing, unlike the trafficking of her body under slavery. Somiela also provides the vehicle for a meditation on the substance and nature of freedom. Her manumission occurs on 1 December 1834, when slaves were officially emancipated at the Cape. And though she wakes up a free woman, she is not joyful; instead, she wistfully reflects on her freedom:

> How did she feel? Did she feel free? Any different from yesterday? December 1st didn't spell freedom for all slaves. For the majority it was only a freedom on paper. There were four more years. They would be bound by the same stringent laws. Despite the title of apprentice, they would still belong to owners who would work them all day and herd them into their kraals at night. No, she didn't feel particularly free. She was free to leave Zoetewater, but not free to enjoy it while others were still in bondage. (272)

Liberation, here, is conceived of as a force which is brought to fruition only when all members of a group are collectively free from oppression. Though Somiela is free to leave the site of her enslavement, her enjoyment of the rights bestowed by freedom is dependent on the emancipation of her entire community. She is free to leave without them, but while her family and loved ones are still in bondage, her freedom remains restricted. Her freedom, in other words, is bound up with the liberation of every person in the oppressed group.

Slavery's haunting in *Unconfessed*

In Yvette Christiansë's *Unconfessed* the reader encounters Sila van den Kaap, a historical figure whose story lay in fragments in an archive, where it was discovered by the author. Sila, an enslaved woman, was sentenced to death in 1822 for murdering her son (Christiansë 2009), but under British Amelioration laws her sentence was commuted to a lengthy imprisonment on Robben Island. Published in 2006, at a time when South Africa was entering what critics have called the post-transitional period, *Unconfessed* employs a completely different narrative strategy to *The Slave Book*. Where the latter runs chronologically through two years of the life of Somiela, the former has a postmodern narrative structure, relying on a circular, fragmented narrative related almost entirely in the first person by Sila. Having experienced unspeakable cruelty, Sila is a traumatised, unreliable narrator who often repeats her telling of trauma, making for a choppy, uneasy narrative that is, at times, difficult to follow. Christiansë (2009) found the records of Sila's trial for the murder of her son in the Western Cape Archives in Cape Town, and the overwhelming silence of Sila van den Kaap in the official record haunted the author. In the colonial court records, 'Sila is structurally muted in that, although we have words from her, the state never granted her full subjectivity, and her utterances remained for them, utterly illegible' (Christiansë 2009, 1). It is in her attempt to imaginatively create for Sila such subjectivity that Christiansë recreated her experience in the novel *Unconfessed*. However, Christiansë (2009) cautions against the idea of 'recovering' a subject who exists in the archive as a mere trace, stripped of full personhood by colonial law and logic. Yet the world of Sila, rendered in fiction, functions as a kind of remedy to this silence around Sila's life and experiences. The novel allows Sila to narrate and reflect upon her childhood in Mozambique, the experience of being sold from one slave owner to another at the Cape, and repeatedly having her children sold on by cruel slave owners.

On Robben Island, where Sila is sentenced to hard labour in the lime quarry, she is also repeatedly raped by prison guards who prostitute her to other guards and visitors to the island. These acts of violence and violation compound the trauma inflicted by being captured in Mozambique, sold off as a child, and abused by various slave masters. The novel illustrates the fact that 'for women, sexual exploitation marked the very definition of slavery, as it did not for men' (Lerner in Baderoon 2011, 217). The reader is confronted with an inescapable truth of the colonial era: 'Enslaved and Khoisan women's bodies were designated as available to access with impunity' (Baderoon 2014, 84). Depictions of Sila's body being used by male warders for purposes of prostitution highlight the sexualised and racialised objectification of black women's bodies in the final years of slavery at the Cape. Abrahams (1998) notes that, as the transnational practice of British slavery drew to a close, a moral panic arose around black male sexuality and its ostensible encroachment on white womanhood, which had to be protected at all costs against the threat of black masculinity. In contrast to this racialised construction of white womanhood as pure and in need of safeguarding, black femininity was constructed as the opposite: degenerate, hypersexual and always-already sexually available. For Abrahams (1998, 229), this conceptual split between black women and white women became the bedrock for a discourse around black women's sexual degeneracy:

> Black women ... were [seen as] more savage than the men, so bestial that even their own men would choose a white woman in preference to them. This was the genesis of a process that culminated in the Victorian ideal of white womanhood. White women were to be increasingly denied sexual expression, while for Black women, sexuality came to be seen as a defining characteristic.

Sila's imprisonment, then, sees her body being used and sold as currency, a practice enabled by the slavocratic ideology of the black woman's body being always available for sex – and, because of its 'bestiality', un-rapeable. The sexual violence perpetrated on Robben Island shows the ways in which rape and sexual violence against black women in slavocratic economies became normalised – with traces of such sexual violence still visible and recurrent in contemporary South Africa.

Whereas Jacobs's *The Slave Book* gives a panoramic, yet detailed, view of historical events over a relatively short period of two years, the strength of *Unconfessed* lies in its uncovering of the thoughts and feelings of the enslaved woman, giving the reader insights into her interior world. Sila's narrative remakes the slave as human, transmutes the enslaved person from mere object into a thinking, feeling subject, thus recuperating a denied humanity. That Sila's experience is recorded at all is due to the fact of her trial for the murder of her son; significantly, she did not defend herself during court proceedings, but uttered repeatedly that, as she slit her nine-year-old son's throat, she felt '*hartzeer en verdriet*' [heartsore and grief] (Christiansë 2009, 17; Baderoon 2011). Christiansë (2009, 18) points out that the word '*hartzeer*' is 'strange and, especially in its transliteration, doubly foreign. The word seeps out across the official documents. It will not be contained.' It is the excess of the word '*hartzeer*' which calls into question the logic of a colonial law that accommodates slavery, showing up the 'law's prerogative over life and death and the monopoloy over the definition of crime and gift [*sic*], crime and accusation'. As a creative writer, Christiansë is engaged here in the work of 're-memory' – a form of 'literary archeology [which] invites the creative writer or artist to journey to a site to see what remains were left behind and to reconstruct the world that these remains imply ... to yield up a kind of truth' (Morrison 1995, 92). Gqola (2010) has adapted the idea of re-memory as a tool for reconstructing South African slave history to imply more than mere recollecting, recalling or reconstructing – re-memorying is itself a commentary on the disjunctures between memory and dominant narratives of history. The act of re-memorying, whether by an individual or collective, works against wilful forgetting or what Gqola (2010, 8) calls 'un-remembering' – political acts of excluding subjects from history's construction. Re-memorying politically counters un-remembering – a 'calculated act of exclusion and erasure.' Re-memorying is thus a mode of engagement with history's lacunae for postcolonial artists such as Christiansë; her novel performs the political and aesthetic work of re-memory in order to create a subjective life for Sila, whose silence screams through the archive.

Sila's fictional narrative addresses several phantoms: her son Baro, who inhabits Robben Island as a ghost; the demons she believes roam the island; and former lovers and family members from whom she has been wrenched away. *Unconfessed* is often compared with Toni Morrison's *Beloved*; however, the presence of the dead child is not a spiteful one which terrorises; it is, instead, a soothing presence that comforts Sila. Whenever she addresses the child, the narrative becomes a vehicle for layered storytelling, where each re-telling produces multiple, and complex, meanings.

Sila repeatedly appeals to Baro's senses as a means of engaging him. 'Stay here and let me tell you what is to be seen,' she tells the phantom child when she first encounters him on the island (37). Her monologue continues: 'Do not be afraid to look at this place' (37). Then she ruminates: 'When I came here ... Hmph! I could not look at anything but what was right in front of me. It was my shame, you see. How good it would be to tell you your mother never had shame ...' (37–38). Shame here is bound up with maternity – not only the act of infanticide, but the very conditions that have made Sila a mother. As Wicomb (1998) has noted with respect to the descendants of slaves, shame is inscribed in the very materiality of the body – in the mark of miscegenation which colours the skin. In this regard, Wicomb (1998, 92) argues: 'Miscegenation, the origins of which lie within a discourse of "race", concupiscence, and degeneracy, continues to be bound up with shame, a pervasive shame exploited in apartheid's strategy of the naming of a Coloured race ...'

The shame Sila experiences is multilayered: the shame of miscegenation, the shame of being enslaved, the shame of having murdered her son. Yet, in speaking this shame, she breaks the taboo of not naming it. Sila reflects on the nature of her shame, and the blindness it results in by 'not look[ing] at anything but what was right in front of me' (37). In the same monologue, Sila tells Baro about this blindness wrought by shame: 'How much better it would be if I could say my rage had made me blind when I came here' (38). Sila's realisation reveals a consciousness that the shame of the enslaved woman is misguided and misdirected; manifesting as internalised hatred, it should be projected outwards, a rage towards those who enslave others. Her lesson to

Baro is thus not to look away from her or the place where she finds herself, but to squarely face it by gazing directly at the conditions she is forced to endure. This unflinching gaze at the face of history, rather than a shameful averting of eyes from the horrors of slavery, is what Baro must cultivate.

Sila's speech, poetic, self-referential and lyrical, is rich with sensory description. As the novel progresses, her exhortations that Baro should use his senses to engage with her, and to interpret the world around him, become more urgent: '*Look at me when I am speaking to you!*' (139) and, 'You have been asleep and now you have woken, but you must open your eyes and your ears' (139). These speech acts become all the more poignant when the reader learns of Sila's partial deafness, the result of a violent beating by a slave owner, and her failing eyesight, because the limestone that she quarries on Robben Island 'beats you in the eyes' (45). Sila tells Baro: 'my ears are awake' (148), reassuring him that 'even with my bad ear – I can hear a prisoner calling out from the Black Hole for more water, or food, or to have the irons taken off of his ankles before they rub down right to the bone' (47).

Sila's articulations around hearing and sight imply that there are different modes of acquiring knowledge and processing information, and seeing and hearing operate on a literal as well as a figurative level. Sila is metaphorically blind when she arrives at Robben Island because her shame makes her unable to look at herself or her surroundings. Blindness is a cloak she wilfully drapes around herself, a protective mechanism to blot out not only shame but also the harsh, dehumanising conditions of her confinement. Her hearing functions similarly: it is not always related to the actual capacity to hear, and even with her 'bad ear', Sila is able to 'hear' shackled prisoners calling, an atunement not only to sound but also to injustice. Hence the association of hearing and seeing with being 'awake' (148). Her ears, though deaf, are 'awake', and the state of consciousness she wants Baro to inhabit is one of being 'woken' (139), now that his ears and eyes have been opened. The words Sila addresses to Baro also read as directives to people who are even more distant from her. Baro is often told to visit future generations, and to either warn or curse them. Thus, when she addresses him, she is also addressing succeeding generations. Through Baro, Sila directs slave descendants to look at the horrors of history and to excise the shame bound up in hybrid identities.

Sila's poetic of the senses evokes sentience, which may be seen as another strategy to restore subjectivity in a human being who has been reduced to an object through slavery. The poetic language of the senses also evokes memory and place – both geographical and psychological. For Baderoon (2014, 217), Sila's speech is 'poetic form as map and memory'. Through her use of language, Sila crafts relationships with women that provide a space of nurturance. Sila's speech creates pockets of space, places of intimacy with others within an extremely brutal setting. In these spaces of intimacy she accesses full humanity, even as she is reduced, in her own words, to a category of women who are regarded as 'poese [cunts] up to our chins' by the men who rape them (312). Sila accesses this humane space through love and fellowship with other enslaved women who see and appreciate her own humanity. One of these instances is with the older woman Alima, who becomes a mother figure to her, and to whom she describes the sadness stirred by a childhood memory involving her senses:

> Alima, Roosje, Mars, they were already grown when they were taken. Not like me. What I remember is very thin. What I had was feelings. A smell of something would make my head spin like nobody's business. I could just be walking, or in the kitchen, making bread and then something would be like a smack. For a long time the smell of summer made me sad even though it was warm and easier for living. It was Alima who saw this and understood how, on a hot day, when the air was wet and covered your skin with drops of sweat, how it made me cry for back there. She said, do not hold your tears. Let them come. (112)

Here we see Sila transported, through sensory memory, back to a place where she was human. Poetic language is the vehicle that transports here there. These memories are borne through the senses of smell and touch – the feeling of humidity against her skin. Though her memory is 'very thin', the place where she comes from reminds her of a time before slavery, when she did not exist as a mere object, 'a cow or a horse' (30), or 'a present one person buys for another' (100). These memories, connected to place, create the space in which Sila inhabits her subjectivity and where it is co-constructed through Alima's recognition of her pain. The 'allusive and poetic form' that her speech takes 'signals a register different from that which describes the brutality of slavery and the silence and entrapment of Black women within it' (Baderoon 2011, 218). Her personhood is affirmed by Alima, who recognises the sadness in Sila's remembering, and allows her to weep for her lost humanity.

Another place where personhood is restored is the intimacy experienced with another prisoner on Robben Island – a woman, Lys, who provides love, protection and sexual pleasure to Sila at a time when both of them are repeatedly being raped. Sila meets Lys when she first arrives on the island, and as she explains to Baro: 'I liked her, from the first day I liked her' (51). The women's relationship is characterised by laughter and mutual support. They share a bed at night, with their bodies 'like two shells that fit each other' (290). As narrated to Baro, Lys is the person who teaches Sila how to survive the island by making the brutal conditions of imprisonment bearable. Sila repeatedly refers to Lys as 'my good day' (283), and addressing her directly, says: 'You are my good, quiet day, Lys. You make a place for my back to rest and all aching stops, and when my face relaxes I know that it was pulled up, strained. You are my good day, and my quiet, Lys' (198).

As women trapped in a system which values them only as objects and, under capitalism, locates their worth in their productive and reproductive functions, the very act of loving one another, both emotionally and physically, is subversive. If their bodies are meant only to work for the profit of their slave owners, stealing time to embrace and take pleasure in each other's bodies transgresses the discursive and legal codes that define them. Sila's description of their bodies coming together in bed at night foregrounds pleasure and joy:

Lys and I save our laughter for when the night is curled around itself. Then we start. First one, then the other. We just start a little laugh, then it is big but we keep our blankets against our mouths. We come together in one bed so that our laughter does not have even the space of the small room to cross. I lie against her back or I feel her against my back and we laugh as if we are two little girls put to bed early by our mother just so that we can learn how it is to have a world that is our own. (152)

The two characters are here engaged in what Halberstam (2005) would call queer place-making practices, in which queer people reconfigure space through their embodiment of queer subjectivities that co-constitute each other. If 'queer' 'refers to the nonnormative logics and organisations of community, sexual identity, embodiment, and activity in space and time' (Halberstam 2005, 6), Lys and Sila are disrupting and queering normative space, in which they are designated labourers and bodies to be raped. In reconstituting oppressive space through queer place-making, the two women use their bodies to 'speak in languages other than those imposed on them by their owners' (Baderoon 2011, 218). Queer love restores their humanity in the recesses of intimate space, providing sustenance for surviving the harsh conditions of imprisonment and enslavement. The 'place' created through the laughter, physical pleasure and warmth between two similarly raced and gendered bodies creates a space for each woman to be restored unto herself, and be fully human, albeit momentarily. In the passage above, Christianse depicts a double recuperation – of slave women's personhood, but also of queer practices that have been excised from formal accounts of history.

In the same way as Rushdy theorises an intertextuality between American neo-slave narratives and the political and cultural movements of the 1960s, *The Slave Book* and *Unconfessed* resonate with events and identity formation practices in transitional and post-transitional South Africa. Both novels are set in a transitionary period where the conditions of slavery are slowly being ameliorated, working towards an end point, in 1838, where slavery is formally abolished. Harries (2013) refers to the amelioration of slave laws and practices as a 'negotiation' between Britain and its allies, thereby conjuring the language of the negotiated settlement South Africa would stage more than a century later as it transitioned from apartheid to democracy. However, as both novels show, power and privilege have ways of reconfiguring themselves when they are threatened. As official slavery ends, a four-year apprenticeship period is instated at the Cape, ostensibly as a way of 'skilling' workers, but in fact further exploiting them economically by keeping them on as indentured labour, a thinly disguised continuation of slavery. The hunger for labour that instituted the prize negro system was another way in which power replicated itself, while ostensibly reconfiguring society to progress towards more just social relations between oppressors and oppressed.

Published in 1998 and 2006 respectively, *The Slave Book* and *Unconfessed*, whether self-consciously or not, intervene in a discourse of what I term rainbownationalism – a discursive nationalism which has its genesis in the utterances of the then chair of the Truth and Reconciliation Commission, Archbishop Desmond Tutu. Whereas Gqola (2004, 6) uses the term 'rainbowism' to denote how the construct of the rainbow nation was 'central to shaping identities in a post-apartheid South Africa', she makes the pointed observation that 'the mere evocation of the identity "rainbow nation" in the print and electronic media, as well as in popular culture, also worked to silence dissenting voices on the (then) state of race and racism in South Africa'. I use rainbownationalism to signify the unificatory, nation-building ideology which sought to heal a divided, deeply scarred nation after 50 years of apartheid and its concomitant human rights abuses against black South Africans. As a surface discourse, it may have held fleeting potential for healing divides, but what it obscured was emerging forms of inequality, predicated no longer on race, but on a widening economic divide. Rainbownationalism, for example, papered over cracks formed after an unheralded transition from an economic system which favoured reconstruction and redistribution, in favour of the Gear (Growth, Employment and Redistribution) macro-economic policy, which liberalised trade. It further obscured the continued inequality wrought through a negotiated settlement in terms of which black citizens were expected to forgive their white compatriots for decades of political and economic domination, with no change being made to the material base upon which such domination rested. The two neo-slave narratives I have discussed can be seen to interrupt rainbownationalism's seamless narrative of progression into a fictive racial harmony dependent on forgetting the nation's past. Rainbownationalism obscures continuing injustice and exploitation during the transition to democracy, much in the same way as amelioration discourse obscured the continuation of slavery under the apprenticeship and prize negro phenomenon.

The Slave Book and *Unconfessed* mark turning points in the production of South African slave literature: with the publication of these novels, the slave experience had, for the first time, been creatively imagined and remembered by black women. Gqola (2010, 10–11) names this kind of memory – a reminder from the past to the present – postcolonial memory; citing Barnor Hesse she characterises it as follows:

> Postcolonial memory recognizes that slave pasts cannot only be addressed through 'abolitionist, curatorial, or aesthetic memories' (Hesse 2002: 165) since it is not concerned with slavery in the past, but with the ongoing effects and processing of that historical consciousness. It is concerned with how the haunting shadow of the past … shape today's experiences. Like Hesse, '[w]hat I call postcolonial memory takes the form of a critical excavation and inventory of the marginalized, discounted, unrealized objects of decolonization and the political consequence of these social legacies'.

The memory produced by the neo-slave narratives of Jacobs and Christiansë reaches from the past into the future; it asks today's South Africans to no longer look away in blindness forged by shame. Christiansë self-consciously references such memory, as Sila, at the end of the novel, orders Baro to travel into the past in order to tell future generations of the horror of slavery:

> Take care, boy. If there is a place where generations gather, warn them!
> Tell them, I am sending you to say we are a trapped people, we are a wounded people, we long for freedom, we long for things we

have been taught to admire and desire, we long for the courage to desire such things, and we are a jealous people. Tell them, that is the worst thing. We have been taught hunger. And I mean *all* of us. No one is safe. (279–280)

Sila's warning to future generations is both prescient and timely. Looking away from one of the founding practices of the South African nation – slavery – requires a forgetting that allows dominant nationalisms to recreate and perpetuate the same erasures of black women's subjectivities, experiences and foundational labour in their building of this country. Where the United States of America periodically revisits the idea of providing reparations to the descendants of slaves, in South Africa this has never even been a consideration. Yet, without a reckoning of the exploitative, racist and sexist capitalist practices upon which this nation has been built, and which continued through the apartheid years, the gnawing hunger born of the deprivations of slavery continues to grow. As structural disparities grow between those who have and those who do not, between those who own land and those who do not, political instability increases too. In the words of Sila, 'no one is safe'.

6

Black Women Writing 'New' South African Masculinities: Kagiso Lesego Molope and Zukiswa Wanner

In South African history, 1976 stands as the year when young black South Africans reignited the fight against apartheid with renewed vigour. The 1976 uprising started in Soweto on 16 June, when apartheid police lashed out at children protesting the introduction of Afrikaans as a compulsory medium of instruction in black schools. At least four children, including 13-year-old Hector Pieterson, were killed by police bullets, thus unleashing student protests across the country. In the ensuing violence, police killed over a thousand people – most of them children of school-going age. In its aftermath, South African police increasingly used the uprising as an excuse to target children in repressing anti-apartheid protests, since the youth had become the vanguard in protest action for a free South Africa. As in other historical eras, black women were uniquely affected, not only by this renewed phase of apartheid brutality but also by the protests that met increased state repression. Two years after the uprising, in a speech to commemorate Women's Day on 9 August, Makhosazana Njobe (1978, 12) described to exiled South Africans the conditions black women were facing inside the country:

> Our women live in perpetual anxiety of husbands and children who disappear from homes, sometimes without trace. Our children are detained in solitary confinement without any change of clothes for days, some are cold bloodedly murdered; children of 7 years old are interrogated for hours, tortured and even made to appear in the racist courts of law as accused … In fact hundreds of them have their young and tender bodies riddled with bullets from the fascist police guns.

Apartheid's blatant brutality against children led a number of black South African women to leave the country and join Umkhonto we Sizwe (MK), the ANC's armed wing, which was engaged in armed struggle against the state. According to Thenjiwe Mtintso, an MK commander, a 'sizeable amount' (in Pillay 1992, 18) of women entered the army in 1976 in response to the uprising and subsequent massacre of children. Women soldiers would eventually make up about 20 per cent of MK's numbers (Pillay 1992). Young women who had witnessed the events of the 1976 uprising, or who were subsequently detained and tortured by police, led the influx into the armed wing of the ANC. Makhosazana Njobe (1978) reported to the women in exile that the 1976 massacres had led to a reinvigoration of the struggle against apartheid, and that young women, especially, were eager to participate as soldiers in the fight against apartheid. Njobe (1978, 14) then warned the government that 'the 1956 babies [participants in the pass law protests] are now 22 years and older. When next the women come to the Union Buildings, we shall not witness music by our women but sounds from the barrel of a gun.'

Several girl children born in 1976 both inside the country and in exile, would also eventually engender a renaissance in black women's literary production. They make up a significant part of what Pumla Gqola (2013, 1–2) has identified as a set of 'brilliant' black women artists who are 'achieving the previously unimaginable' – creatively rendering not only critiques of oppression, but imagining new worlds and ways of being in them; worlds that are 'new, more exciting, more pleasurable'. In the realm of poetic expression, I have elsewhere documented an explosion of creativity in black women's poetry in the post-transitional era (Boswell 2016). The term 'post-transitional' has been theorised by literary critics as denoting South Africa in the period after the extended transition to democracy. The post-transitional is contested terrain, where meaning is fluid, incomplete and provisional. The term denotes temporality, while also pointing to a larger set of values and aesthetics that are emerging as a new cultural formation in literary production. Ronit Frenkel and Craig MacKenzie (2010) conceive of the post-transitional as South African literature that is not as obviously tethered to the past and to history in the way

apartheid writing was, though it may still seek ways of reformu-
lating the past and processing it in new ways. Where apartheid
and transitional literature tends to cluster around four nodes –
'race, history, space/place and nation' (Frenkel and MacKenzie
2010, 2) – post-transitional literature contests or ignores apartheid
racial taxonomies, and also unhinges, to an extent, binaries such
as victim/perpetrator, black/white, good/bad. Meg Samuelson
(2008, 132) notes that a key feature of the post-transitional in
South African literature 'is the emergence of the bold new literary
voices of young Black women (for instance, Angela Makholwa,
Kopano Matlwa and Zukiswa Wanner)'. Lynda Spencer (2009)
argues that, whereas more established writers such as Ngcobo,
Tlali and Head have slowly gained recognition and entry into the
South African literary canon, this new cohort of writers suffers
from the same lack of critical attention to their work initially
experienced by more established writers.

It is striking to note, in surveying post-transitional novels
by black South African women writers, that many of the signifi-
cant writers were born in or around 1976. Here, I include Kagiso
Lesego Molope, born in Atteridgeville, and author of three novels:
Dancing in the Dust (2002), *The Mending Season* (2005) and the
young adult novel *This Book Betrays my Brother* (2012); Zukiswa
Wanner, whose fiction includes *The Madams* (2006), *Behind Every
Successful Man* (2008), *Men of the South* (2010), and *London, Cape
Town, Joburg* (2014); Maxine Case, who has published, to great
acclaim, *All We have Left Unsaid* (2006) and *Softness of the Lime*
(2017); and Angela Makholwa, best-selling author of the crime
thrillers *Red Ink* (2007), *The 30ᵗʰ Candle* (2009), *Black Widow
Society* (2013) and *The Blessed Girl* (2017). I extend this cohort to
include Nadia Davids, born in 1977, and author of *An Imperfect
Blessing* (2014); Carol Ann Davids, born in 1970, and author
of *The Blacks of Cape Town* (2013); Cynthia Jele, who wrote
Happiness is a Four-letter Word (2010) and *The Ones with Purpose*
(2018); Shafinaaz Hassim, who has self-published the novel
SoPhia (2012); Shaida Kazie Ali, author of *Not a Fairytale* (2010)
and *Lessons in Husbandry* (2012); and the prolific and acclaimed
Kopano Matlwa, born much later in 1985, and author of the
novels *Coconut* (2007), *Spilt Milk* (2010) and *Period Pain* (2016).

This late transitional fiction includes two works by Rozena Maart: a short story collection titled *Rosa's District 6* (2006), and a novel, *The Writing Circle* (2007). These women's contributions to the South African literary canon are, indeed, deserving of a separate volume of criticism interrogating the post-transitional aesthetic in black women's writing.

This explosion in black women's literary creativity parallels the burgeoning of black women's poetry. If the '1956 babies' grew up to be the women soldiers of MK in the 1970s and 1980s, who ultimately fought for and won national liberation, it would be accurate to say that the 1976 revolution also gifted South Africa with an unexpected flowering of creative, novelistic expression on the part of black women. Yet the South African revolution, from a black feminist, anti-capitalist perspective, is incomplete. Despite having what is regarded as one of the most progressive constitutions in the world, which enshrines gender equality and LGBTIQ rights, women as a collective remain an oppressed group in South Africa. The intersection of patriarchal, white supremacist, capitalist and homophobic discrimination against women manifests in one of the world's highest rates for intimate femicide – half of all women murdered in South Africa are killed by an intimate partner (Abrahams et al. 2009). In 2008, the South African Medical Research Council found that around 30 per cent of men admitted to physically abusing their wives or intimate women partners daily (Gupta et al. 2008), while South Africa was given the title of 'rape capital of the world' by Human Rights Watch in 1995 (Jewkes and Abrahams 2002, 1231).

Post-apartheid South Africa's adoption of a neoliberal economic policy has resulted in the increased feminisation of poverty. Bentley (2004, 247) shows how poverty has entrenched gender inequality, so that 'poverty in South Africa has a gender dimension that challenges the equal status of women in law, and poses a threat to the realisation of their equal human rights in practice'.

A comparative reading of fictional works by black South African women writers reveals a number of ongoing concerns: racialised and gendered power dynamics; all forms of violence against women; black women's identity construction in the changing sociopolitical terrain of democratic, neoliberal South

Africa; and the long shadow cast by apartheid inequality and brutality on women's subjectivities and lived experience. Spencer (2009) has noted that, while black South African women writers of the apartheid era and the transition have finally received critical attention, the new crop of younger black writers are almost invisible in literary criticism. Spencer (2009, 67) defines emerging black women writers as follows:

> [Y]oung, Black writers who would not have had the conditions encouraging writing previously, but are now in the new dispensation, able to find their voice … They are concerned with reinterpreting their experience from a female perspective through prose narratives; in the process they extend the range of female characters and experiences that have been portrayed in fiction by established writers.

Kagiso Lesego Molope's *Dancing in the Dust* (2002) is one such novel that reconfigures black female subjectivity and experience. Published on the cusp of the transitional and post-transitional periods, and performing the function of what Sorcha Gunne (2010, 168) calls '(re)producing a social narrative that explores the past in order to facilitate transition', the novel draws heavily on a gendered experience of apartheid, and resistance to it, as evidenced by the perspective of its teenaged main character, Tihelo, during the 1980s. While Tihelo is reluctantly drawn into student resistance in her township of Mabopane, she slowly becomes radicalised by her own and others' oppression by apartheid police and the structural violence of the apartheid state. Molope employs a device frequently used by black postcolonial women writers, that of a 'dual focus' (see Chapter Three). In so doing, the novel traces the development of two girls who have similar yet divergent paths: Tihelo and her older sister, Keitumetse, whose gendered experience of blackness has a significant impact on the younger girl. Through the figure of Keitsumetse, Molope introduces the topic of sexual and reproductive health rights, and the lack of access for young women during apartheid – a previously unexamined issue in black women's fiction (except for Wicomb's *You Can't Get Lost in Cape Town*). After the teenaged Keitumetse becomes pregnant, Tihelo helps to procure for her older sister a potion guaranteed to induce abortion, but with results that are almost fatal. After a long hospitalisation, Keitumetse recovers from her horrific abortion experience. Through Keitumetse, Molope articulates a strong call for safe sex for young women and the right to obtain a safe abortion: when questioned by Tihelo about whether she feels guilt about the abortion, Keitumetse is clear that she regrets neither the pregnancy nor the abortion. The assertion by a young black woman that an abortion is a legitimate and logical choice for an unplanned pregnancy registers an insistence on the well-being and safety of the black girl. Keitumetse's refusal to internalise abortion stigma reveals her to be a critically conscious young woman aware of her right to sexual and reproductive health.

In *Dancing in the Dust*, Molope also gestures to a more complex view of race than binary oppositions of black and white, troubling notions of blackness through the figure of Tihelo. As a light-skinned girl, Tihelo is obsessed with the colour of her skin, and her othering by the community, which makes her feel like she never quite fits in. The family secret of her mixed-race origins is revealed at the end of the novel, as is her biological parentage. Tihelo is not singled out for mockery by her community, which knows the circumstances of her birth, but is protected by neighbours from the hurtful facts of her origins. She is accepted by her family and community, and after learning the truth about her biological parents, accepts herself and refashions her concept of self, signing a letter to her white biological mother as 'Tihelo Masimo, Revolutionary' (189). The end of the novel thus signals an integration by Tihelo of her racial ambiguity, gesturing towards a future where apartheid categorisations of race will be less salient than the chosen identities and transgressive practices of self-naming.

Similar reconsiderations of racial identity and categorisation, with which the power structures are imbued, are found in two novels that soon followed *Dancing in the Dust*. *The Madams* (2006) by Zukiswa Wanner and Kopano Matlwa's *Coconut* (2007) both subvert and invert apartheid racial scripts, while showing the lingering effects of the brutal policy on black women's identity formation. Certain of their black women protagonists could be read as having fulfilled Tihelo's dream of escaping the oppression of the apartheid township. Wanner's characters, Thandi and Nosizwe, are comfortably upper-middle class, residing in the leafy suburbs of Johannesburg with full access to designer clothes and shopping trips to Paris, and mingling with white suburban friends. When Thandi, the narrator, expresses guilt about her need to employ a domestic worker, her neighbour Lauren intones: 'Ours is a capitalist nation, my darling ... and you'll just have to live with the pecking order' (xi). Capitalism, together with its conspicuous consumption, is uncritically embraced by these characters. Wanner, however, playfully deconstructs apartheid's hegemonic racial order when Thandi decides to hire a white working-class domestic worker as a 'White Economic Empowerment' project – thus subtly satirising the post-apartheid economic policy of Black Economic Empowerment. For Thandi, a white domestic worker is a vehicle for transposing the race relations she sees in the home of her friend and neighbour, the left-leaning Lauren, whose racism is, however, all too apparent in her treatment of her domestic worker, Ma Rosie. The utopian 'new' South Africa has thus delivered affluence to the fortunate few black women who have escaped the poverty and degradation of the townships, but the economic levelling with whites has not eliminated the scourge of that pernicious brand of white South African racism displayed by urban progressives.

Similarly, race and two young women's racial subjectivities are a significant preoccupation in Kopano Matlwa's *Coconut*. This debut novel explores the interiority of two young black women, Ofilwe, called 'Fifi' by her white friends, and Fikile, known as 'Fiks', whose social positions are on opposite sides of the economic divide. The novel points to the way in which economic inequality has become the new divide by foregrounding the experiences of two young black women whose class position radically forecloses possibilities that might otherwise be open to them. A 2005 study of poverty and inequality in South Africa found that, after ten years of democracy, Africans had generally grown poorer, with the income gap between rich and poor continuing to widen. Economic inequality had effectively increased, making South Africa one of the countries with the largest inequality gaps in the world (Hoogeveen and Özler 2005). Through the characters Ofilwe and Fikile – who respectively live in a gated community in the northern suburbs of Johannesburg and a one-roomed backyard shelter in a nearby township – Matlwa sketches a poignant depiction of life on opposite ends of the neoliberal wealth spectrum. Both girls, who are united by their racial identity, suffer the devastating effects of overt as well as covert racism in a democratic South Africa, suggesting that class mobility and wealth may ultimately not be enough to buffer young black women from the effects of racism. Ofilwe, despite living in an opulent setting and attending a prestigious private school, cannot escape the racial taunts of her white friends, who mock her about her father's wealth, her accent, and her African facial features. Daily life, for her, is filled with the humiliations of post-apartheid racism, and however subtle this may be in comparison, for example, to the indignities experienced by Tlali's protagonist in *Muriel at Metropolitan* (1975), it is nevertheless devastating to her developing psyche.

Ofilwe's life intersects briefly with Fikile's when the latter waits on Ofilwe and her family at the upmarket, predominantly white restaurant where, on Sundays, the family enjoys brunch together. Fikile lives in abject poverty in a distantly located township, where she shares a bed with her uncle, who sexually abuses her. Her ambition to become wealthy and successful is encoded in her imaginative project, 'Project Infinity', an aspirational plan whereby she hopes to achieve affluence. The veneer of middle-class respectability she acquires through expensive clothing, weaves, make-up and blue-tinted contact lenses, comes at a steep price – Fikile is shown shoplifting items of clothing she needs to fit into her place of employment. She internalises the racism she is exposed to in the restaurant where she is employed, so that she considers herself to be unlike other black people in the township of Mpe Batho – in her view, 'hopeless, shortsighted people' (118). With her blue contact lenses and skin-lightening cream, what Fikile unashamedly aspires to is whiteness, a goal that is futile in its unattainability. She uses the very circumstances of her poverty to fuel her dreams, musing that 'they can serve as a constant reminder to me of what I do not want to be: Black, dirty and poor' (118). Though Ofilwe and Fikile are separated by class, what binds them is a similar obsession with aspirational whiteness in post-apartheid South Africa. Spencer (2009) reads this aspiration to an acceptable subject position within the shifting racial and economic order of South Africa as 'enclosed with whiteness; [yet] their journeys ultimately end in entrapment because of the ways in which freedom has been encoded' (Spencer 2009, 68). Ofilwe and Fikile struggle to navigate a world that locates them both between two problematic identities: an 'essentialising 'Africanness' and 'aspirational whiteness' (Spencer 2009, 69).

Trapped in the unattainable aspiration towards whiteness, what is tragic about their encounter is that each projects her loathing of blackness onto the other, with each displaying a palpable disdain for the other girl. *Coconut* suggests that the class chasm between the two young women is insurmountable, foreclosing the possibility of friendship or solidarity between the girls on the basis of their shared gender and racial identities. South Africa's inequality dooms the two to being locked into a dynamic of disdain and disgust.

A significant phenomenon in this cluster of literature by black women, which proliferated around 2006/7, is an emerging queer aesthetic as gay, lesbian and queer characters were included in some of their work. Molope's *Dancing in the Dust*, for the first time in this body of literature, depicts a nascent same-sex attraction between Tihelo and her older comrade, Dikeledi. Tihelo ruminates on their friendship, confessing: 'I had to admit she was really beautiful when she smiled. I had never seen her face glow like that … That was a big moment for me, I could have watched her smile forever' (109). The relationship is, however, doomed. Tragically, Dikeledi does not survive the youth uprising of the 1980s and is killed during a massacre when police open fire on protesting students. The savagery of the state in the dying days of apartheid seems to foreclose the possibility of a sustaining, nurturing and sensual love between the two young women: indeed, in keeping with the time, and given the brutality rained on young black bodies by the apartheid regime, Tihelo's first sexual encounter is a horrific sexual assault by policemen while she languishes in an extended period of detention. She is tortured psychologically by police who comment on her 'unspoilt' state of virginity and persistently issue threats of rape. This experience turns fifteen-year-old Tihelo from a young woman who was once proud of her body into a girl who 'want[ed] to be out of my body, and I stopped enjoying the beauty of my body at that room' (166–167). In a socially just society, Tihelo may have been free to investigate her attraction to Dikeledi through a healthy, consensual mutual exploration of their bodies and their sexuality. This possibility, too, is violently stolen from her by apartheid law and its patriarchal, masculinist brutality. Ten years later, Molope would explore same-sex attraction and queer identity among young black women in greater depth in *This Book Betrays my Brother*.

In Wanner's *The Madams*, the white domestic worker, Marita, whom Thandi employs to make a political point to her white neighbour, turns out to be a lesbian who openly engages in a relationship with another woman, but not before struggling to 'come out'. After Marita expresses anxiety about how her sexual orientation will affect her relationship with her black best friend, the neighbour's domestic worker, Ma Rosie, Thandi encourages her to embrace her sexual orientation by asserting that many black South Africans in the township of Alexandra are gay or lesbian, and in any case, 'Jesus loves everyone, so she [Ma Rosie] cannot say she is a Christian if she does not accept that you love and are giving love, whoever it is that you love' (152). Thandi's deployment of the Christian ideology of love and acceptance, her reassurance that there are 'many homosexuals in Alex' (152), as well as her expression of happiness on Marita's behalf, seem to hold the didactic aim of representing same-sex love as acceptable, or even desirable, for the collective well-being of women.

Assessing black novels of the early and mid-2000s, Pumla Gqola (2009b) reads them in relation to Njabulo Ndebele's foundational 1986 essay, 'The Rediscovery of The Ordinary: Some New Writing in South Africa' (discussed at some length in Chapter Two). She makes the case that such post-transitional literature has finally heeded Ndebele's call, with its textured depictions, having 'turned inwards to amplify the details of everyday life' (Gqola 2009b, 62). She goes on to argue as follows:

In the works of daring novelists such as Kagiso Lesego Molope (2002) and K. Sello Duiker (2001), readers are witnesses to the play of memory, sexuality and identity in path-breaking ways, all the while never losing sight of the characters' emotional landscapes. Kopano Matlwa's debut novel, *Coconut* (2007), explores the psychic torment of gendered Blackness in South Africa in a way that inverts Fanon's *Black Skin, White Masks*, according to Lynda Spencer, while Mtutuzeli Nyoka's powerful *Speak to the Silent* (2004) explores the places where intimacies and violence meet against the backdrop of a nation in transition. (Gqola 2009b, 62)

Though for Gqola (2009b) the black literary turn away from Ndebele's 'spectacular' signals a richer textual engagement with the quotidian, the 'spectacular' has not disappeared from South African political life. Gqola contends that it has moved away from the literary sphere to the political imaginary, where a kind of hegemonic masculinity which she dubs 'spectacular masculinity' has gained prominence. She uses the term 'the masculine spectacular' to denote a hypervisible, public performance of patriarchal masculinity, 'where such performance hints at masculine violence or a contest between forms of manhood' (Gqola 2009b, 64). Accordingly, I will now examine the construction of black masculinities, and black women's entanglements with such masculinities, in Molope's *This Book Betrays my Brother* (2012) and Wanner's *Men of the South* (2010) in order to explore their engagement with hegemonic, alternate and queer masculinities as South Africa's democracy enters its second decade.

Both the transition to democracy and the post-transition held the promise not only of political freedom but also the freedom to imagine and enact new forms of citizenship, and to do so through reconfiguring individual subjectivities and collective identities. The type of nation that might thus emerge after apartheid was predicated upon types of subjectivities – whether masculine, feminine, queer or racialised – that could be generative of a 'nation in formation'. The transitioning nation would also produce new subjectivities – the result of increased political freedom and expanding conceptions of citizenship and personhood, untethered from the ideological strictures of formal apartheid.

These two novels, which I examine in greater depth below, speak profoundly to the ways in which black women writers were articulating and critiquing the types of masculinities produced within the emerging democratic nation. Though completely different stylistically and thematically, they share a concern with highlighting an emerging hegemonic black masculinity, which, while still encumbered by structural oppressions such as homophobia, racism and xenophobia, nevertheless continue to position black women as subservient, and, indeed, inferior, to black men. Both Kagiso Lesego Molope and Zukiswa Wanner inscribe and also critique black masculinities, with Wanner offering, through her fiction, imaginings of alternative black masculinities that are less toxic and punitive towards not only black women but also black men.

New nation, new masculinities: *This Book Betrays my Brother* and *Men of the South*

Kagiso Lesego Molope's second novel, *This Book Betrays my Brother* (2012) is narrated from the point of view of a protagonist, Naledi, who, like that of Farieda Karodia's *Daughters of the Twilight*, is barely fourteen years old. Naledi, who is the subject of Molope's bildungsroman, is likewise on a path to profound danger and disillusionment as she becomes conscious of the gender hierarchy that structures her world. The girl narrator is a naïf, growing up in the seemingly idyllic world of a successful black nuclear family whose affluence enables it to shrug off and transcend its working-class origins – all of which is made possible by the transition to democracy. Naledi's parents are successful business people who have moved out of the location where they both were born. They now live in middle-class affluence that affords them a luxurious home with every modern convenience, as well as private schooling for their two children, and several domestic helpers who are employed in their home and at the family business.

Through the figure of Naledi, who unselfconsciously narrates the world she encounters and the gender order that structures it, the reader is introduced to the ways in which the community – and

Naledi's own nuclear family – construct and perform gender. What is evident from the outset is the premium placed on men and boy children in this particular social milieu; for example, Naledi takes it as a given that her brother is more wanted, valued and cherished than she is as a girl child. We learn early on that her elder brother Basimane's birth was seen as an unparalleled blessing to the extended family: '[a] son, in my mother's family, had been in people's wishes for many years' (7).

His birth had filled the extended family with the sense that a promise would be fulfilled through his presence, as 'Basimane was made of everything strong, beautiful and promising ...' Thus, Basi is 'as special as raindrops on dying crops' (10), auguring life and replenishment on a withered and dying extended family, with one aunt, a former political prisoner, declaring that his birth was like 'the first glimmer of light in a dark cell' (9–10). Here, Aunt Tumo likens Basi to a saviour figure who will liberate and bestow favour on the family, in much the same way as the liberation movement provided an oppressed country with hope and, ultimately, liberation. Basimane is thus cast as the family's last and great hope, a figure who will deliver, on the personal level, an approximation of the political freedom that enabled the transition to democracy in the country. In this post-transitional novel, he is from the moment of his birth regarded as the embodiment of a 'spectacular' masculinity that promises to build a new nation predicated on freedom. The type of freedom imagined by his extended family is, clearly, contingent on his maleness. No girl child born into this family holds the same promise for the family – freedom, actualisation and political liberation is thus inextricably bound up with masculinity – a type of hegemonic masculinity that Basimane has no choice but to grow into as he develops from a boy to a young man. Molope here gestures to the ways in which nation-building remains enmeshed with patriarchy, the 'one-eyed' vision of the nation referred to by Elleke Boehmer (see Introduction and Chapter Three). Notably, this post-transitional novel seems, then, to critique the idea that democracy has rid itself of the oppression of patriarchy and sexism in its articulation of a 'new' nationalism upon which the ideological foundations of post-apartheid South Africa are seen to rest.

Unlike the girl narrators in the fiction of Agnes Sam and Farida Karodia (see Chapter Three), Naledi is, at first, seen to lack critical consciousness: a child narrator, she merely relays the social order she is born into without much thought for racial or gender injustice. She simply narrates the ways in which her brother is revered, and what his gender enables him to achieve – achievements and praise that are unavailable to her as a girl. Naledi, does not, however, criticise the advantages his maleness bestows on her brother – the gender order is a structure she accepts and within which she happily lives. As a literary strategy, this uncritical girl narrator allows the reader to experience Naledi's world and her place in it without too much mediation by a developing political or feminist consciousness – we are simply shown 'what is'. The reader learns that in the township where Naledi and her brother had originally lived, girls play games that do not allow them to venture beyond the street they live in; by contrast, boys have the freedom to explore as far as their legs (and later, cars) can take them:

> Boys, on the other hand, are allowed to go. They kick off their shoes, roll up their pants and run away. They move through Kasi in groups like lion packs hunting. What they do together stays secret for the most part – unless you are like me and you're lucky enough to have a brother who trusts you and lets one or two secrets slip. (17–18)

This seemingly value-free description by Naledi of the different ways in which boys and girls in the location spend their free time nevertheless reveals a great deal. Boys have the freedom to roam and explore their environment, while girls are expected to stay close to home where they are more likely to be under the surveillance of parents and other members of the community. Boys are allowed to keep their activities and adventures a secret – it is, in fact, expected that they will keep these experiences from women.

In addition to setting up the gender order, this paragraph also foreshadows the event that the plot builds up to: the rape of a 16-year-old girl, Moipone, by Basimane, which Naledi witnesses but later denies out of loyalty towards her brother and family.

The boys in the novel have the same untrammelled freedom to 'explore', abuse and violate women's bodies as they display in exploring the woods. Women's bodies are thus equivalent, in the prevailing gender order, to territory available to be explored and conquered through sexual violence: street harassment is pervasive and normalised in the novel, with rape a trope – one which Anne McClintock (1994) shows to be prevalent in colonial writing about the conquest and invasion of terra nullius, or seemingly uninhabited land. Molope uses this colonial trope of women's-bodies-as-territory to demonstrate the incomplete decolonial and democratic project: in the purportedly 'free' South Africa, women's bodies are as open to violence and sexual assault as they were during the colonial period and the apartheid era.

Naledi's inability to speak out in solidarity with Moipone after witnessing the rape is the novel's central conflict, which haunts the narrator several years later as she reaches adulthood. In the extract quoted above, Naledi's simile likens the roaming bands of boys to 'lion packs hunting' (18), thus gesturing to the predatory nature of the boys' developing masculinity. Indeed, Basimane, despite his proclaimed concern for women and women's rights, and his ambition to become a human rights lawyer fighting for women's rights, is revealed to be a sexual predator who preys on Moipone, luring her away from a party and into a room at his home where he knows no one will interrupt the rape. It is only fifteen years later, after she herself has been raped, that Naledi is able to see herself as a 'sister' who should be in solidarity with Moipone: 'Are we sisters? I think so. We move like impalas among hunting lions' (184). The likening of women – herself and Moipone – to prey, vulnerable at any moment to predators, reinforces the opening scenes where boys are likened to lions. Viewed superficially, the image carries positive connotations of strength and bravery, and resonates with that of the 'Young Lions' of the liberation movement, but the shadow side of the image reveals sexual violence to be so ingrained in South African culture that it is normalised among young boys – with rape almost a rite of passage into manhood.

Incidents of verbal, sexual and physical violence against women by both men and boys dominate the novel, reinforcing the idea of gender-based violence as quotidian and rape culture as normalised in South African culture through the enactment of violent masculinities. Molope describes, early in the novel, a scene of sexual harassment that establishes just how normative this behaviour is:

> As we drove that day the usual group of men were loitering on the front stoep, calling over every girl who had walked by and hissing at the ones who ignored them. I had seen them make girls cry. They would curse a girl, or reveal some deeply personal and shaming gossip about her, and she would burst into tears as soon as she was out of sight. (66)

Despite this type of harassment being directed at 'every girl', the problem of sexual harassment is not seen as pressing, or even problematic, by the community. For example, Basimane's friend Five Bop verbally harasses a girl passing by him in the street. The act is witnessed by Naledi and Basimane's mother, who does not chide him, but indulgently and 'light-heartedly' laughs at this behaviour (67). This tolerance for male sexual violence is further internalised by Naledi, who has been led to believe that a boy twisting her wrist until it hurts and the skin underneath turns red is just a normal game between boys and girls: 'I got used to it, and the more a boy twisted my wrist, the more I thought he liked me' (101). Male violence towards women being equated with being 'liked' or desired becomes a normative ideology in this construction of gender relations between boys and girls. As the novel progresses, these incidents of violence, which permeate the novel, become more ominous. Naledi's best friend, Olebogeng, or Ole, is a queer teenager the same age as Naledi. Because of her sexual orientation, Ole is repeatedly threatened with rape in the streets, and Naledi is reminded of the time one of the boys called out to her friend, 'this one just needs to be raped. That will fix her' (161). Sexual violence, and the threat of sexual violence, are thus woven into the fabric of the narrative, and the unceasing violence against women culminates in the spectacle of the rape of Moipone, narrated in realist mode by Naledi.

As with Sam's 'Jesus is Indian' and Karodia's *Daughters of the Twilight*, Molope employs what Flockemann (1992, 37) has referred to as the 'dual focus' (see Chapter Three) of girl narrators, pairing Naledi's point of view with that of her best friend, Olebogeng. While Ole's voice and point of view are not nearly as prominent as Naledi's, it is significant that she is a queer black girl, perhaps the first such character in the fictional work of a black South African woman; through Ole, the reader is given insight into the subjectivity and experiences of a queer girl growing up in a township in post-apartheid South Africa. As suggested above, Molope's main protagonist in *Dancing in the Dust*, Tihelo, articulates a queer desire which is never, however, actualised; her sexual development is brutally damaged and shut down as a result of the sexual assault she suffers at the hands of police while in detention. In contrast, *This Book Betrays my Brother* features a queer black girl who not only desires women, but is able, within the constraints of sexism, homophobia, racism and patriarchy, to exert agency and act upon her desires. Additionally, she presents in a way that marks her as queer, so that she is visibly othered in the novel and cannot, and does not want to, 'pass' for straight. Despite Ole's voice being fairly muted – Naledi remains the first-person narrator throughout – her dialogue and verbal sparring with Naledi becomes a discursive site of consciousness-raising for Naledi and, arguably, for the reader too. Ole becomes the voice of the subaltern in Naledi's comfortable, middle-class existence, forcing Naledi to reckon with the experiences of a working-class, queer black girl. The friendship develops until the poignant moment when Ole comes out to Naledi by declaring her love for a girl – an utterance Naledi, in her self-centredness, glosses over as she continues talking about her own preoccupation with boys. This coming-out scene works, in a sense, to normalise same-sex desire and relations, as Naledi takes in the information but does not give it a second thought. The way she thinks and feels about her best friend does not change – Ole's sexual orientation is just another facet of her personality, a bit of information that Naledi absorbs and quickly processes within her cognitive framework.

Ole's queerness surfaces at key moments throughout the novel, partly to disrupt Naledi's sense of comfort regarding the gender status quo. Ole represents an alternative form of femininity to Naledi's passive docility; moreover, her treatment by boys and men pricks Naledi's conscience and raises her consciousness about patriarchy and violence. When, later on, Ole tells her about the rape threats, Naledi is shocked. The revelation engenders introspection on the part of Naledi about her heterosexual and class privilege:

> I realised for a moment, and perhaps for the very first time, how terrifying it must be to be her, walking around Kasi every day. I couldn't imagine being her, with the knowledge of unidentified dead bodies and Vera-the-Ghost and hearing people's contempt for her spoken out loud. And it was really shameful, I suddenly felt, that having been such close friends for most of our lives, I was only now thinking about it. (162)

Here Naledi registers, for the first time, the danger of queer feminine embodiment, and her own obliviousness to the plight of a girl who is ostensibly her best friend. Ole is, moreover, the one who urges Naledi to corroborate Moipone's story about being raped by Basimane, which Naledi tentatively does, but then retracts under pressure from her family. This effectively ends the girls' friendship – after Naledi's retraction, she never sees or speaks with Ole again; indeed, choosing to defend her brother destroys any possibility of friendship or solidarity not only with Ole, but also Moipone.

Another device used by Molope to explicate the pervasiveness of gender-based violence is the figure of Vera-the-Ghost referred to in the passage above; she appears in the form of a woman who haunts the township and its surrounding roads. As Naledi's father tells the story, she is the spirit of a very beautiful young woman who died violently under mysterious circumstances: '[P]eople say she disappeared after going out to buy vegetables on a Sunday morning ... Some say that she was killed in her own house, but that her body was never found. Her husband cleaned the place until it was spotless' (156). Other versions of the urban legend hold that Vera-the-Ghost was a young woman kidnapped and gang-raped at a party by a group of men (Mhlongo 2013). The figure of the ghost first makes its presence felt as Naledi is about to embark on an important adolescent rite of passage. She is about to attend a social at her brother's school, where, for the first time, she will socialise with teenaged boys without a chaperone. The event might be said to mark her departure from girlhood and entry into adolescence, as she is seen to be entering the terrain of heterosexual dating. It is no coincidence that her mother spots Vera-the-Ghost as Naledi is preparing for the social. With the spectre of gender-based violence appearing at this pivotal moment, the implication is that Naledi is being inaugurated into a world of looming danger, with the possibility of being raped or murdered by a stranger or an intimate partner. If a ghost is evidence of a haunting, a way in which that 'which appears to be not there is often a seething presence' (Gordon 1997, 7) – a 'presence' that dominant discourses attempt to obscure – Vera-the-Ghost signifies the gross injustice of women being subjected to sexual and other physical violence by both strangers and intimate partners alike. The ghost of gender-based violence is the spectre that haunts contemporary South Africa as much as it did during slavocratic and apartheid times.

The second time Vera-the-Ghost appears, Naledi's mother has a much more frightening and visceral experience with it. She encounters it alone at night, and this time the spectral appearance seems far more threatening. This second sighting occurs just after Basimane has been accused of raping Moipone – yet another haunting that signifies the ever-present danger to women from even their intimate partners. The ghost seems to be haunting the denial that cloaks Basimane, and the automatic defence his family mounts without so much as a question as to the possibility that he is guilty of the rape. This interpretation of the haunting is confirmed by Aus Johanna, a domestic worker in the household who cautions Naledi that 'there's a reason why most ghosts are women' (171). Women are at risk of the most gruesome forms of violence from men who may be either strangers or partners, and if, as Niq Mhlongo (2013) posits, the figure of the ghost in African storytelling has didactism as its purpose, the lesson Vera-the-Ghost holds for all women in the locations of South Africa is that they could be harmed at any time, by any man, even, as Aus Johanna puts it, 'someone she knew so well' (171). This realisation nullifies for Naledi the closely-held belief that her adored brother, Basimane, is not like the other boys who sexually harass girls in the street and threaten them with rape. For Naledi, Vera-the-Ghost destroys this myth, showing Basimane to be exactly like every other man who has verbally, physically or sexually harassed women.

Vera-the-Ghost may also be figured as the ghost of the sexual abuse of black women by black men in apartheid South Africa. This is poignantly highlighted by Zoë Wicomb in *David's Story* (see Chapter Four) – the unresolved, unspoken mass atrocity that has still not been addressed by society at large or nation-building mechanisms like the Truth and Reconciliation Commission. Indeed, this culture of denial and forgetting, which elides black women's experiences and narratives of rape, produced the rape culture that enabled a rape-accused to become president of the South African nation. It is little wonder, then, that *This Book Betrays my Brother* ends ominously, with Basimane's mother speculating on her son's fate 'with unwavering confidence. "He can be president, if he wants to be"' (185). Several inferences may be drawn from his mother's perception of Basimane as capable, despite the rape accusation, of ascending to the highest office in the new democracy. One is that the heroic, patriarchal, nationalist brand of masculinity (Boehmer 1991) that is deployed in nation-building, and displayed both by then President Jacob Zuma and Basimane, is a desirable brand of masculinity which younger men should emulate. The articulation of this type of masculinity often finds expression in 'war talk' which normalises violence, thus contributing to rape culture: 'violent masculinities create a public consciousness in which violence is not just acceptable and justified, but also natural and desirable' (Gqola 2015, 152). Both Gqola and Mmatshilo Motsei (2007) attribute this normalisation of spectacular masculine violence and rape culture to the utterances and threats made against Jacob Zuma's rape accuser, Fezekile Kuzwayo, by crowds of Zuma supporters outside the court where the rape trial was heard. In a similar manner to the way in which Kuzwayo was blamed for trying to destroy a powerful man through a false rape accusation, Moipone is accused of lying, wanting to trap Basimane, and is ultimately blamed for what transpired between her and Basimane. Analysing the discursive constructs around the rape victim in the Zuma trial, Motsei

(2007, 147) posits that 'the prevailing tendency to blame the oppressed for the consequences of their oppression is common-place ... For a woman accusing a man of rape ... she is blamed for something beyond her control'. In drawing parallels between the aftermath of the Zuma rape charge and the rape of Moipone, Molope shows how the boy who was 'the first glimmer of light in a dark cell' (9) becomes a sexual terrorist whose violence is excused and even condoned under a patriarchal nationalist order which constantly remakes itself and, indeed, thrives on such displays of violent masculinity.

Towards a new vision of masculinity: *Men of the South*

In contrast with Molope, Zukiswa Wanner interrogates black masculinities emerging in South Africa in the wake of the transition to democracy by portraying, in *Men of the South* (2010), the variegated, heterogeneous nature of such masculinities; critiquing certain types of masculinity; and offering versions of black masculinity that are less toxic to women as well as men.

Wanner interweaves the stories of three black male characters living in contemporary Johannesburg and Cape Town, deftly showing how their performances and iterations of masculinity construct not only their own subjectivities, but also co-construct one another's masculinities. The tryptich form of the novel introduces us to three young black men whose lives intersect at various points: Mfundo, a jazz musician who came of age in Soweto during apartheid; Mzilikazi, a '100 percent Zulu boy', who, for much of his youth and young adulthood, carries the secret that he is gay; and Tinaye, a British-born Zimbabwean who struggles to obtain permanent residency, and, therefore, gainful employment in South Africa. The contestation between differing – and shifting – forms of masculinity provides the central thrust of the novel.

The notion of hegemonic masculinity, as defined by Morrell (1998), is central to my argument. Accordingly, masculinity as a collective identity is always socially constructed, and always fluid:

There is not one universal masculinity, but many masculinities. These are not fixed character types but configurations of practice generated in particular situations in a changing structure of relationships. Class and race factors are constitutive of the form that masculinity takes. This means that in any society there are many masculinities, each with a characteristic shape and set of features. The contours of these masculinities change over time, being affected by changes elsewhere in society and at the same time, themselves affecting society itself. (Morrell 1998, 605)

Morrell argues further that, within the framework of masculinities, dominant and subordinate masculinities operate within a matrix of power constructed through nodes of difference such as race, sexual orientation and nationality. Contestations exist between different types of masculinity in any given society, with those belonging to the category of dominant masculinity displaying 'hegemonic masculinities'. Since masculinity is socially constructed, imbued with power, and always contested, hegemonic masculinity, while resting on the ability to assert power over women, also 'silences and subordinates other masculinities, positioning these in relation to itself such that the values expressed by these other masculinities are not those that have currency or legitimacy' (Morrell 1998, 605).

Men of the South explores such contestations of masculinity between three male characters as they come into their own – or fail to do so – as mature black men during the first years of democracy in South Africa. Though the three men's stories are given equal weight in the novel, Mfundo's character functions as a pivot around which the other two revolve. Mfundo's story is the first to be encountered, and his experiences and articulation of masculinity become a baseline against which Mzilikazi and Tinaye's versions of manhood are measured. Thus, the lives and experiences of Mzilikazi and Tinaye are set against the backdrop of Mfundo's hegemonic masculinity.

Mfundo's story is a first-person narrative in which life only really starts on the day he first meets his partner, a woman called Slindile. This meeting, an important origin story of his life, occurs on 11 February 1990 – the day Nelson Mandela was released after 27 years of imprisonment. Using this day as a marker establishes Nelson Mandela's release and the political events which would flow from it – the Codesa negotiations and the first democratic election in 1994 – as a starting point, not only of the new South African nation, but also in the life of Mfundo. Much as Basimane's birth was 'the first glimmer of light in a dark cell' (Molope 2012, 9), signifying hope and a new freedom for his extended family, Mfundo's meeting Slindile on this significant date seems to augur well for the couple, who will be building their lives together as politically liberated citizens in the newly developing democracy. The promise the relationship holds, given its auspicious start, is not, however, brought to fruition. This is partly due to the toxic masculinity displayed by Mfundo, who jettisons a promising career as a jazz musician by assaulting a famous American singer, then later destroys his relationship with Slindile by assaulting her. Well aware of the deficiencies of his performance of masculinity, Mfundo sets down the two models of township masculinity that he draws on:

> There were two types of them [that is, men], you see. There were the happy-go-lucky men in the neighbourhood who would send me to buy them loose skyfs at the nearest spaza shop as they sat drinking at all hours of the day. Then there were the salt-of-the earth type of men like my father and Mzi's father, who looked after their families and came home on time. But these men were dictatorial. Their wives feared them, their children feared them. I never wanted to use either of the two groups as a role model. What examples of men do I see? I once asked Mzilikazi. How am I to turn into a better man if these are the only men I'm encountering? (17)

Mfundo shows an awareness that he needs to and wants to be a 'better man' than the men he encounters around him, but he does not know how to become such a man due to the lack of 'role models for ghetto boys' (20). Though in the developing democratic nation, Mfundo seems set to be the type of man who embodies hegemonic masculinity due to the intersection of his race, class, cisgender and heterosexual identities, he nevertheless wishes to craft a new type of masculinity for himself, as no satisfactory mode of being a black, heterosexual man is available to him. Neither of the two dominant modes of being a man he has encountered in the township appeals to him. Both are violent, resting on the control of women, children and other men deemed 'lesser' (that is, younger, queer, effeminate and foreign men). However, even though Mfundo sets out to cobble together a way of being a man in the world which transcends the narrow models available to him, he fails miserably.

The first major obstacle to creating the life he could have under a new democratic dispensation surfaces when he loses his job after the assault and 'joined the ranks of the forty percent or so of this country's unemployed' (53). Though Slindile is a doctor who is comfortably middle class, this puts the couple, who by now have a baby, under considerable financial strain, resulting in vitriolic arguments. After becoming unemployed, Mfundo embraces his role as a stay-at-home father to his infant daughter, becoming a 'Domestic God' (55) who enjoys cooking, baking, doing the laundry, and other household chores. However, Slindile resents his lack of income and its effect on their lifestyle; in a gender role-reversal characteristic of Wanner's fiction, Slindile undervalues his unpaid domestic and parenting labour, and the contribution this makes to their lives. When Slindile berates Mfundo, demanding that he 'be the man of the house for once', Mfundo assaults her with 'fists of fury' (57). The assault spells the end of their relationship, so that Mfundo has lost not only his livelihood, but also the woman he deeply loves and a stable family life.

Mfundo's catastrophic descent into chaos, unemployment and homelessness is cemented when he returns to Soweto, where he'd grown up, becoming one of the men who drinks all day, whom he'd so despised as a younger man. He seems doomed to fall back into one of the two models of manhood, having failed to forge a new type of masculinity that reconfigures gender roles and casts him as the nurturer rather than the financial provider. It is ironic that his woman partner is the chief agent of rejection of this model of masculinity, preferring a 'real man' (57) who is the archetypal provider over one who prefers to be a full-time caregiver to their child.

Another form of masculinity is presented through Mfundo's best friend, Mzilikazi, a self-identifying queer Zulu man. Though Mzilikazi narrates his own section of the novel, explaining how he came to accept his sexual orientation, being '100% gay' (85), the reader first encounters him through the homophobic lens of Mfundo. In relation to Mzilikazi, Mfundo displays hegemonic masculinity when he first discovers that his best friend has been having sexual relations with another man, a mutual acquaintance Mfundo describes as 'that thuggish guy in the hood' who 'has tons of babies with different women to whom he refers as bitches' (20). Mfundo discovers this secret when he inadvertently walks in on Mzilikazi and his lover, saying in dismay, 'finding out the way I did was pretty tough on me' (29). Mfundo goes so far as to compare being gay with having a chronic, life-altering illness: 'Finding out Mzi was gay was similar to learning that someone close to you is HIV positive ... It can have quite a devastating effect' (29–30). In demonstrating the deeply entrenched stigma attached both to being queer and HIV positive, Wanner also interrogates an enduring myth about queer male identity: that gay men are responsible for 'spreading' HIV. In so doing, Wanner exposes a myth concerning HIV and its conflation with queer male identity, a hegemonic and deleterious ideology theorised by Leo Bersani (1987) during the early stages of the AIDS epidemic in the USA. Bersani argues that at the outset of the pandemic in the USA, public discourse constructed gay men as the embodiment of the disease in the same way as nineteenth-century women sex workers came to signify venereal disease. Female sexuality was represented as 'intrinsically diseased' (Bersani 1987, 211), a trope that would be resurrected more than a century later to 'infect' the bodies of gay men who were similarly cast as spreading HIV through ostensible displays of promiscuity. Through the narrative of Mzilikazi, Wanner brings this trope of the 'infectious' gay body to light in order to debunk pernicious and enduring myths about gay men.

Mzilikazi tackles these stereotypes head-on, reclaiming the abject aspects of his queer subjectivity: 'If there is anything like a 100% Zulu boy who is cosmopolitan, I am he. I am also 100% gay ... I am gay, ungqingili, a fag, is'tabane, a queen. Hundred percent Zulu Queer. I am as attracted to men as other men are to women' (85). In this initial self-description, Mzilikazi juxtaposes 'Zulu boy' with '100% gay'; this amounts to a contradiction in homophobic ideologies of homosexuality as 'unAfrican' (Msibi 2011). Mzilikazi's declaration challenges homophobia as often articulated on the African continent, and as embodied in the figure of Mzilikazi's father, who, in a jarring scene, laments the protection of LGBTIQ rights by the new South African Constitution. As his infuriated father watches a television news clip depicting the legalisation of same-sex marriage by the Constitutional Court, he says to Mzilikazi: 'Do they realize this is Africa, coming to pollute this continent with their Eurocentric ideas?' (122). Mzilikazi's self-naming at the opening of his section of the novel functions to counter the pernicious myth that homosexuality is unAfrican, by consolidating both Zulu and gay identity within one black man's subjectivity. Mzilikazi further lists a string of derogatory monikers for homosexuals, claiming them as part of his identity and thus subverting their power to diminish and harm the intended targets of hate speech. Significantly, the Zulu term 'ungqingili', which Mzilikazi uses to refer to himself, is a homophobic slur brought to the nation's awareness when soon-to-be president Jacob Zuma used it during a 2006 speech in Stanger: he denounced homosexuality as unAfrican and declared that, as a young man, he would have struck down any such person had he encountered them. Though Mzilikazi uses this term as a self-descriptor, it is also used ironically as an intervention into the homophobic discourse produced, in part, by Zuma. The use of the phrase '100% Zulu boy' is, as (Stobie 2011) suggests, 'an implicit rebuke' to Zuma, who proudly claims '100% Zulu' identity while at the same time being homophobic. Here, Wanner enters the public national debate through fiction, interrogating the use of the slur, subverting its meaning and stripping it of its associations with moral degeneracy. Moreover, by describing his attraction to men as having equal weight to that of a heterosexual man's attraction to women, Mzilikazi decentres heterosexuality as normative, giving same-sex attraction and sexual orientation equivalent value within his world view. Mzilikazi further layers the meanings of his queer subjectivity by describing additional, equally important constituent parts of his identity:

> I am a father and a divorcee. I am also a rural-born, kasi-bred Zulu man who can stick-fight and slaughter with the best of them. In other words, reincarnate him and I could probably

out-Zulu Shaka Zulu. So no more talk of homosexuality being un-African, if you please. (87)

In this self-portrait, Mzilikazi invokes the iconic masculinity of the Zulu king and legendary warrior Shaka Zulu, jesting that he could 'out-Zulu' him. Consolidating this figure of dominant, powerful masculinity with male-gendered performative practices such as stick-fighting and cattle-slaughtering produces for Mzilikazi a dominant masculinity that dovetails comfortably with his queer masculinity that is, however, perceived as subordinate within the hegemonic gender order. For Mzilikazi, there are no contradictions inherent in these seemingly disparate strands of identity – he embodies the seamless co-existence of these masculine elements, and lives a successful life imbued with political and sexual autonomy. Yet this freedom only comes after he divorces his wife and moves away from his family to Cape Town – the only space in the country where he feels 'really and truly free' (127). Yet despite this purported freedom, he is unable to come out to his father or to take his partner home to meet his parents and extended family. Thus, even though he fully embraces his queer Zulu identity, it is an identity that he can only fully inhabit in certain spaces – neither his parental nor ancestral home is included among these.

When his father dies, Mzilikazi faces a reckoning and the impossibility of fully inhabiting his queer identity when he returns to his rural home for the burial. Looking at his partner, he laments the fact that they cannot hold hands or show affection at a time of great loss, and asks 'would we always be exiles in our own land?' (148). Despite the relative freedom to forge his own destiny and live as an openly gay man with his partner in Cape Town, being queer in the emerging South African democracy still implies a type of exile, the withholding of a fully integrated notion of citizenship. Aspects of Mzilikazi's subjectivity will always have to remain hidden, Wanner's novel implies, especially from other, older men such as his father and uncles. Here, hegemonic masculinity still dominates, defines and structures alternate forms of masculinity such as queer black manhood, constricting the lives and citizenship of men like Mzilikazi.

The novels of both Wanner and Molope comment on developing masculinities in post-apartheid South Africa, thereby signalling the dangers of valorising black hegemonic masculinity. Whereas Molope offers no alternative forms of masculinity to the type she interrogates through the figure of Basimane, Wanner does offer alternatives. In *Men of the South*, her character Mfundo explores a different way of being a man: he embraces his role as a stay-at-home parent who looks after his infant daughter and invests himself in domestic labour. Mzilikazi, too, constructs an alternative lifestyle to the dominant model of masculinity available to him as a Zulu man. This includes a loving relationship with a male partner, which, ironically, is the most stable romantic relationship of those engaged in by the three male characters in the novel. Nevertheless, both characters attempting an alternative to violent, hegemonic masculinity fail at fully actualising a different vision of masculinity in their lives. Ironically, it is a woman, Mfundo's intimate partner, who shows the most disdain for his softer iteration of masculinity, and which indirectly leads to him to choose a more violent articulation of being a man. Similarly, it is Basimane's mother and the host of aunts surrounding him who protect him when he is accused of rape, thereby upholding a standard of violent masculinity that is central to South Africa's rape epidemic. While Wanner offers glimpses of what an alternative, non-hegemonic, non-violent man may look like in the developing South African democracy, the structured gender order is seen to militate against individual men making the subjective, personal changes necessary for engendering non-normative, non-violent masculinities.

Conclusion: Towards a Black South African Feminist Criticism

This book has aimed to show the ways in which black South African women writers have made visible their standpoint on apartheid and the emerging democratic South African nation. During the apartheid era, two pioneering black novelists, Miriam Tlali and Lauretta Ngcobo, inserted into the national discourse a counter-hegemonic vision of the nation, and black women's place in it, by critiquing the nationalism that was dominant at the time. Tlali and Ngcobo's singular contribution in their novels was to analyse the construction and use of apartheid space, with Ngcobo's *And They Didn't Die* (1990) offering an alternative vision by reconfiguring space for a more just and equitable South African social order. Exemplars of a critical black geography (McKittrick and Woods 2007), their novels critique the dominant mode of apartheid spatiality, making visible the lives of those who inhabit its fissures and margins.

Writing during the late-apartheid era, both Farida Karodia and Agnes Sam focus on daughterhood and South African Indian identity, producing subaltern voices that question the constructs of race and femininity, as well as emergent discourses foundational to a democratic nation. Karodia's *Daughters of the Twilight* (1986) and Sam's 'Jesus is Indian' (1989) pay particular attention to the ways in which contact with colonial power and the apartheid system position the Indian girl protagonists in a liminal space between their 'Indianness' and colonial culture. These writings also examine the ways in which the girls negotiate their identity within the racial tumult of the apartheid years, thus anticipating young women's struggles in the democratic nation.

I have also argued that, in the post-apartheid transitional period from white domination to democracy, Zoë Wicomb and

Sindiwe Magona used the discursive space opened up by the transition to interrogate androcentric nationalist rhetoric by calling into question the patriarchal, unitary nature of nationalism in their respective novels, *David's Story* (2000) and *Mother to Mother* (1998). Wicomb achieves this in *David's Story* by decentring the notion of a cohesive truth – which was pivotal to the nation-building project of the TRC. She further achieves this by recreating in her text the silences around discourses of rape within the ANC's military wing – silences reproduced by the TRC through the glaring omissions in its final report. Wicomb succeeds in drawing attention to these elisions in women's experiences without speaking the unspeakable act of rape. In turn, Magona fractures emerging, hegemonic forms of a unitary nationalism by relating the story of a young freedom fighter responsible for the political killing of a white woman, from the perspective of his mother. In doing so, she decentres the narrative of the black male militant as an agent of history, a heroic figure in the liberation of South Africa, and creates a more textured story of the interconnected lives of the son, his mother, Mandisa, and the white people who have shaped their destinies.

A relatively new genre in black South African women's writing is also examined: the neo-slave narrative, which is told here from the perspective of authors who are conceivably descended from slave populations at the Cape. In a comparative reading of Yvette Christiansë's *Unconfessed* (2006) and Rayda Jacobs's *The Slave Book* (1998), I argue that both novels point to the political economy of South African slavery while at the same time offering a critique of democratic South Africa's embrace of neoliberal economic policies. Both writers use the neo-slave tale as a generative narrative for a 'new' South African nation that includes women as full citizens. The country's entry into democracy offers a vantage point to reassess slave ancestry, heritage and political economy.

I conclude my analysis with a comparative reading of Zukiswa Wanner's *Men of the South* (2010) and Kagiso Lesego Molope's *This Book Betrays my Brother* (2012), which examines the writers' engagements with black masculinities, focusing on their treatment of violent and hegemonic masculinities. Both writers, in their critique of hegemonic black masculinities, gender-based violence, and homophobia, propose alternative forms of masculinity that are crucial for the development of a nation that has been damaged by high levels of violence against women and homophobia.

While the works I have examined differ both stylistically and in the periods they depict, what they share is a subaltern perspective on the nation and a commitment to interrogating hegemonic discourses of citizenship, whether these relate to apartheid or African national patriarchy. As cultural and subversive texts, their efficacy lies in an uncompromising willingness to challenge dominant narratives that construct hegemonic forms of national identity whose meaning is co-constructed with the oppositional 'other'. Often, this 'other' is gendered woman. The texts surveyed here refuse this sublimation of black woman as other, and insist upon inserting the figure of the black woman into national discourse. Given the different types of patriarchal nationalism faced in different periods in South African history, the writers whose texts are examined here use a variety of literary strategies to contest dominant nationalisms.

In her analysis of gender in African women's writing, Juliana Makuchi Nfah-Abbenyi (1997, 263) posits that African women writers specifically concerned with gender, and the historical deployment of gender as a social category in colonial and postcolonial Africa, not only create worlds within the text, but are also engaged in the project of 'fictionalized theory or ... theorized fiction'. Accordingly, African feminist novels are not just fiction, but also function as theoretical texts:

> The theory is embedded in the polysemous and polymorphous nature of the narratives themselves. These texts reinscribe and foreground teleological, ontological, and epistemological insights and praxes relevant to the specific histories and politics that preceded the fictional texts. (Nfah-Abbenyi 1997, 262–263)

Similarly, the fictional texts examined in this book are located within the realm of theory, and in interrogating the logic of patriarchal nationalisms – be these Afrikaner or emerging postcolonial African nationalisms – the authors effectively theorise a black, feminist praxis for engaging with and subverting these nationalisms.

I return here to the question that opens this book concerning the utility of theory. Following on what Gqola (2008, 51) names 'creative theorisation in the arena of African feminist imagination', I propose that the works of Tlali, Ngcobo, Karodia, Sam, Magona, Wicomb, Christiansë, Jacobs, Wanner and Molope produce a black South African feminist theory that has also utility as literary criticism. I define this black South African feminist literary theory as both the theorisation of black women's positionality in relation to structures of domination such as apartheid and black patriarchy, and a method for reading transgressive, feminist literature produced by other black women writing subjects. This black South African feminist criticism is thus an approach to reading black South African feminist fiction, one with a feminist ethical dimension.

Why theorise from a specifically South African standpoint and not a pan-African or transnational black feminist perspective, especially when a wealth of African feminist theoretical perspectives exist, from which one might draw? Chikwenye Okonjo Ogunyemi, for example, as early as 1985, offered the concept of womanism as an analytical lens for reading African women's fiction. She defines womanism in the work of African women writers as explicitly contrasted with white, western feminism:

> While the white woman writer protests against sexism, the Black woman writer must deal with it as one among many evils; she battles also with the dehumanisation resulting from racism and poverty. What, after all, is the value of sexual equality in a ghetto? ... The politics of the womanist is unique in its racial-sexual ramifications; it is more complex than white sexual politics, for it addresses more directly the ultimate question relating to power: how do we share more equitably the world's wealth and concomitant power among the races and between the sexes? (Ogunyemi 1985, 68)

Ogunyemi's analysis of the conditions under which African women write, and why they write, integrates Kimberlé Crenshaw's (1989) idea of intersectionality into the understanding of writerly subjectivity, before Crenshaw's theory was posited. While a womanist analysis of black South African women's writing, one which is 'conscious of Black impotence in the context of white patriarchal culture, [and thus] empowers the Black man' (Ogunyemi 1985, 68), may apply to the early writings of Head, Tlali, Ngcobo and Karodia, by the early transitional period, womanism could no longer be used as an adequate paradigm for critically assessing black women's writing. Even before the end of formal apartheid, as the writing of Sam, Wicomb and Magona demonstrates, black women writers were shifting their political engagement to include a critique of black masculinity and its iterations as nationalism. A black South African feminist literary theory, then, accounts for the ways in which not only colonisation, but also the singularly destructive inhumanity of apartheid inflected and structured people's lives, and continues to shape collective and individual futures. It exists on a spectrum between womanist literary expression and what Simidele Dosekun (2007, 46)) terms 'radical African feminism'; both an ideology and a movement, it 'pursues substantive equality between men and women in Africa where gender inequality persistently reigns'. Significantly, 'this feminism is not just for women. Its purpose is not to replace men with women, nor even to merely include more women in men's worlds. Its purpose, rather, is to transform the very structures of our societies which produce and perpetuate gender inequalities in the first place.' A black South African feminist literary theory incorporates aspects of both womanism and radical African feminism, often shifting strategically, as history and politics dictates, to incorporate elements of each.

Black South African feminist literary theory is seen, therefore, to operate on two levels. Firstly, it examines the actual production of fiction which itself theorises black women's lived experiences and strategies for emancipation. Secondly, as a form of feminist literary criticism, it offers useful entryways into analysing texts.

Black South African feminist fiction as literary theory

Black South African women's feminist fiction writing may be reconceptualised as a form of theory. In fiction that also functions as black South African feminist theory, experiences and events are narrated from the perspective of black women, providing access to their interior lives. Black women are portrayed as thinking subjects and not mere ciphers or physical objects. In this way, the writers foreground the subjugated knowledges of black women which were suppressed by hundreds of years of colonialism and many decades of apartheid. In these fictional works, black South African feminist theory locates black women historically, allowing insights into the forces of oppression that operate against them, as well as opportunities they are able to take advantage of within the matrix of power in which they are situated. In such representations, black South African feminist theory both historicises and situates black women as subjects constrained by the politics of their respective social locations. Yet, significantly, black women are also represented as agentic beings, able to navigate and negotiate the constraints they face. This leads me to another characteristic of black South African feminist theory: creative re-visioning.

I have previously introduced (Boswell 2017) the concept of creative re-visioning: a subject's ability to re-envision and reimagine what is possible for her to achieve within her life-time, given the constraints under which she operates, and the low expectations the society in which she is located has of her. At the time, I argued that the writers I interviewed – Miriam Tlali, Lauretta Ngcobo, Gladys Thomas and Sindiwe Magona – were engaged in a creative re-envisioning of their lives in the very act of being writing subjects. Since the societies in which they were born and raised deemed them only fit for domestic labour, and educated them accordingly, their acts of creatively re-visioning themselves as writers in possession of creative agency marked a radical shift in their subjectivities. I now extend this argument to encompass the subjectivities of the black women characters these writers bring to life in their fiction. These thinking subjects, located within the historic constraints of their specific social situ-ations, provide alternative forms of consciousness and counter-narratives, as well as a creative re-visioning of black women's lives and subjectivities on the page. The subjectivities constructed in *Muriel at Metropolitan, And They Didn't Die, 'Jesus is Indian', Daughters of the Twilight, David's Story, Mother to Mother, The Slave Book, Unconfessed, This Book Betrays my Brother* and *Men of the South* are constantly engaged in renegotiating the bounds of what is possible for black women to achieve within the systems in which they are embedded, a prime example being Mhlophe's character who re-orders and subverts the politics of the toilet she has appropriated. These self-directing women characters interrogate and push against the structures that hold them back, a process that in turn engenders further agency. And while the women do not always end up in a world with a restored, more just, social order, they nevertheless continue to fight against discourses and practices which deny them agency and humanity.

An additional characteristic of a black South African feminist theory produced by black women's fiction is found in the way it responds to, and positions, black women in relation to their particular experience of oppression. It recognises that black women experience intersecting forms of oppression: their situation cannot be accounted for by merely considering the effects of one system of oppression upon them. As is made clear in the novels I have examined, the black women protagonists who inhabit the worlds created by Tlali, Magona, Sam, Karodia, Wicomb, Ngcobo, Christiansë, Jacobs, Wanner and Molope negotiate overlapping forms of oppression, including oppression by white supremacist capitalist ideology and black patriarchy. The authors position their women characters between these systems, often offering, through their characters' struggles, models for simultaneously negotiating the discourse and practices of multiple systems of oppression.

A final characteristic of a black South African feminist literary theory is its insistence on imagining social worlds where justice, humanity, and agency are freely available to oppressed citizens. Through critiquing dominant structures within their society, and using their creative fiction to imagine different worlds, these authors are engaged in a transgressive process of reshaping the world. The degree to which they imagine an alternative to their present world may vary, yet each author, in exposing fallacies and contradictions in masculinist nationalisms at different historical moments, begins the work of transforming society. Thus, Miriam Tlali reveals the unworkability and unviability of the apartheid system that needs the black bodies it continuously abjects in order to maintain itself, and gestures to a world without the dreaded pass laws and artificial boundaries within which the protagonist finds herself. Lauretta Ngcobo, in her imaginative, feminist utilisation of space in *And They Didn't Die*, shows a model for black women's resistance by demonstrating the ways in which black women have literally reconfigured the oppressive spaces in which they find themselves, by working collectively and using their bodies to shelter each other. Agnes Sam and Farida Karodia uncover the value the young girl with a developing political consciousness holds in an emerging post-apartheid nation. Zoë Wicomb, in *David's Story*, points to the dangers inherent in inaugurating a new nation when it has a reductive understanding of 'truth'. She also demonstrates how national unity is built upon the bodies of black women guerillas whose stories of rape and abuse were ultimately subsumed by nation-building discourses at the Truth and Reconciliation Commission. Wicomb thus indirectly opens up a discussion of what the alternative might look like: how a more inclusive discourse around reconciliation might work to forge deeper reconciliation and healing. Sindiwe Magona, in similar fashion, points to the incomplete project of national reconciliation undertaken by the TRC; in failing to account for the structural violence committed against black South Africans during apartheid, it circumvents the opportunity to produce meaningful reconciliation, one which factors in the different types of structural violence and loss endured by South Africa's citizens. Yvette Christiansë and Rayda Jacobs show us the systemic roots of rape in the very founding of the nation, and the role of systematic rape in the formation of nation's political economy. Zukiswa Wanner and Kagiso Lesego Molope critique hegemonic forms of black masculinity that produce sexual violence and other forms of gender-based violence, as well as homophobia, and point to alternative forms of masculinity that are neither toxic nor desirous of dominance over 'the other' – whether women, children or queer subjects.

Black South African feminist criticism as an analytical method

The novels surveyed in this book produce not only a black South African feminist theory, but also a mode of criticism, a lens which offers literary critics ways of interpreting black women's writing that refuses to reduce such writing to mere description. As an analytical and theoretical practice, this form of criticism is the antithesis to conventional modes of knowing and knowledge production. The latter enables, for example, the esteemed South African writer, Nadine Gordimer (1985, xi), to state the following in her preface to Ellen Kuzwayo's *Call Me Woman* (1985): 'Fortunately, although she is not a writer, she has the memory and the gift of unselfconscious expression that enable her to tell her story as no-one else could.' Gordimer conceives of Kuzwayo as no more than a stenographic recorder of her own life, reliant on memory rather than artistry or creative agency in constructing her life story. Rather than thoughtful, crafted writing, Kuzwayo's autobiography is mere 'unselfconscious expression', an example of simple, everyday storytelling: for Gordimer, Kuzwayo is categorically 'not a writer'.

A black South African feminist criticism as a method of engaging with black, women-authored texts, takes as its point of departure the intrinsic value of a black woman – her life shaped by oppressive forces such as slavery, apartheid, colonialism, capitalism and patriarchy – sitting down to write from her uniquely gendered, classed and racialised position. Whether fiction, autobiography or poetry, such work should be approached as containing possible insights and perspectives not available elsewhere. Additionally, it attends to the political discourses that shape black women as speaking subjects, noting the dominant discourses of the time as well as the location of a text in its representation of these women. This form of criticism notes, too, that power structures often intersect, so that apartheid and black patriarchy, for example, are seen to work together in shaping black women's lives. It is painstakingly alert to these forces, the way they operate, and the way they are depicted textually.

A black South African feminist criticism is attentive to the historiography of black women's existence within past and present South African societies, and notes the ways in which historical constraints have impeded the lives of black subjects represented in texts it seeks to elucidate. It carefully seeks out and closely observes the subjectivities of black women in relevant texts, utilising, again, the unique vantage point afforded by black women's subjugated knowledges. It searches for these knowledges wherever they may be found; it notes the absence of such unique ways of knowing where lacunae exist; and it embeds interpretations of black women's subjectivities in its critique of the work under scrutiny. It is similarly attentive to formulations of black women's agency in relation to oppressive structures, as portrayed in literary texts. Importantly, it extrapolates meaning from the presence – or, indeed, absence – of such agency in literary texts. This opens up new ways not only of seeing the South African nation, but also of reconceptualising knowledge, in order to re-centre those most oppressed, and the valuable knowledge they offer. Such a politics of reading opens up unprecedented ways of refiguring the nation as a more just, equitable place, where black women will finally be able to feel themselves at home.

Select Bibliography

Interviews

Christiansë, Yvette. Interview by author. Tape recording. New York, 27 July 2012.

Magona, Sindiwe. Interview by author. Tape recording. Cape Town, 17 July 2006.

Ngcobo, Lauretta. Interview by author. Tape recording. Durban, 11 July 2006.

Thomas, Gladys. Interview by author. Tape recording. Cape Town, 19 July 2006.

Tlali, Miriam. Interview by author. Tape recording. Johannesburg, 4 July 2006.

Secondary sources

Abrahams, Naeemah, Rachel Jewkes, Lorna J Martin, Shanaaz Mathews, Lisa Vetten, and Carl Lombard. 2009. 'Mortality of Women from Intimate Partner Violence in South Africa: A National Epidemiological Study.' *Violence and Victims* 24 (4): 546–556.

Abrahams, Yvette. 1998. 'Images of Sara Bartman: Sexuality, Race, and Gender in Early Nineteenth-Century Britain.' In *Nation, Empire, Colony: Historicizing Gender and Race*, edited by Ruth Pierson and Nupur Chaudhuri, 220–236. Bloomington: Indiana University Press.

Adhikari, Mohamed. 2005. *Not White Enough, Not Black Enough: Racial Identity in the South African Coloured Community*. Athens, Ohio: Ohio University Press.

Adichie, Chimamanda. 2009. 'The Danger of a Single Story.' TEDGlobal 2009. Accessed 13 March 2020. https://www.ted.com/talks/ chimamanda_ngozi_adichie_the_danger_of_a_single_story.

Ali, Shaida Kazie. 2010. *Not a Fairytale*. Cape Town: Penguin Random House.

———. 2012. *Lessons in Husbandry.* Cape Town: Penguin Random House.

Althusser, Louis. 1971. 'Ideology and Ideological State Apparatuses (Notes toward an Investigation).' In *Lenin and Philosophy and Other Essays,* edited by Louis Althusser, 127–188. New York: Monthly Review Press.

ANC (African National Congress). 1997. '"Apology Tendered to Premier Phosa," Press Release Issued by Department of Information and Publicity.' African National Congress. Accessed 12 May 2004. http://www.anc.org.za/show.php?doc=ancdocs/pr/1997/pr0807a. html.

Anderson, Benedict. 1991. *Imagined Communities: Reflections on the Origin and Spread of Nationalism.* New York: Verso.

Baderoon, Gabeba. 2011. '"This is Our Speech": Voice, Body and Poetic Form in Recent South African Writing.' *Social Dynamics* 37 (2): 213–227.

———. 2014. *Regarding Muslims: From Slavery to Post-Apartheid.* Johannesburg: Wits University Press.

Barnard, Rita. 2007. *Apartheid and Beyond: South African Writers and the Politics of Place.* Oxford: Oxford University Press.

Beal, Jo. 1990. 'Women and Indentured Labour in Colonial Natal, 1860–1911.' In *Women and Gender in Southern Africa to 1945,* edited by Cherryl Walker, 146–167. London: James Currey.

Bentley, Kristina. 2004. 'Women's Human Rights and the Feminisation of Poverty in South Africa.' *Review of African Political Economy* 31 (100): 247–261.

Bersani, Leo. 1987. 'Is the Rectum a Grave?' *October* 43: 197–222.

Bethlehem, Louise. 2001. '"A Primary Need as Strong as Hunger": The Rhetoric of Urgency in South African Literary Culture under Apartheid.' *Poetics Today* 22 (2): 365–389.

Bhabha, Homi K. 1984.'Of Mimicry and Man: The Ambivalence of Colonial Discourse.' *October* 28: 125–133.

———. 1990. 'Introduction: Narrating the Nation.' In *Nation and Narration,* edited by Homi K Bhabha, 1–7. London: Routledge.

———. 1992. 'The World and the Home.' *Social Text* (31/32): 141–153.

———. 1994. *The Location of Culture.* London: Routledge.

Biko, Steve. 1978. *I Write What I Like.* Oxford: Heinemann.

Boehmer, Elleke. 1991. 'Stories of Women and Mothers: Gender and Nationalism in the Early Fiction of Flora Nwapa.' In *Motherlands: Black Women's Writing from Africa, the Caribbean and South Asia,* edited by Susheila Nasta, 2–23. London: The Women's Press.

Boswell, Barbara. 2016. '"Conjuring up Her Wholeness": Post-Transitional Black South African Women's Poetry and its Restorative Ethic.' *Scrutiny2* 21 (2): 8–26.

———. 2017. 'Overcoming the "Daily Bludgeoning by Apartheid": Black South African Women Writers, Agency, and Space.' *African Identities* 15 (4): 414–427.

Bragard, Véronique. 2008. *Transoceanic Dialogues: Coolitude in Caribbean and Indian Ocean Literatures.* Brussels: PIE Peter Lang.

Brink, André. 1982. *A Chain of Voices.* London: Faber and Faber.

Burton, Antoinette. 2010. '"Every Secret Thing?" Racial Politics in Ansuyah R. Singh's "Behold the Earth Mourns"' lecture, 11 March.

Carter, Perry L. 2006. 'The Penumbral Spaces of Nella Larsen's Passing: Undecidable Bodies, Mobile Identities, and the Deconstruction of Racial Boundaries.' *Gender, Place and Culture* 13 (3): 227–246.

Case, Diane. 1986. *Love, David.* Cape Town: Dutton.

Case, Maxine. 2006. *All We Have Left Unsaid.* Cape Town: Kwela Books.

———. 2017. *Softness of the Lime.* Cape Town: Umuzi.

Chapman, Michael. 1996. *Southern African Literatures.* London: Longman.

Christiansë, Yvette. 2006. *Unconfessed.* New York: Other Press.

———. 2009. '"Heartsore": The Melancholy Archive of Cape Colony Slavery.' *S&F Online* 7 (2). Accessed 13 March 2020. http://sfonline. barnard.edu/africana/christianse_01.htm.

Cock, Jacklyn. 1989. *Maids and Madams: Domestic Workers under Apartheid.* London: The Women's Press.

Crenshaw, Kimberlé. 1989. 'Demarginalizing the Intersection of Race and Sex: A Black Feminist Critique of Antidiscrimination Doctrine, Feminist Theory and Antiracist Politics.' *University of Chicago Legal Forum 1989:* 139–168.

Davids, Carol Ann. 2013. *The Blacks of Cape Town.* Cape Town: Modjaji Books.

Davids, Nadia. 2014. *An Imperfect Blessing.* Cape Town: Umuzi Random House.

Davies, Carole Boyce. 1986. 'Finding Some Space: Black South African Women Writers.' *A Current Bibliography of African Affairs* 19 (1): 31–45.

———. 1991. 'Private Selves and Public Spaces: Autobiography and the African Woman Writer.' *CLA Journal* 34 (3): 267–289.

———. 1994. *Black Women, Writing and Identity: Migrations of the Subject.* London: Routledge.

Daymond, Margaret. 1990. Afterword. In Lauretta Ngcobo, *And They Didn't Die*, 247–273. New York: The Feminist Press at the City University of New York.

———. 1996. 'Inventing Gendered Traditions: The Short Stories of Bessie Head and Miriam Tlali.' In *South African Feminisms: Writing, Theory, and Criticism*, edited by Margaret J Daymond, 223–240. New York: Garland.

Daymond, Margaret, Dorothy Driver, Sheila Meintjes, Leloba Molema, Chiedza Musengezi, Margie Orford and Nobantu Rasebotse, eds. 2003. *Women Writing Africa: The Southern Region*, Vol. 1. New York: The Feminist Press at the City University of New York.

De la Rey, Cheryl and Floretta Boonzaier. 2002. 'Constructing Race: Black Women Activists in the Western Cape.' In *Discourses on Difference: Discourses on Oppression*, edited by Norman Duncan, Pumla Dineo Gqola, Murray Hofmeyr, Tamara Shefer, Felix Malunga and Mashudu Mashige, 77–89. Cape Town: CASAS.

Dike, Fatima. 1979. *The First South African*. Johannesburg: Ravan Press.

———. 1987. 'The Sacrifice of Kreli.' In *Theatre One: New South African Drama*, edited by Stephen Gray, 33–79.

Dosekun, Simidele. 2007. 'Defending Feminism in Africa.' *Postamble* 3 (1): 41–47.

Ebrahim-Vally, Rehana. 2001. *Kala Pani: Caste and Colour in South Africa*. Cape Town: Kwela Books.

'Effects of Apartheid on the Status of Women in South Africa, 1980: Extracts from Paper Prepared by the Secretariat for the World Conference of the United Nations Decade for Women, Copenhagen, July 1980.' Accessed 12 March 2005. http://www.anc.org.za/ancdocs/history/women/effects.html.

Erasmus, Zimitri. 2001. 'Introduction: Re-Imagining Coloured Identities in Post-Apartheid South Africa.' In *Coloured by History, Shaped by Place: New Perspectives on Coloured Identities in Cape Town*, edited by Zimitri Erasmus, 15–28. Cape Town: Kwela Books.

Flockemann, Miki. 1992. 'Not-Quite Insiders and Not-Quite Outsiders: The "Process of Womanhood" in *Beka Lamb*, *Nervous Conditions* and *Daughters of the Twilight*.' *The Journal of Commonwealth Literature* 27 (1): 37–47.

———. 1998. 'Asian Diasporas, Contending Identities and New Configurations: Stories by Agnes Sam and Olive Senior.' *English in Africa* 25 (1): 77–86.

Frenkel, Ronit. 2010. *Reconsiderations: South African Indian Fiction and the Making of Race in Postcolonial Culture*. Pretoria: Unisa Press.

Frenkel, Ronit and Craig MacKenzie. 2010. 'Conceptualizing "Post-transitional" South African Literature in English.' *English Studies in Africa* 53 (1): 1–10.

FSAW (Federation of South African Women). 1954. 'Women's Charter.' April 1954. Accessed 3 January 2004. http://www.anc.org.za/ancdocs/history/women/wcharter.html.

Gaitskell, Deborah and Elaine Unterhalter. 1989. 'Mothers of the Nation: A Comparative Analysis of Nation, Race and Motherhood in Afrikaner Nationalism and the African National Congress.' In *Woman-Nation-State*, edited by Nira Yuval-Davis and Floya Anthias, 59–78. London: Palgrave Macmillan.

Goetz, Annemarie, and Shireen Hassim, eds. 2003. *No Shortcuts to Power: African Women in Politics and Policy Making*. London: Macmillan.

Gordimer, Nadine. 1985. Preface. In Ellen Kuzwayo, *Call Me Woman*, xi–xii. San Francisco: Aunt Lute Books.

Gordon, Avery. 1997. *Ghostly Matters: Haunting and the Sociological Imagination*. Minneapolis, MN: University of Minnesota Press.

Govinden, Devarakshanam. 2008. *'Sister Outsiders': The Representation of Identity and Difference in Selected Writings by South African Indian Women*. Pretoria: Unisa Press.

Gqola, Pumla Dineo. 2001. 'Contradictory Locations: Blackwomen and the Discourse of the Black Consciousness Movement (BCM) in South Africa.' *Meridians: Feminism, Race, Transnationalism* 2 (1): 130–152.

———. 2003. 'Shackled Memories and Elusive Discourses? Colonial Slavery and the Contemporary Cultural and Artistic Imagination in South Africa.' PhD. diss., Ludwig-Maximilians-Universität München.

———. 2004. 'Where Have all the Rainbows Gone?: Memory.' *Rhodes Journalism Review* (24): 6–7.

———. 2008. '"Crafting Epicentres of Agency": Sarah Bartmann and African Feminist Literary Imaginings.' *Quest: An African Journal of Philosophy* XX: 45–76.

———. 2009a. '"Pushing Out From the Centre": (Black) Feminist Imagination, Redefined Politics and Emergent Trends in South African Poetry.' *XCP: Cross Cultural Poetics* 21/22: 214–38.

———. 2009b. '"The Difficult Task of Normalizing Freedom": Spectacular Masculinities, Ndebele's Literary/Cultural Commentary and Post-apartheid Life.' *English in Africa*, 36 (1): 61–76.

———. 2010. *What is Slavery to Me? Postcolonial/Slave Memory in Post-Apartheid South Africa*. Johannesburg: Wits University Press.

————. 2013. *A Renegade Called Simphiwe*. Johannesburg: Melinda Ferguson Books.

————. 2015. *Rape: A South African Nightmare*. Johannesburg: Melinda Ferguson Books.

Gray, Stephen. 1980. 'An Interview with Fatima Dike.' *Callaloo* 8/10: 157–164.

Gupta, Jhumka, Jay G Silverman, David Hemenway, Dolores Acevedo-Garcia, Dan J Stein and David R Williams. 2008. 'Physical Violence Against Intimate Partners and Related Exposures to Violence among South African Men.' *CMAJ* 179 (6): 535–541.

Halberstam, J. 2005. *In a Queer Time and Place: Transgender Bodies, Subcultural Lives*. New York: New York University Press.

Hansen, Thomas. 2013. *The Melancholia of Freedom: Social Life in an Indian Township in South Africa*. Johannesburg: Wits University Press.

Harries, Patrick. 1981. 'Slavery, Social Incorporation and Surplus Extraction: The Nature of Free and Unfree Labour in South-East Africa.' *The Journal of African History* 22 (3): 309–330.

————. 2000. 'Culture and Classification: A History of the Mozbieker Communities at the Cape.' *Social Dynamics* 26 (2): 29–54.

————. 2013. 'Negotiating Abolition: Cape Town and the Trans-Atlantic Slave Trade.' *Slavery & Abolition* 34 (4): 579–597.

Hassim, Shafinaaz. 2012. *SoPhia*. Crown Mines: World Flute Press.

Hassim, Shireen. 2002. 'A Conspiracy of Women: The Women's Movement in South Africa's Transition to Democracy.' *Social Research: An International Quarterly* 69 (3): 693–732.

————. 2004. 'Nationalism, Feminism and Autonomy: The ANC in Exile and the Question of Women.' *Journal of Southern African Studies* 30 (3): 433–456.

————. 2005. 'Nationalism Displaced: Citizenship Discourses in the Transition.' In *(Un)Thinking Citizenship: Feminist Debates in Contemporary South Africa*, edited by Amanda Gouws, 55–70. Burlington: Ashgate Publishing.

Head, Bessie. 1968. *When Rain Clouds Gather*. London: Heinemann.

————. 1971. *Maru*. Oxford: Heinemann.

————. 1973. *A Question of Power*. Oxford: Heinemann.

————. 1977. *The Collector of Treasures and Other Botswana Village Tales*. Oxford: Heinemann.

————. 1981. *Serowe: Village of the Rain Wind*. Oxford: Heinemann.

———. 1984. *A Bewitched Crossroad: An African Saga.* Johannesburg: Ad. Donker.

———. 1990. *A Woman Alone: Autobiographical Writings*, edited by Craig MacKenzie. London: Heinemann African Writers Series.

———. 1993. *The Cardinals, with Meditations and Short Stories.* Cape Town: David Philip.

Hoogeveen, J, and B Özler. 2006. 'Poverty and Inequality in Post-Apartheid South Africa: 1995–2000.' In *Poverty and Policy in Post-Apartheid South Africa*, edited by Haroon Bhorat and Ravi Kanbur, 59–94. Pretoria: HSRC Press.

hooks, bell. 1990. *Yearning: Race, Gender and Cultural Politics.* Boston: South End Press.

———. 1991. 'Theory as Liberatory Practice.' *Yale Journal of Law and Feminism* 4 (1): 1–12.

———. 1994. *Teaching to Transgress: Education as the Practice of Freedom.* New York: Routledge.

Hoza, Mfusi Cynthia. 2012. 'Patriarchal Self-Inflated Pompous Image Deflated: A Feminist Reading of Swartbooi's *UMandisa.*' *South African Journal of African Languages* 32 (1): 63–70.

Hunter, Eva. 1994. '"We Have to Defend Ourselves": Women, Tradition, and Change in Lauretta Ngcobo's *And They Didn't Die.*' *Tulsa Studies in Women's Literature* 13 (1): 113–126.

Jabavu, Noni. 1960. *Drawn in Colour: African Contrasts.* London: John Murray.

———. 1963. *The Ochre People: Scenes from a South African Life.* London: John Murray.

Jacobs, Rayda. 1998. *The Slave Book.* Cape Town: Kwela Books.

Jameson, Fredric. 1971. *Marxism and Form.* Princeton: Princeton University Press.

Jayawardena, Kumari. 1986. *Feminism and Nationalism in the Third World.* London: Zed Books.

Jele, Nozizwe Cynthia. 2010. *Happiness Is a Four-letter Word.* Cape Town: Kwela Books.

———. 2018. *The Ones with Purpose.* Cape Town: Kwela Books.

Jewkes, R and N Abrahams. 2002. 'The Epidemiology of Rape and Sexual Coercion in South Africa: An Overview.' *Social Science & Medicine* 55 (7): 1231–1244.

Johnson, David. 2012. 'Representations of Cape Slavery in South African Literature.' *History Compass* 10 (8): 549–561.

Kaplan, Caren, Norma Alarcon and Minoo Moallem. 1999. 'Introduction: Between Woman and Nation.' In *Between Woman and Nation: Nationalisms, Transnational Feminisms, and the State,* edited by Caren Kaplan, Norma Alarcon and Minoo Moallem, 1–16. Durham: Duke University Press.

Karodia, Farida. 1986. *Daughters of the Twilight*. London: The Women's Press.

———. 1988. *Coming Home and Other Stories*. Heinemann Educational Books.

Keegan, Timothy. 1996. *Colonial South Africa and the Origins of the Racial Order*. Charlottesville: University of Virginia Press.

Kuzwayo, Ellen. 1985. *Call Me Woman*. San Francisco: Aunt Lute Books.

Layoun, Mary. 2001. *Wedded to the Land? Gender, Boundaries, and Nationalism in Crisis*. Durham: Duke University Press.

Lenta, Margaret. 2010. '*A Chain of Voices* and *Unconfessed*: Novels of Slavery in the 1980s and in the Present Day.' *JLS/TLW* 26 (1): 95–110.

Lewis, Desiree. 2001. 'Constructing Lives: Black South African Women and Biography.' In *Apartheid Narratives*, edited by Nahem Yousaf, 163–190. Amsterdam: Rodopi.

———. 2002. *Gender and Women's Studies in South Africa: A Review Report*. Cape Town: African Gender Institute.

———. 2007. *Living on a Horizon: Bessie Head and the Politics of Imagining*. Trenton, NJ: Africa World Press.

Lim, Shirley Geok-lin. 1993. 'Asians in Anglo-American Feminism: Reciprocity and Resistance'. In *Changing Subjects: The Making of Feminist Literary Criticism*, edited by Gayle Greene and Coppelia Kahn, 240-252. London: Routledge.

Lockett, Cecily. 1989. '"The Fabric of Experience": A Critical Perspective on the Writing of Miriam Tlali.' In *Women and Writing in South Africa: A Critical Anthology*, edited by Cherry Clayton, 275–285. Marshalltown: Heinemann.

Maart, Rozena. 2006. *Rosa's District 6*. Cape Town: David Philip.

———. 2007. *The Writing Circle*. Toronto: TSAR Publishers.

Mabuza, Lindiwe. 1989. *One Never Knows: An Anthology of Black South African Women in Exile*. Johannesburg: Skotaville Publishers.

MacKenzie, Craig. 1990. Introduction. In Bessie Head, *A Woman Alone: Autobiographical Writings*, edited by Craig MacKenzie, ix–xix. Oxford: African Writers Series.

Magona, Sindiwe. 1998. *Mother to Mother*. Cape Town: David Philip.

Makholwa, Angela. 2007. *Red Ink: A Novel*. Singapore: Singapore Books.

———. 2009. *The 30ᵗʰ Candle*. Johannesburg: Pan MacMillan.

———. 2013. *Black Widow Society*. Johannesburg: Pan MacMillan.

———. 2017. *The Blessed Girl*. Johannesburg: Pan MacMillan.

'Malibongwe Conference Programme of Action.' January 1990. Accessed 10 December 2003. http://www.anc.org.za/ancdocs/history/women/pr900118.html.

Mandela, Winnie. 1984. *Part of My Soul Went with Him, edited by Anne Benjamin*. New York and London: Norton.

Mashinini, Emma. 1989. *Strikes Have Followed Me All My Life: A South African Autobiography*. London: The Women's Press.

Masola, Athambile. 2017. 'Reading Noni Jabavu in 2017.' *Mail & Guardian*, 11 August 2017.

Matlwa, Kopano. 2007. *Coconut*. Johannesburg: Black Bird Books.

———. 2010. *Spilt Milk*. Johannesburg: Jacana Media.

———. 2016. *Period Pain*. Johannesburg: Jacana Media.

Matthews, James and Gladys Thomas. 1972. *Cry Rage*. Cape Town: Spro-Cas Publications.

Mazibuko, Lita Nombangu. 1997. 'Truth and Reconciliation Commission Victim Hearing Transcript. July 29, 1997.' Accessed 12 January 2010. www.justice.gov.za/trc/special/women/mazibuko.htm.

McClintock, Anne. 1995. *Imperial Leather: Race, Gender and Sexuality in the Colonial Contest*. London: Routledge.

McKittrick, Katherine. 2006. *Demonic Grounds: Black Women and the Cartographies of Struggle*. Minneapolis: University of Minnesota Press.

McKittrick, Katherine and Clyde Woods. 2007. 'No One Knows the Mysteries at the Bottom of the Ocean.' In *Black Geographies and the Politics of Place*, edited by Katherine McKittrick and Clyde Woods, 1–13. Boston: South End Press.

Meer, Fatima. 1969. *Portrait of Indian South Africans*. Durban: Avon House.

———. 1985. 'Women in the Apartheid Society.' Accessed 3 January 2004. http://www.anc.org.za/ancdocs/history/misc/fatima.html.

Meintjes, Sheila. 1997. 'Dealing with the Aftermath – Sexual Violence and the Truth and Reconciliation Commission.' *Agenda* 36: 7–18.

Meintjes, Sheila and Beth Goldblatt. 1996. *Gender and the Truth and Reconciliation Commission: A Submission to the Truth and Reconciliation Commission*. Johannesburg: Centre for Applied Legal Studies and Witwatersrand University Press.

Mesthrie, Rajend. 2005. 'Assessing Representations of South African Indian English in Writing: An Application of Variation Theory.' *Language Variation and Change* 17 (3): 303–326.

Mhlongo, Niq. 2013. 'Niq Mhlongo on *Way Back Home.*' *Times Live*, 30 October. Accessed 30 January 2019. www.niqmhlongo. bookslive.co.za.

Mhlophe, Gcina. 1987. 'The Toilet.' In *Sometimes When it Rains: Writing by South African Women,* edited by Ann Oosthuizen, 1–7. London: Pandora Press.

———. 2002. *Love Child.* Pietermaritzburg: University of KwaZulu-Natal Press.

Mofokeng, Boitumelo. 1989. 'Where Are the Women? Ten Years of *Staffrider.*' *Current Writing* 1: 41–42.

Molope, Kagiso Lesego. 2002. *Dancing in the Dust.* Toronto: TSAR Publishers.

———. 2005. *The Mending Season.* Oxford University Press.

———. 2012. *This Book Betrays my Brother.* Cape Town: Oxford University Press Southern Africa.

Morrell, Robert. 1998. 'Of Boys and Men: Masculinity and Gender in Southern African Studies.' Journal of Southern African Studies 24 (4): 605–630.

Morrison, Toni. 1987. *Beloved.* New York: Plume.

Motsei, Mmatshilo. 2007. *The Kanga and the Kangaroo Court: Reflections on the Rape Trial of Jacob Zuma.* Melbourne: Spinifex Press.

Motsemme, Nthabiseng. 2002. 'Gendered Experiences of Blackness in Post-Apartheid South Africa.' *Social Identities* 8 (4): 647–673.

———. 2004. '"The Mute Always Speak": On Women's Silences at the Truth and Reconciliation Commission.' *Current Sociology* 52 (3): 909–932.

Motsemme, Nthabiseng and Kopano Ratele. 2000. 'Losing Life and Remaking Nation at the Truth and Reconciliation Commission.' Presentation at Discourses on Difference and Oppression Conference, 19–22 July, Makhado, Venda.

Msibi, Thabo. 2011. 'The Lies We Have Been Told: On (Homo) Sexuality in Africa.' *Africa Today* 58 (1): 55–77.

Narismulu, Priya. 1998. '"Here be Dragons": Challenging "Liberal" Constructions of Protest Poetry.' *Alternation* 5 (1): 191–214.

Ndebele, Njabulo. 1986. 'The Rediscovery of the Ordinary: Some New Writings in South Africa.' *Journal of Southern African Studies* 12 (1): 143–157.

————. 1989. 'The Writers' Movement in South Africa.' *Research in African Literatures* 20 (3): 412–421.

Nfah-Abbenyi, Juliana Makuchi. 1997. *Gender in African Women's Writing: Identity, Sexuality, and Difference.* Bloomington: Indiana University Press.

Ngcobo, Lauretta. 1981. *Cross of Gold.* London: Longman.

————, ed. 1987. *Let It Be Told: Essays by Black Women in Britain.* London: Pluto Press.

————. 1989. 'Introduction.' In Miriam Tlali, *Soweto Stories.* London: Pandora Press.

————. 1990. *And They Didn't Die.* New York: The Feminist Press at the City University of New York.

Nixon, Rob. 1993. 'Border Country: Bessie Head's Frontline States.' *Social Text* 36: 106–137.

Njobe, Makhosazana. 1978. 'Speech of the Struggling Women of South Africa Read by Makhosazana Njobe on the Commemoration of August 9th 1978, South Africa's Women's Day.' *Mayibuye*, August 1978. Accessed 10 April 2005. http://disa.nu.ac.za.

Ntantala, Phyllis. 1993. *A Life's Mosaic: The Autobiography of Phyllis Ntantala.* Berkeley: University of California Press.

Oliphant, Andries and Ivan Vladislavic. 1988. *Ten Years of Staffrider.* Johannesburg: Ravan Press.

Ogunyemi, Chikwenye Okonjo. 1985. 'Womanism: The Dynamics of the Contemporary Black Female Novel in English.' *Signs: Journal of Women in Culture and Society* 11 (1): 63–80.

Opland, Jeff. 2007. *The Nation's Bounty: The Xhosa Poetry of Nontsizi Mgqwetho.* Johannesburg: Wits University Press.

Perkins, Kathy, ed. 1998. *Black South African Women: An Anthology of Plays.* London: Routledge.

Pillay, D. 1992. 'Women in MK – Thenjiwe Mtintso.' *Work in Progress*, 80.

Pirbhai, Mariam. 2009. *Mythologies of Migration, Vocabularies of Indenture: Novels of the South African Diaspora in Africa, the Caribbean and Asia-Pacific.* Toronto: University of Toronto Press.

Plaatje, Sol. 1930/1978. *Mhudi*, edited by Stephen Gray. London: Heinemann.

Promotion of National Unity and Reconciliation Act, No. 34, July 26, 1995. Accessed 10 May 2004. http://www.doj.gov.za/trc/legal/act9534.htm.

Raman, Parvathi. 2003. 'Yusuf Dadoo: Transnational Politics, South African Belonging.' Paper presented at the Workshop on South

Africa in the 1940s, South African Research Centre, Kingston, September 2003.

Ramphele, Mamphela. 1993. *A Bed Called Home: Life in the Migrant Labour Hostels of Cape Town.* Cape Town: David Philip.

Ray, Sangeeta. 2000. *En-Gendering India: Woman and Nation in Colonial and Postcolonial Narratives.* Durham: Duke University Press.

Reddy, Jayapraga. 1987. *On the Fringe of Dreamtime and Other Stories.* Johannesburg: Skotaville Publishers.

Rive, Richard. 1982. 'Books by Black Writers.' *Staffrider* 5 (1): 12–15.

Rolfes, Chloe. 1981. 'Miriam Tlali: Feted, Berated then Banned'. Fairlady, 4 November, 63.

Ross, Fiona C. 2003. *Bearing Witness: Women and the Truth and Reconciliation Commission.* London: Pluto Press.

Rushdy, Ashraf. 1999. *Neo-Slave Narratives: Studies in the Social Logic of a Literary Form.* Oxford: Oxford University Press.

Said, Edward. 1994. *Culture and Imperialism.* New York: Vintage Books.

Sam, Agnes. 1989. *Jesus is Indian and Other Stories.* London: The Women's Press.

Sambureni, Nelson. 1995. '"We Are Not Children. We Are Asking for the Managers to Listen to our Problems": Some Aspects of the 1973 Durban Strikes.' *African Historical Review* 27 (1): 196–213.

Samuelson, Meg. 2007. *Remembering the Nation, Disremembering Women?: Stories of the South African Transition.* Pietermaritzburg: University of KwaZulu-Natal Press.

———. 2008. 'Walking through the Door and Inhabiting the House: South African Literary Culture and Criticism after the Transition.' *English Studies in Africa* 51 (1): 130–137.

Schmidt, Elizabeth S. 1983. 'Now You Have Touched the Women: African Women's Resistance to Pass Laws in South Africa 1950 – 1960.' Accessed 2 April 2005. http://anc.org.za/ancdocs/history/misc/schmil23.html.

Shell, Robert. 1994. *Children of Bondage: A Social History of the Slave Society at the Cape of Good Hope, 1652–1838.* Hanover: Wesleyan University Press published by University Press of New England.

Sikakane, Joyce. 1977. *A Window on Soweto.* London: International Defence and Aid Fund.

Spencer, Lynda. 2009. 'Young, Black and Female in Post-Apartheid South Africa: Identity Politics in Kopano Matlwa's *Coconut.' Scrutiny2* 14 (1): 66–78.

Spivak, Giyatri. 2001. 'Can the Subaltern Speak?' In *The Norton Anthology of Theory and Criticism*, edited by Vincent B Leitch, 2197–2208. London: WW Norton and Company.

Swartbooi VNM. 1934. *UMandisa*. Alice: Lovedale Press.

Thomas, Gladys. 1992. *Avalon Court: Vignettes of Life of the 'Coloured' People on the Cape Flats of Cape Town*. Johannesburg: Skotaville Publishers.

Tlali, Miriam. 1975. *Muriel at Metropolitan*. Johannesburg: Ravan Press.

———. 1980. *Amandla*. Johannesburg: Ravan Press.

———. 2004. *Between Two Worlds*. Peterborough, Ontario: Broadview.

TRC (Truth and Reconciliation Commission). 2001a. *Truth and Reconciliation Commission of South Africa Report*. Vol. 1–5. London: Palgrave Macmillan.

———. 2001b. 'Amnesty Committee Decision: Application in Terms of Section 18 of the Promotion of National Unity and Reconciliation Act, No. 34 of 1995.' Accessed 11 May 2004. http://www.justice.gov.za/trc/decisions%5C2001/ac21273.htm.

Wakoko, Florence and Linda Lobao. 1996. 'Reconceptualizing Gender and Reconstructing Social Life: Ugandan Women and the Path to National Development.' *Africa Today* 43 (3): 307–322.

Walker, Cheryl. 1995. 'Conceptualising Motherhood in Twentieth Century South Africa.' *Journal of Southern African Studies* 21 (3): 417–437.

Wanner, Zukiswa. 2006. *The Madams*. Cape Town: Oshun.

———. 2008. *Behind Every Successful Man*. Cape Town: Kwela Books.

———. 2010. *Men of the South*. Cape Town: Kwela Books.

———. 2014. *London, Cape Town, Joburg*. Cape Town: Kwela Books.

Wheeler, John H. 1961. 'Apartheid Implemented by Education in South Africa.' *The Journal of Negro Education* 30 (3): 240–258.

Wicomb, Zoë. 1987. *You Can't Get Lost in Cape Town*. London: Virago Press.

———. 1996. 'To Hear a Variety of Discourses.' In *South African Feminisms: Writing, Theory, and Criticism 1990–1994*, edited by Margaret J Daymond, 45–56. New York: Garland Publishing.

———. 1998. 'Shame and Identity: The Case of the Coloured in South Africa.' In *Writing South Africa: Literature, Apartheid, and Democracy, 1970–1995*, edited by Derek Attridge and Rosemary Jolly, 91–107. Cambridge: Cambridge University Press.

———. 2000. *David's Story*. New York: The Feminist Press at City University of New York.

Wilentz, Gay. 1992. *Binding Cultures: Black Women Writers in Africa and the Diaspora*. Bloomington: Indiana University Press.

Wisker, Gina. 2001. '"A Gesture of Belonging": Creativity and Place in South African Women's Writing.' In *Apartheid Narratives*, edited by Nahem Yousaf, 143–162. Amsterdam: Rodopi.

Woodward, Wendy. 1993. 'The Powers of Discourse: The Identity of Subaltern Women under Colonial Law in *Nervous Conditions* and *Daughters of the Twilight*.' *Journal of Literary Studies* 9 (1): 80–91.

Worden, Nigel. 1985. *Slavery in Dutch South Africa*, African Studies Series, 44. Cambridge: Cambridge University Press.

Xaba, Makhosazana. 2009. 'Noni Jabavu: A Peripatetic Writer Ahead of Her Times.' *Tydskrif vir Letterkunde* 46 (1): 217–219.

Yuval-Davis, Nira and Floya Anthias, eds. 1989. *Woman-Nation-State*. London: Palgrave Macmillan.

Zinn, Maxine Baca and Bonnie Thornton Dill. 1996. 'Theorizing Difference from Multiracial Feminism'. *Feminist Studies* 22 (2): 321–331.

Index

Notes: *The context of entries is South Africa and the subject is black women and black women's writing, unless indicated or obviously otherwise. These terms are not separately indexed. Prepositions in subheadings are ignored in the alphabetical arrangement.*